THE DESIGN DIRECTORY OF

Bedding

—m—

THE DESIGN DIRECTORY OF

Bedding

Written and Illustrated by

Jackie Von Tobel

GIBBS SMITH
TO ENRICH AND INSPIRE HUMANKIND
Salt Lake City | Charleston | Santa Fe | Santa Barbara

First Edition
13 12 11 10 09   5 4 3 2 1

Cover background fabric by Robert Allen: Abberley in Lagoon.
www.robertallendesign.com, Licensed by the **ROBERT ALLEN** Group, Inc.
On the end sheets: adapted from "Birds & Branches" from the Jackie Von Tobel Collection
by Adaptive Textiles.

Published by
Gibbs Smith
P.O. Box 667
Layton, Utah 84041

Orders: 1.800.835.4993
www.gibbs-smith.com

Designed and produced by TTA Design
Printed and bound in China
Gibbs Smith books are printed on either recycled, 100% post-consumer waste, FSC-certified
papers or on paper produced from a 100% certified sustainable forest/controlled wood source.

Library of Congress Cataloging-in-Publication Data

Von Tobel, Jackie.
  The design directory of bedding / Jackie Von Tobel ; illustrations by Jackie Von Tobel. — 1st ed.
    p. cm.
  ISBN-13: 978-1-4236-0444-0
  ISBN-10: 1-4236-0444-X
  1. Bedding. 2. House furnishings. 3. Interior decoration—Amateurs' manuals. I. Title.
  TT399.V693 2009
  646.2'1—dc22
                        2008054230

For my Dad

Acknowledgments

I could not have completed this book without the unwavering support of my wonderful husband, Arnie, my daughter, Angelica, and my two boys, JT and Geordie. Thanks to my sisters Julie, Vickie, Trudi, and Valorie, and my good friends Denise and Tim.

Contents

Introduction

Over the past few years, I have made the transition from designing soft treatments to also writing about them. In my practice as an interior designer, one of the most common requests I received from clients was for a beautiful bedroom. They wanted a haven away from the hustle and bustle of life, a place where they could relax and revitalize, a private sanctuary that reflected their personality but above all would lull them softly to sleep in luxurious comfort.

This second volume of The Design Directory is my tribute to the personal retreat—the bedroom. From the day my sister Julie and I received our first polka-dot chenille ballerina bedspreads, I was constantly redecorating my bedroom. I draped my bunk beds, made canopies out of flowery bed sheets, and upholstered cardboard cartons into sumptuous doll beds. As I grew into a designer, my passion for creating custom bedding and bedroom design motivated me to look for knowledge and fresh ideas.

I have spent years researching bedding design and collecting ideas from around the world. This book contains the fruit of that research, including basic design fundamentals, thousands of inspirational ideas, and detailed resources, all of which combine to create the most complete directory of bedding design ideas and instruction ever assembled.

The Design Directory of Bedding is the must-have resource for designers, workroom professionals, and do-it-yourselfers. Concise, straight-to-the-point lists, definitions, and descriptions of design fundamentals and components provide a comprehensive education on bedding design. More than 1,000 individual components and complete designs illustrated in this book are meant to encourage your creativity and enable you to stretch your design boundaries.

Standardized definitions of design terminology will help you communicate effectively within the industry.

Black-and-white line drawings of every color illustration in this book are available on the enclosed CD-ROM. You can download them to your computer or print them and personalize with color for your project. Also included on the CD-ROM are detailed workroom worksheets and service request forms.

I have been encouraged and motivated by the hundreds of design professionals and homeowners with whom I have associated. I am very happy to share this information and inspiration with you so that you can put your personal touch to your creations to make them uniquely your own.

Jackie Von Tobel

How to Use This Book

The *Design Directory of Bedding* helps simplify the complicated process of design in order to assist you in creating a beautiful, personal, and comfortable bedroom that is as attractive as it is functional. Within the pages of this book you will find hundreds of creative ideas and applications that will be a springboard for your own creativity and unique designs. Each section of the directory will assist you in making decisions critical to your success:

Design: Using the fundamentals and calculations outlined in the first chapter, measure your bed, analyze your space and calculate the basic proportions, then lay out and construct your design.

Fabric: Choose the fiber, weave, pattern, hand, and colors of the fabrics you will use.

Components: Choose the separate bedding elements that will complete your ensemble.

Style: Choose from the many complete designs in the book or choose a combination of components to create a new look that is all your own.

Embellishments: Apply finishing touches that will personalize your design.

Hardware: If your design calls for hardware, choose the appropriate type and style of hardware or mounting technique for your design.

Workroom: Communicate your designs effectively and accurately to your workroom to ensure that your bedding is properly made.

On the inside back cover you will find a CD-ROM that contains black-and-white line drawings of all the illustrations shown in this book. Also on the CD are the worksheets.

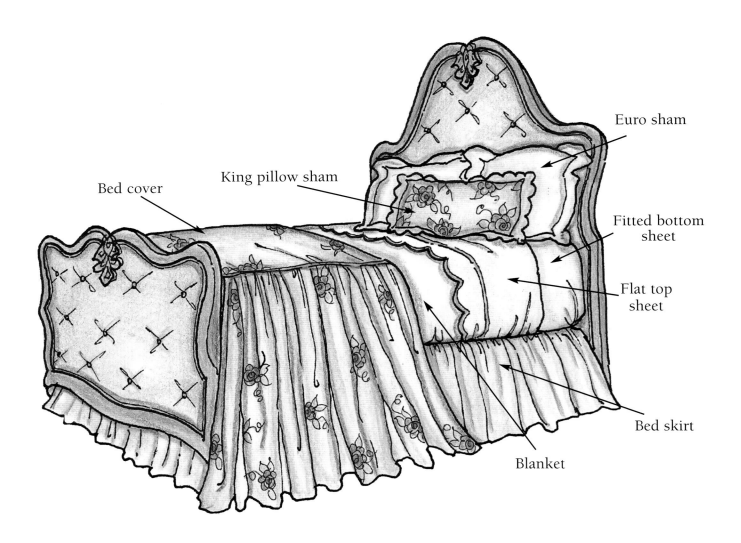

Bed cover

King pillow sham

Euro sham

Fitted bottom sheet

Flat top sheet

Bed skirt

Blanket

Typical Bedding Ensemble

Bedding ensembles today can vary greatly, from a simple, clean, contemporary design to a multilayered traditional scheme complete with elaborate canopy and draperies; but the basic elements of the ensemble remain the same:

- **Bed Linens:** top sheet, bottom sheet, pillowcases, thermal blankets

- **Bed Covers:** duvet, coverlet, comforter, bedspread, fitted bed cover, box spring cover

- **Pillow Covers:** pillowcases, pillow shams, decorative pillows, neck rolls, bolsters

- **Bed Draperies:** coronas, crowns, pediments, cornices, bed drapes

- **Canopies:** full canopy, partial canopy, open canopy, half tester, full tester

- **Bed Skirts:** full skirt, pieced skirt

Bedding Design Fundamentals

When designing bedding, basic design fundamentals should always inform your choices. By combining your knowledge of these principles with knowledge of the products and options available, you will be able to create beautiful designs that will meet your functional and aesthetic needs.

The basic design fundamentals are separated into five categories:

Features and Functions: The features and functions of the many separate elements of bedding are the beneficial attributes that can be achieved with their application.

Principles: The design you choose for your bedding should meet your functional needs in an appropriate, attractive manner. The principles of design are used to evaluate the functional and aesthetic needs of your bedroom as well as the finished bedding.

Elements: The elements of design are the set of physical tools or raw materials with which the principles of design can be applied.

Rules of Thumb: Rules are a set of tools that help you calculate correct proportions for your bedding.

Specifications: The specifications for soft treatments for the bedroom are a list of rules and guidelines that should be applied during the fabrication of your bedding to ensure quality in construction.

The Features and Functions of Bedding

The features and functions of the many separate elements of bedding are the beneficial attributes that can be achieved with their application.

Design

- Create a sense of style and visual interest.
- Add softness and warmth.
- Complement the style, line, and scale of the bed.
- Complement the architectural style, line, and scale of the room.
- Establish, continue, or reinforce a decorative theme.
- Create a focal point.
- Bring focus to architectural details.

Function

- Provide comfort by utilizing soft fillers and fibers.
- Provide orthopedic support for improved health.
- Allow for temperature control, adding warmth in winter and promoting coolness in summer.
- Create privacy through the use of drapery.
- Provide dust and pest control.

Camouflage

- Hide exposed hardware and unattractive metal bed frames.
- Hide the box spring.
- Soften hard lines.
- Hide architectural flaws.

Illusion

- Manipulate the appearance, style, and size of the bed.
- Balance the proportions of the room.

Energy Efficiency

- Reduce drafts.
- Help to maintain an appropriate temperature.

The Principles of Bedding Design

The design you choose for your bedroom should meet its functional needs in an appropriate, attractive manner. The principles of design are used to evaluate the functional and aesthetic needs of your bedroom as well as the finished bedding.

Proportion: Proportion is the relationship of the individual parts to the whole bedding ensemble when comparing sizes and shapes. The proportions must be manipulated to create a harmonious balance between all of the components used and the overall size and scale of the design.

Scale: Scale is the relative size of an element, whether it refers to the scale of the entire bedding ensemble or the scale of the pattern on the fabric. You must consider the relationship of the scale of the room to the bedding ensemble to be used in it. You must also consider the scale of the patterns of different fabrics to be used on the bedding in order to produce a harmonious balance among them.

Balance: Balance is the state of evenness, stability, or equilibrium among the design elements used in your design. There are two types of balance:

Symmetrical: Both sides of the design are the same, or mirrored.

Asymmetrical: The two sides are somewhat different, yet they are balanced by a central element, or equilibrium.

Radial: The elements radiate from a central point outward in spokes or concentric circles.

Rhythm: The connection of elements within the design scheme used to create balance and harmony. There are three types of rhythm:

Transition: The use of elements such as trim, color, or lines to create visual movement.

Gradation: Shapes made to decrease and increase in size, or colors made to grow darker or lighter in a specific order to create visual movement.

Repetition: A color, texture, or element is used repeatedly.

Emphasis: The use of colors, patterns, or elements to create a focal point in the design.

Harmony: Composed of unity and variety. Design elements should be applied to the design to create a sense of unity among the components; however, it must also be imparted with enough variety within those components to create a pleasing balance, or harmony.

The Elements of Bedding Design

The elements of design are the set of physical tools or raw materials with which the principles of design can be applied.

Space: Space sets the limits on the functional and decorative boundaries of your designs. Use pattern, color, line, and opacity to manipulate the visual interpretation of the design.

Light: There are ways to visually alter and manipulate the intensity of the light that reaches the bed.

Line: Line creates direction, harmony, and balance in your design. Use it to manipulate the scale and visual appearance of the bed. Vertical line adds height while horizontal line adds width.

Color: Use the choice of color to manipulate the visual impact of the design scheme.

Texture: The surface smoothness or roughness of the elements can affect the visual interpretation of the treatment. Smooth and shiny surfaces can be more formal and sophisticated, while rough surfaces can impart a casual, comfortable feel.

Pattern and Ornamental Decoration: The inclusion or omission of specific pattern and ornamentation can create or reduce drama, excitement, or visual attention to the design.

Form and Shape: The overall form and shape of the design can be altered and adjusted to create the balance needed to create harmony within the bedding ensemble.

Rules of Thumb

While good design sometimes calls upon us to think outside the box, there are certain rules of thumb that enable you to calculate the proper proportions to use as a starting point.

The Rule of Halves: Equal vertical halves are not pleasing to the eye. Never cut the bed in half by designing any element to be exactly half of the length or width of the design. For example, when calculating the drop of a coverlet over the mattress, the coverlet should leave a third of the bed skirt exposed, not half.

The Rule of Threes or Odd Numbers: The human eye finds objects grouped together in threes or in odd numbers, such as three or five, to be the most visually pleasing. In design, using three elements allows for one to be used as a statement, another as a contrast, and a third as a complement. This rule can be used to choose the placement and number of individual elements in a bedding ensemble.

The Rule of Fifths and Sixths: When calculating the dimensions of your design, ratios of three and five are the most visually pleasing. By using these ratios mathematically, you can calculate good starting points for the lengths and widths of your design. In bedding, this is particularly important for drapes, canopies, or coronas.

For Example

If you have a bed drape that will be 96" finished length mounted at the ceiling and you want to calculate the proper length for a valance or cornice, review the following information:

Finished length of the drape = 96"
    96" divided by 5 = 19 1/4"
    96" divided by 6 = 16"

The finished length of the valance or cornice according to this rule of thumb should be somewhere between 16" and 19" in order to ensure that it is in good proportion. This range of measurements can also be used to determine the long and short points of hems or tails.

To calculate swags and cascades using this rule, review the following:
Swag drop = 1/5 total length of the treatment
Cascade = 3/5 of the total length of the treatment

Specifications for Bedding Fabric and Construction

Bedding design and construction require careful planning and execution to produce long-lasting, comfortable products. Bedding is the only product in interior design that is designed to come in direct contact with a person's bare skin. This presents some specific challenges and requirements that must be met when specifying fabrics and construction.

Fabric Considerations and Preparation

When choosing fabrics and fiber content to use in bedding construction, several key considerations should be addressed:

- Durability and washability of fabric are key issues in bedding design.
  - If you specify washable fabrics such as cotton or cotton blends, they should be prewashed before construction.
  - When prewashing, always test a small piece of fabric first for color fastness.
  - For delicate or loosely woven fabrics such as linens and some cottons, you must serge raw edges before prewashing to avoid excessive raveling.
  - Delicate fabrics such as silks should not be used in high wear-and-tear areas or where they will come in contact with body oils, as they will stain.
  - When applying trim to bedding, make sure it is able to be dry-cleaned. If it cannot be cleaned, ensure that it can be easily removed before the bedding is washed or dry-cleaned.
- Consider the tactile qualities of the fabrics you specify and their comfort factor. Itchy or scratchy fabrics, such as wool and rough linens, should be used cautiously. Allergies and skin sensitivity should be taken into consideration.
- Match the fabric repeat and plot the pattern placement to best complement the design and the room.
- Plot the fabric's pattern placement on the treatment before construction and make note on your work orders.
- On textured fabrics, such as velvet, specify the direction of the nap, as it will affect the color of the finished design. Make sure the nap falls in the same direction on all pieces.

Quality Construction

- All seams should be serged and finished with an overlock stitch.
- If using an open-pressed seam, the selvages should be overlocked for a finished look and to prevent raveling.
- On high-stress areas, such as the top of bed covers, a second-row, or security stitch, might be appropriate.
- Plot your seams carefully. Where possible, do not place seams in the center of the top or sides of your bed covers. Run a full width of fabric down the center and make up the shortfall by running two sections on either side of the center width.
- When constructing bed covers with multiple sections of fabric, use a single base section to anchor the individual pieces. This prevents sagging, bunching, and stretching.
- Always take care to match the pattern carefully to disguise the seams.
- Coordinate the color of thread to be used with the fabric on the treatment. Use several colors, if necessary. Clear monofilament thread should be used as a second choice.
- Trim should be topstitched through the face fabric only, never through the lining.

Hem Construction

- Rolled hems on items such as bed skirts or ruffled pillows should be double turned and blind stitched.
- Avoid topstitching unless it is an integral part of your design.
- Standard hems on bed skirts should be double turned and blind stitched to the lining.
- For sheer fabrics used on bed skirts or drapes, a lingerie hem is appropriate.
- Use drapery weights or string weights in the hem to control the hang of your drapery panels or scarves. They can also be used in bed skirts if needed.

Appropriate Linings

✣ Specify lining where it is appropriate, such as on bed skirts. In many cases, using a contrasting fabric as lining can make the item reversible. Consider this option to add versatility and flexibility to your design.

✣ Bump or felted interlining can be used very effectively in place of batting for a lightweight coverlet. It will also add a rich, sumptuous feel to pillow shams and cases when used in the face.

✣ In most cases, lining fabric is not suitable for the underside of duvets, comforters, or coverlets. A quality custom design should specify a contrasting, coordinating, or solid fabric for this purpose.

Fabric

Fabric is a manufactured product that is constructed of fiber, weave, color, pattern, and finish.

Fiber

Fibers are natural, such as silk, linen, or cotton, or man-made, such as polyester, nylon, or rayon. Fabric can be made exclusively of natural or man-made fibers or a combination of the two, such as polyester and cotton. The qualities of the individual fiber are integral to the performance of the finished fabric. Those qualities should be taken into consideration when choosing the right fabric for your application.

Fiber Characteristics

Fabric	Special	Resistance characteristics	Resistance to deterioration	Soil resistance to fading by sun	Flammability	Care
COTTON	Drapes well	Poor to fair	Good to very good	Fair unless treated	High unless treated	Washable
Acetate	Drapes well	Poor to fair	Fair to good	Fair to good	Burns quickly unless treated	Dry clean
Acrylic	Drapes well, may stretch	Very good	Very good	Good	Melts or burns	Washable
Modacrylic	Drapes well, may stretch	Very good	Very good	Good	Will not flame	Washable
Nylon	Builds up static	Fair to good	Fair to good	Good to very good	Melts	Washable, press on low
Polyester	Wrinkle resistant, may stretch	Good to very good	Good	Good	Melts & drops off in flame	Washable
Rayon	Drapes well, tends to stretch unless modified	Poor to fair	Fair to good	Fair to good	Burns like paper unless treated	Washable or Dry clean depending on label

Weave

The fabric weave refers to the method or type of loom used to weave the weft and warp yarns together to produce the woven length of fabric. The many complex and different methods of weaving create specific types of fabric.

Plain weave: Each filling yarn passes over and under each warp yarn with each row alternating.

Satin weave: The face of the fabric consists of only the warp or the weft threads, giving the fabric a very smooth and lustrous surface.

Twill weave: Similar to plain weave, but the warp yarns skip at regular predetermined intervals, creating a diagonal rib in the weave.

Basket weave: Two or more warp yarns cross alternately side by side, with two or more filling yarns. It resembles a plaited basket.

Jacquard weave: Intricate patterns created on a Jacquard loom.

Rib weave: A plain weave type formed with heavy yarns in the warp, or filling direction.

Dobby weave: A decorative weave characterized by small designs or geometric figures being woven in the fabric structure.

Leno weave: The warp yarns are arranged in pairs. One yarn is twisted

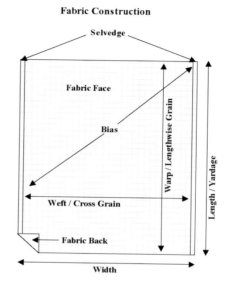

Fabric Construction

Selvedge · Fabric Face · Bias · Warp / Lengthwise Grain · Length / Yardage · Weft / Cross Grain · Fabric Back · Width

around the other between picks of the filling yarn.

Oxford weave: A group of fabrics made with modified plain weave or basket weave. Usually made for shirting materials.

Cut pile: The face of the fabric is composed of cut ends of pile yarn, such as in velvet or velveteen.

Uncut pile: A pile of yarns consisting of loops, as in terry cloth.

Double knit: A type of circular knit fabric of double thickness.

Chenille: Fabric of soft wool, silk, cotton, or rayon yarn with protruding pile.

Coloring

Coloring is the process of applying pigments or dyes to fibers or finished fabrics using dyeing or printing processes.

Dyeing Methods

Piece Dyeing: The dyeing of woven lengths of finished fabric.

Solution Dyeing: The addition of dyes or pigments to the viscose solution that forms the extruded fiber. This process locks the color into the fiber, making it resistant to sun fading.

Stock or Fiber Dyeing: The dyeing of natural fibers before they are spun into yarn.

Yarn Dyeing: The application of dye to a finished length of yarn.

Printing Methods

Hand Printing: Batik, silk screen, stenciling, hand painting, or block printing.

Semiautomated and Rotary Screen Printing: Multiple semiautomated screens are used to apply multiple colors and patterns to the fabric face.

Roller Printing: A series of engraved copper rollers apply the color and pattern to the fabric.

Finishes

Fabric finishes are treatments or processes that complete a textile. The average fabric used in interior design has a combination of six finishes. Finishes that are applied to the fabric after it has been colored fall into two categories: standard and decorative.

Standard: Standard finishes add to a fabric's durability or lend it the ability to perform in a certain way. The most common of these finishes are:

Antibacterial: Suppresses mold and mildew and delays decay; applicable in health care.

Antistatic: Inhibits static.

Fabric care: Makes the fabric easier to care for, such as permanent press or wrinkle resistance.

Flame retardant: Slows the rate of ignition and flame spread and helps the fabric to self-extinguish.

Insulating: Usually a foam product is sprayed onto the back of the fabric to insulate from temperature or noise; e.g., insulated blackout lining.

Laminating: The process of joining two fabrics together; e.g., vinyl laminated with a knit backing in upholstery fabric.

Mothproofing: Protects from insect infestation.

Soil repellent: Protects the surface of the fabric from dirt and stains.

Water absorbent: Improves the absorbent qualities of the fabric.

Water repellent: Makes the fabric less water absorbing; e.g., patio furniture upholstery fabric.

Decorative: Decorative finishes create a specific decorative look or improve the feel or appearance of fabric. The most common of these finishes are:

Antiwrinkling: Makes the fabric more wrinkle resistant and helps it retain its shape.

Brightening: Brightens the colors in the fabric and makes them last longer.

Calendaring: A starch, glaze, or resin is forced deep into the fabric with a heavy roller to achieve a specific effect.

Chintz: A calendared finish that uses a glaze to add shine to a fabric.

De-lustering: Removes the shiny finish from fabrics in which it would not be appropriate.

Embossing: Uses an engraved roller to calendar the fabric, producing a permanent three-dimensional design.

Etching or burn-out: Uses an acid compound to burn or etch the fiber to reveal a sheer pattern.

Flocking: A decorative pattern is made with small fibers bonded to the fabric.

French wax: The shiniest, highest-gloss finish.

Lustering: A method that gives a luster to the fabric without the addition of resins or starches.

Moiré: Embossing that leaves a watermark pattern on the fabric.

Napping: The fabric's fibers are brushed to create a fuzzy finish or short pile.

Panné: An embossing technique presses down the fibers of a velour or velvet in a particular direction to create a pattern.

Plisse: An acid is applied to cause the yarns to pucker into a plaid or all-over wrinkle.

Post finishing: Some specialty finishes can be applied to fabrics after they have been manufactured. These include flame retardant, lamination, paper, foam, and latex backing.

Resin: Resin is applied as a glaze or as a base for waterproofing or soil repellent finishing.

PATTERN

The pattern can be woven into the fabric, as with a jacquard weave, or it can be printed onto it. In the case of a combination print, a woven jacquard pattern in the fabric is covered with a printed pattern on top.

Pattern Repeat: The repeat denotes the size of the print and the repetition and should be appropriate for the scale of the length of the treatment. Avoid using large repeats on small areas; they should be used on large areas with a wide exposure.

Pattern Match: The pattern ends and begins at the selvage edge of the fabric, usually cut in half. Make sure that all patterns match across the widths of the item and at the leading edges of panels, as well as in all other applications of the fabric in the room.

Pattern Direction: The pattern is woven into or printed onto the fabric. The standard direction is parallel to the length of the fabric. If the pattern is "railroaded," it runs perpendicular to the length of the fabric.

Types of Pattern

Small/Mini Patterns: Tiny all-over motifs are often seen by the eye as texture, not pattern. They can be used to blend colors and give the illusion of tactile dimension.

Large Patterns: Large motifs will cause a space to look smaller. They create a focal point and command attention. Large patterns appear to advance visually.

Directional Patterns: Stripes, checks, and plaids create a directional flow. They can be manipulated to provide horizontal, vertical, and diagonal emphasis. These patterns must be matched precisely and can be subject to pattern drifting or weave warping.

Optical Patterns: Patterns such as moirés, geometrics, and dots can create the illusion of movement. These patterns can imitate depth, projection, and three-dimensional texture.

Random Pattern: A pattern that has an asymmetrical or nonbalanced configuration. This can range from a large-scale floral bouquet to a contemporary squiggle pattern. These patterns create excitement and energy. Although they appear random, they possess a horizontal repeat that must be matched.

Regulated Pattern: A pattern is considered regulated when it repeats on a regular basis, either horizontally or vertically. This can include stripes, plaids, checks, or geometrics. These patterns provide structure and formality to a design.

Pattern Direction

Railroaded Pattern: The pattern runs horizontally from selvage to selvage. Railroaded patterns are used primarily for upholstery and can make pattern matching a challenge.

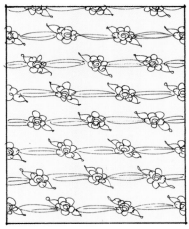

Railroaded

Typical Pattern: The pattern runs vertically along the length of the fabric. This is typical for most drapery and upholstery fabrics.

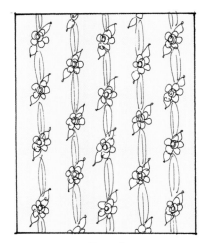

Typical

Pattern Dominance: Many fabrics have a motif that includes a primary and secondary pattern. It is important to choose which one you want to highlight when plotting your pattern placement.

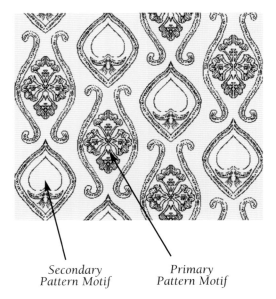

*Secondary
Pattern Motif*   *Primary
Pattern Motif*

Pattern Repeats and Pattern Matching

Vertical and Horizontal Repeats: The distance between the full repeat of the pattern on the face of the fabric going in either a horizontal or vertical direction.

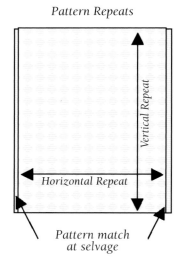

Pattern Repeats

Vertical Repeat

Horizontal Repeat

*Pattern match
at selvage*

Print-on-Print Repeats: In fabrics such as woven damasks, which have a printed pattern on the face, there are two patterns that must be matched: the base pattern of the damask as well as the printed pattern. Failing to match the ground pattern and printed pattern will result in an off-matched ground pattern that will be obvious when constructed into bedding.

Small-Pattern Repeats: Very often a fabric with a small pattern that seems to have little or no repeat will have a larger full-length repeat. This can result in a striping effect when it is used in length. The only way to check for this patterning is to inspect a generous length of the fabric.

Balanced Pattern Match: The pattern that is repeated is a whole motif that is balanced on both selvage edges of the fabric. In this case, the seam runs through the field of the fabric or a secondary pattern when joining cuts, and there are no seams running through the primary motif.

Halved Pattern Match: The pattern that is to be repeated is cut in half at each selvage edge of the fabric. In this case, the seam will run through the center of the primary motif when joining cuts.

Half-Drop Repeat or Drop Match Pattern: The pattern on one selvage edge of the fabric panel will not match straight across to the other edge. The pattern on the right edge of the fabric will be half its height up or down from the left edge. Therefore, additional fabric is needed to match the pattern, as half of the repeat is wasted in making matching cuts.

Straight Repeat or Straight Match Pattern: The pattern is positioned in a straight line across the width of the fabric and is the same on the right side of the fabric as on the left.

Half-Drop Pattern Repeat   *Straight Match Pattern Repeat*

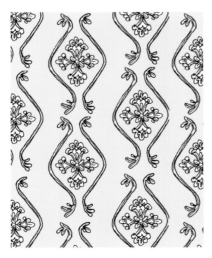

Fabric Widths

Knowing the accurate bolt width and usable width of the fabric you are using is key to estimating the correct amount of yardage you will need.

Bolt Width: The measure of the fabric from selvage edge to selvage edge.

Usable Width: The measure of the fabric from selvage allowance to selvage allowance.

Selvage Allowance: The portion of the fabric from the selvage edge inward to the line on which the pattern match is centered. This line is where the seam must be placed in order to match the pattern properly. The fabric past that line to the selvage edge is rough and is not meant to be seen.

While the majority of home décor fabrics are woven at 54" wide, there are many exceptions. The selvage allowance, or unusable edge of the fabric, can also vary in width as much as $1/2$" to $1^1/2$". Some woven fabrics, such as rayon and silk velvets, have a very wide selvage edge that must be subtracted from the usable width of the fabric. It is important to know what the "usable" width of your fabric is after selvage and seam allowances are deducted.

Typical Widths

Standard drapery and upholstery fabric . . . . .54" wide
Drapery sheers . . . . .54"–60"–106" wide
Extra-wide drapery sheers . . . . .108"–118"–126" wide
Extra-wide jacquards . . . . .114"–116" wide
Some high-end silks and linens . . . . .42"–45" wide
Dress-making fabric . . . . .45"–58" and 60" wide
Quilting cottons . . . . .45" wide
Knits . . . . .60" wide
Drapery lining . . . . .48"–54"–60" wide
Extra-wide drapery lining . . . . .115"–126" wide

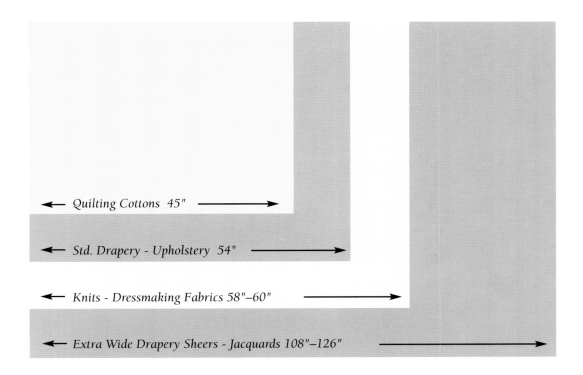

← Quilting Cottons 45" →

← Std. Drapery - Upholstery 54" →

← Knits - Dressmaking Fabrics 58"–60" →

← Extra Wide Drapery Sheers - Jacquards 108"–126" →

LINING

Lining is used in a variety of applications in designing bedding. It is a tool that allows you to manipulate the fabric in your treatment and add performance.

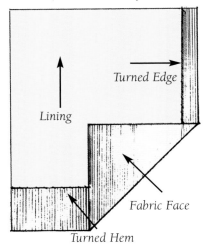

Turned Edge

Lining

Fabric Face

Turned Hem

❧ Lining adds body, volume, and thermal stability to fabrics.

❧ It protects the face fabric from slipping and puckering.

❧ It stabilizes fabric and reduces droop.

❧ It reduces color bleed-through.

❧ It provides a clean, finished, professional look.

❧ It adds stability and strength.

Types of Lining

White polyester-cotton lining: This is standard in most workrooms unless otherwise specified. The degree of quality and pliability can change dramatically from vendor to vendor. Get a sample of your workroom's "standard lining" to see if it is acceptable to you. White lining keeps the color true on the face fabric.

Ivory or cream-colored lining: This has a softer look than white and can subtly change the color of the face fabric.

Self-lining or colored linings: Use this when any part of the lining can be seen. Remember to consider the view of the treatment from all positions. In many cases, using self-lining or contrasting lining can make the item reversible and add to its versatility.

French or black lining: This can be used as a lining or interlining for a blackout look or to eliminate color and pattern bleed-through. When using a light-colored face fabric, black lining can turn the face fabric slightly gray.

Blackout lining: This is used to achieve maximum light blocking. Pin or needle holes can show through the treatment during daylight hours. Glue baste the widths of blackout lining together before sewing to avoid pin holes. In the past, blackout lining was stiff, heavy, and hard to work with. Many vendors are offering a new breed of soft, pliable blackout and thermal linings that have a wonderful hand and are easy to sew with. These are a good solution when draping a window that is behind or next to the bed.

Thermal suede lining: This is heavier than regular lining and has a rubber backing for insulation. This is another good option if draping a window behind the bed.

Lining color should be consistent on all items in the ensemble.

INTERLINING

Interlining is a layer of specialty fabric placed between the face fabric and the lining of the treatment. In recent years, the practice of interlining has become very popular.

There are many reasons to use an interlining:

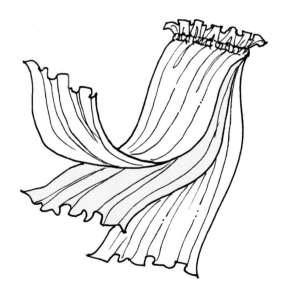

- ⚜ To add richness and fullness to your design.

- ⚜ To prolong the life of the item.

- ⚜ To add a thermal layer to the item for reducing cold or heat.

- ⚜ To create a blackout effect without using stiff blackout lining.

- ⚜ To add bulk and volume to a thin fabric.

- ⚜ To stabilize a loosely woven fabric.

- ⚜ To eliminate pattern or color bleed-through.

- ⚜ To impart body, strength, and stability to silks.

Types of Interlining

Most interlinings are 100-percent cotton goods that have been felted or flannelled. Heavyweight and flannelled interlinings can substitute for batting in thin coverlets or quilts. They are also suitable for quilted facings on pillow fronts.

- English bump is a thick but soft interlining. It imparts a fluffy, heavy look to the fabric.

- Heavyweight flannel is heavier than regular interlining, but not as heavy as table felt.

- Table felt is a very thick, heavy interlining. It imparts a heavy, stiff look to the fabric.

- Lightweight interlining is used in valances, swags, cascades, and tails.

How to Use Interlining

- Always interline silk. Use bump for a thick, fluffy look or lightweight interlining for a crisper, lighter look.

- Let interlining rest for twenty-four hours after it is cut before you begin fabrication. Interlining stretches when it is rolled on the tube at the mill. It returns to original size when unrolled and allowed to rest.

- Do not seam interlining. Join the selvages by overlapping to reduce bulk.

- There are many new types of interlinings and dual-purpose linings available today that can address any particular challenge you may face when constructing your design. Check with your supplier or workroom, or consult the resource directory at the back of this book to familiarize yourself with the many options available.

Key Fabric Terms

Bias cut: Fabric is cut at a 45-degree angle to the fabric weave. This cut of fabric has give to it, allowing swags to drape better and enabling cording to hug curves. Prints should be checked before cutting on the bias. Some upright prints can be cut on the bias and look great; others can't.

C.O.M.: (aka COM) Customer's own material.

Crinoline (aka buckram): A heavily sized or stiff fabric used as a foundation for pleats in draperies.

Crosswise grain (aka fillers, woof, weft): The threads of a woven fabric that run perpendicular to the selvages. The fabric has a slight give in the crosswise grain.

Cut allowance: The amount of fabric added to finished measurements for hems and headings.

Cut width: The complete amount of fabric needed for treatment width, including hems, and/or any other allowances.

Drapability: The ability of a certain fabric to hang in pleasing folds.

Drop match: A drop match is one in which the pattern will NOT line up perfectly to be seamed at the selvage when the width is cut straight across by the print. The pattern repeat does not match until halfway down the vertical pattern repeat. Therefore, additional yardage is required. Add one-half pattern repeat per cut. This is commonly found in fabrics that coordinate with wallpaper. It is usually (but not always) designated in the sample books as a drop match.

Dye lot: A batch of fabric printed at the same time. Each time a new printing is done the fabric is classified with a new dye lot. Fabrics from different dye lots can vary in color. If color matching is important for your project, always get a cutting of the dye lot you will order from.

Fabrication: The process of manufacturing raw goods into a finished product.

Face fabric: The decorative fabric on a treatment that "faces" into the room. The lining is behind it.

Facing: A piece of fabric is stitched to a raw edge and turned to the back side to form a finished edge. The diagonals of jabots or cascades are sometimes faced to show a contrast in the angles.

Finish: Product applied to fabric as a protection against watermarks and fading.

Flame-retardant fabric: Fabric that will not burn. It can be inherently flame retardant, which means the actual fiber from which it was made is a flame retardant fiber, e.g., polyester, or it can be treated to become flame retardant, which usually changes the fibers and makes the fabric stiff.

French seam: A way of stitching fabric together with the seam hidden from view. Used on sheer fabrics.

Grain: The direction of threads in a fabric. It can be crosswise or lengthwise.

Hand: The feel of the fabric.

Half-drop match: One in which the pattern itself drops down half the repeat on the horizontal but does match at the selvage. It is a concern when planning cuts for horns, pelmets, empire swags, box pleats, etc., when the same design or motif is needed on each piece.

Lengthwise grain (aka warp): The threads in a woven fabric that run parallel to the selvages. Fabrics are stronger along the lengthwise grain.

Nap: A texture or design that runs in one direction, such as corduroy and velvet. A fabric with a nap will often look different when viewed from various directions. When using a fabric with a nap, all pieces must be cut and sewn together so the nap runs in only one direction.

Pattern repeat (repeat): The distance between any given point in a design and where that exact point first appears again. Repeats can be horizontal or vertical.

Pillowcase (aka pillowslip): The technique where face fabric and lining fabric are seamed together, usually with a 1/2" seam, then turned and pressed so the seam becomes the very edge of the item.

Poplin: Cotton fabric with corded surface.

Railroad: To turn fabric so the selvage runs across the treatment instead of up and down. Sheer fabric of 118" width is made to be used this way so that pinch pleats are put in across the selvage end instead of across the cut end. This can eliminate seams on some treatments.

Right side: The printed side of the fabric that is used as the finished side of an item. The right side generally has the most color and the most finished look to it.

Seam: The join where two pieces of fabrics are sewn together.

Seam allowance: An extra amount of fabric used when joining fabric.

Selvage (also selvedge): The tightly woven edge on the length of the fabric that holds the fabric together.

Straight grain: The lengthwise threads of the fabric, running parallel to the selvages.

Tabling: Measuring a treatment and marking it to the finished length before the final finishing.

Turn of cloth: The minute ease of fabric that is lost from making a fold.

Warp and weft: Refers to the direction of threads in a fabric. Warp threads run the length of the fabric. Warp threads are crossed by the weft threads, which run from selvage to selvage across the width of the fabric.

Width: Refers to a single width of fabric (from selvage to selvage). Several widths of fabric are sewn together to make a panel of drapery.

Wrong side: The back of the fabric. This is the less finished side that may have stray threads or a rougher look to it.

Bedding Basics

Designing for the bedroom requires specific knowledge of many key elements that are unique to bedding.

- Bed Types, Construction, and Sizes

- Mattress Types and Sizes

- Typical Bedding Sizes and Yardage Requirements

- Bed Linens

- Decorative Bedding Design and Construction

- Quilting and Batting Options

- Pillow Insert Options

- Bed Drapery Design and Construction

- Bed Canopy Design and Construction

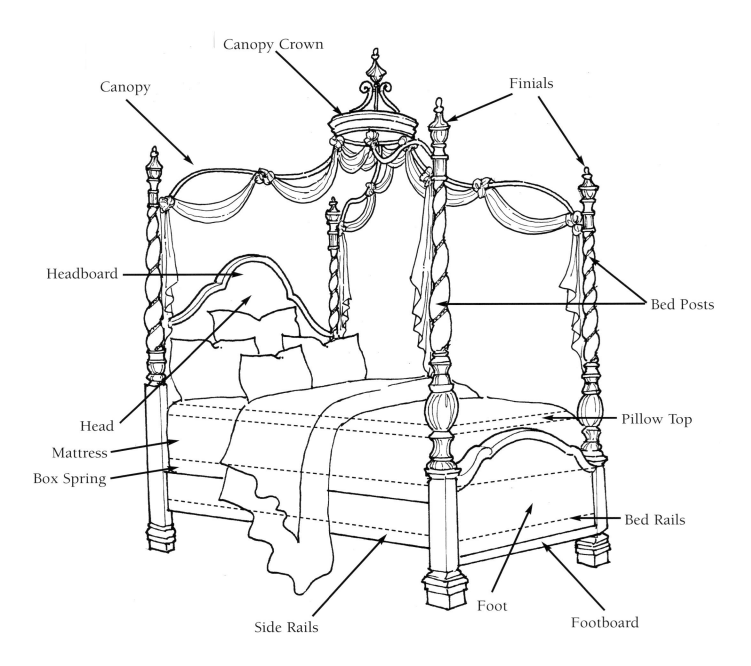

Canopy Crown

Canopy

Finials

Headboard

Bed Posts

Head

Mattress

Pillow Top

Box Spring

Bed Rails

Side Rails

Foot

Footboard

Anatomy of the Bed

The structural elements of the bed have changed very little since the modern raised bed was made popular.

Head: The end of the bed where the head rests.

Foot: The end of the bed where the feet rest.

Canopy: A structural frame suspended on top of the bedposts and usually secured by the insertion of the bed finials into holes at the top of the posts. A canopy can also be independent of the bed frame and can be hung from the ceiling.

Canopy crown: The apex of a raised canopy frame.

Bed posts: Vertical posts placed on either side of the headboard and footboard that extend from the floor to the top of the headboard, footboard, or canopy.

> **Head posts**—the bed posts at the head of the bed
> **Foot posts**—the bed posts at the foot of the bed

Headboard: A solid or openwork panel at the head of the bed.

Footboard: A solid or openwork panel at the foot of the bed.

Side rails: Rails that extend from the headboard to the footboard on each side of the bed in order to support the box spring and mattress.

Bed rails: Flat support rails that rest on top of the side rails, perpendicular to the bed rails, in order to add additional support for the box spring and mattress.

Center supports: Additional feet or leg supports attached to the bed rails to add center support for split box springs or large mattresses.

Finials: Decorative end caps for the bed posts, used to hold a canopy in place on canopy beds.

Mattress Facts

Mattress technology is constantly changing and, as a result, so are the dimensions and features available. Some key facts to consider are the following:

- Twin, full, and queen mattress sets have a single box spring, while king and super king have a split box spring.

- Many mattresses have pillow tops on both sides and can be flipped. A current trend is to have a deep pillow top on one side only or a removable pillow top that can be switched from side to side when you flip the mattress.

- Super king and ultra king mattresses are split into two halves. A flexible spine fills the gap between mattresses, and a single pillow top covers both halves.

- Many mattress sets are extremely heavy, e.g., memory foam units. Consider bedding designs that do not require the movement of the mattress to make the bed when these mattresses are present.

- Adjustable or customizable mattresses such as Sleep Number beds or automated, motorized beds are popular, especially with the aging-in-place and baby boom generations. Consider the unique challenges that these type of beds present.

Typical Mattress Sizes

Common Mattress Sizes in the United States

TYPE	LENGTH	WIDTH
Crib	52"	27"
Daybed	75"	39"
Twin	75"	39"
Twin X-Long (Dorm)	80"	39"
Full (Double)	75"	54"
Queen	80"	60"
Cal Queen	84"	60"
King (Standard/Eastern)	80"	76"
Cal King	84"	72"
Super King	98"	80"

Common Mattress Sizes in the United Kingdom

TYPE	LENGTH	WIDTH
Single	75"	36"
Double	75"	54"
King	78"	60"
Super King	78"	72"

Common Mattress Depths

TYPE	LENGTH
Standard	7"–9"
Double	10"–15"
Extra Deep	16"–22"
Double Pillow Tom	22"–26"

Bed Linens

Bed linens, or bed sheets, include the following practical components:

- Fitted Bottom Sheet
- Flat Top Sheet
- Pillowcases for Face Pillows
- Pillow Covers for Face Pillows
- Mattress Pad or Cover
- Feather Bed
- Mattress Topper

Linens and sheets are constructed to be very durable and long lasting, as they are washed frequently and are used in a high wear-and-tear capacity. At the same time, it is vital for them to be as comfortable as possible for the user. Selecting sheets and bed linens today can be a complicated process due to the plentiful options available.

The two key factors in determining the quality and superiority of one sheet versus another are the type of fiber used and the thread count. *(Content refers to the type of fiber used to weave the yarns that are woven into cloth for the sheet in question.)*

Fibers Used in Sheets and Linens

100-percent cotton: Most cotton fibers are generally about 1" long or shorter. Cotton is available all over the world and is a plentiful renewable resource. Cotton sheets are cool to the touch and do not retain heat. They release moisture and are easily cleaned. Cotton is generally considered the most comfortable fabric used to fabricate bed linens.

Egyptian cotton: The king of all cottons, this variety produces a longer individual fiber, at about $1^{3}/_{8}$" long, which makes for a stronger cloth with a smoother hand. Many of the finest linens in the world are made from 100-percent Egyptian cotton. Egyptian cotton is the name for the variety of these specific plants, which are grown only in Egypt.

Supima cotton: Grown in the southwestern United States and other locations, this extra-long staple cotton boasts the second-longest fibers, at over 1". It also produces a very smooth, strong cloth that is a close second to Egyptian cotton. The name supima refers to the grade of the cotton fibers used.

Pima cotton: A long-fiber cotton that produces superior cloth, it is preferable to standard cotton but not as luxurious as Egyptian or supima. The name pima refers to the grade of the cotton fibers used.

Cotton-polyester blends: Less-expensive sheets are sometimes made with cotton-polyester blends. These sheets tend to wear unevenly and pill on the surface. They do not release moisture as well as cotton and are not as easily cleaned. On the positive side, most cotton-poly blends are generally wrinkle free.

Linen: One of the oldest natural fibers used to produce cloth, linen has also been a long-standing fiber used for bedding, hence the term "bed linens." Linen can be very soft to the touch and comfortable if it is processed properly. Linen sheets used to be the norm in European countries but are giving way to high-quality cottons. Many very high-end bed linens are constructed of linen fiber.

Silk: Silk sheets are a luxurious but not very practical choice. Silk fabric wrinkles and absorbs moisture and body oils and is difficult to clean.

Sateen: This term refers to a weave of fabric, not a fiber. Most sateen sheets are made of 100-percent cotton yarn woven so that one vertical thread is woven over four or more horizontal threads and then under one horizontal thread. Because it has more threads on the surface, it reflects more light and has a greater sheen.

Jersey: Fabric that is knitted rather than woven. Jersey can be made of 100-percent cotton fibers or may contain other fibers such as polyester, lycra, or spandex that are inherently flexible to add stretch to the fabric.

Flannel: Usually produced using 100-percent cotton yarns that have been brushed to produce a very soft, fuzzy hand, which helps to retain warmth. Flannel can pill over time and wear unevenly at high-stress or high wear-and-tear points.

Combed cotton: Cotton that has gone through a process in which the fibers are combed to remove the shorter fibers and all the fibers are put in the same alignment, making for a softer yarn and fabric. Most high-end cotton sheets are combed.

Percale: A particular weave of fabric that is plain, or balanced. This means that the vertical threads, called the warp threads, and the horizontal threads, called the weft threads, cross over each other one at a time in an even, balanced manner. Percale can be 100-percent cotton or a cotton-and-polyester blend. In many cases, a resin finish is applied to the face of the fabric to prevent wrinkling.

Thread Count

This the second key factor in choosing the quality of bed linens. Thread count refers to the number of individual threads woven into one square inch of fabric. The common perception is that the higher the thread count of the fabric, the finer the thread that was used to weave it. Finer threads are thought to produce a softer, stronger, smoother surface on the fabric. The reality is that finer threads are not always as strong as thicker threads and may not last as long. Fine threads woven with long fibers are the best combination. When looking for the finest linens and bed sheets, take notice of a high thread count, but also make sure they are made using a long-fiber cotton such as Egyptian, Supima, or Pima. The combination of a moderately high thread count (more than 300 threads per inch) and high-quality cotton makes for a superior sheet. Ultra-high-thread-count sheets can sometimes be inferior to moderate-thread-count sheets produced with premium fibers.

How to Measure for Bedding

Accurate measuring is essential to produce beautiful bedding.

✦ Set up the bed frame as it will be used by the owner. Make sure it is put together properly and that the mattress in place is the one that will be used.

✦ Make up the bed as it will be used. If the owner will be adding a mattress pad or feather bed, or if they use a heavy duvet or comforter, put it in place. These items can change the dimensions of the bed considerably and must be taken into consideration.

✦ Every mattress has very different dimensions, so do not rely on so-called "standard" measurements. Carefully measure the mattress to be used.

- Always use a cloth measuring tape to measure for bedding. It will drape accurately over the mattress and linens to give you a true measurement. Tape two cloth measuring tapes together to create a single tape capable of spanning the width and drop of the bed, or create your own using a strip of fabric banding marked with inches.

- Allow for take-up when specifying a quilt or duvet. Take-up can vary greatly, from 2" to 12" in width and 2" to 12" in length. It is important that you check with your workroom or refer to the manufacturer for the proper take-up allowance for each specific item.

- List all measurements in total inches, not feet and inches.

- Always measure left to right so you are reading the tape measure in the upright position.

- Every bed is unique and will pose a specific set of challenges that you must address.

- Take a careful look at the mattress and bed frame to determine what questions you need to answer, such as the following:

  - Will the box spring be exposed?
  - Do you need to specify a cover for it?
  - Do you need to split the corners of your bed cover to accommodate bed posts?
  - Do you need to add ties to the split corners so they can be closed after being wrapped around the bed posts?
  - Should you specify boxed corners?
  - How will the bed frame affect your bed skirt? Can you use a continuous skirt with decking or do you need to use a pieced skirt attached directly to the bed frame?
  - Do you need a skirt at all?

- Measure twice, order once!

Common Bedding Dimensions

Measurements vary depending on the manufacturer.

Common Fitted Sheet Dimensions

TYPE	LENGTH	WIDTH
Twin	76"	39"
Twin X-Long (Dorm)	80"	39"
Full (Double)	75"	54"
Queen	80"	60"
King	80"	78"
Cal King	72"	84"

Common Comforter Dimensions

TYPE	LENGTH	WIDTH
Twin	86"	68"
Full (Double)	88"	88"
Queen	94"	86"
King	110"	96"
Daybed	95"–106"	51"–60"

Common Blanket Dimensions

TYPE	LENGTH	WIDTH
Twin	66"	90"
Full (Double)	90"	90"
Queen	90"	90"
King	108"	90"
Throw	50"	60"

Common Duvet Dimensions

TYPE	LENGTH	WIDTH
Twin	66"	88"
Full, Queen	88"	88"
King	104"	88"

Common Bed Pillow Sizes

TYPE	LENGTH	WIDTH
Standard	20"	26"
Queen	20"	30"
King	20"	36"
Euro	27"	27"

Common Decorative Pillow Sizes (in Inches)

SQUARE	RECTANGLE	CIRCLE	BOLSTER
12" x 12"	6" x 16"	12" Diam.	6" x 16"
14" x 14"	7" x 16"	14" Diam.	7" x 16"
16" x 16"	7" x 18"	16" Diam.	7" x 18"
18" x 18"	8" x 24"	18" Diam.	8" x 24"
20" x 20"	9" x 24"	20" Diam.	9" x 24"
22" x 22"	9" x 38"	22" Diam.	9" x 38"
24" x 24"		24" Diam.	
26" x 26"		26" Diam.	
28" x 30"		28" Diam.	
30" x 30"		30" Diam.	

Types of Pillows

There are many different varieties of pillows and pillow inserts available today. Thanks to new technologies, man-made fibers, and space-age foams, there is a pillow for every application. Bed pillows and throw pillows are essentially the same and are only distinguished as belonging in one category or another by their shape, size, and function.

Pillow inserts are grouped into two categories, natural and man-made.

Natural

- Premium white goose down
- Duck down
- Feather-down combinations
- Pillow-in-pillow combinations
- Wool
- Organic all-cotton

Terms and Facts Related to Natural Fills

Down: Refers to the small fibrous clusters that grow under the feathers in geese and ducks. These fibers possess unique characteristics and an appearance that resembles a mature dandelion cluster, which makes down a perfect fiber for pillow fill. Down has a superior loft that allows a pillow to retain its shape and trap air between clusters that provide insulation. Down releases excess moisture that can build up in the pillow, allowing the pillow to "breathe." Down is cool in the summer and warm in the winter. It is considered to be a superior filling agent in pillows as well as comforters, duvets, and upholstery.

Goose down: The down clusters harvested from geese are larger and possess more loft than the down from any other bird. This makes them a superior choice for down fill. Within this category, there are standards that grade the down as superior.

- Large individual clusters.
- Lightness of pigment, with white being the best.
- The term *fill power* is used to denote the quality of the down. The larger and stronger the cluster, the more fill power it possesses.

Hungarian goose down: Widely considered to be the finest quality down clusters, they are larger than the norm and are mostly pure white in color.

Duck down: The clusters of down harvested from ducks are smaller and more coarse than those of geese. Most duck down is collected from ducks raised for food, so they are slaughtered at a young age and the down is not grown to full maturity. Duck down is considered a low-quality down and is sometimes mixed with goose down.

Eider down: This is considered to be the ultimate in duck down. It is from a particular species of duck that produces the largest down clusters.

Feather-down combinations: For most applications, using 100-percent down fill is not appropriate. Down compacts with use and does not hold the shape of the pillow without constant fluffing. Most pillow forms are filled with a combination of down and feathers. The presence of feathers in the mix adds weight, stability, and bulk to the pillow form.

Within the industry, there are several standard mixes available:

% OF FEATHERS	% OF DOWN
0	100
50	50
25	75
90	10

When choosing the mix for your pillow forms, know that the higher the percentage of down to the percentage of feathers, the lighter and fluffier the pillows will be. For most applications, a 25:75 down-to-feather ratio is appropriate. Feather-and-down pillow forms must be covered with tightly woven pillow ticking to prevent the down from "leaking" out of the seams. Feather quills can also poke through the ticking and can be an uncomfortable intrusion to the outside of the pillow. The higher the concentration of feathers in your mix, the higher the occurrence of quill leaking. Be sure the forms you purchase have leak-proof ticking to prevent these problems.

Pillow-in-pillow combinations: New to the market in recent years are combination bed pillows that are constructed with an independently wrapped core of mostly feathers. This core is then encased in a separate wrapping of a higher down count. This feature provides for more weight and support at the center of the pillow while maintaining the light fluffy feel on the outside because of the high volume of down.

Wool-filled: Pillows constructed with 100-percent wool fill are hypoallergenic and very popular with people who seek an organic or green product for their bedding. One of the unique features of wool fill is that it wicks moisture away from the body, keeping your skin dry and comfortable. The wool also provides additional warmth.

Organic cotton: For those with multiple chemical sensitivities (MCS) who seek an allergy-free pillow, organic cotton might be the answer. It contains no bleach, dyes, or polymers and is completely nontoxic and hypoallergenic.

Man-Made Inserts

Polyester fillers: The most widely used pillow inserts are made from a variety of polyester fibers. There are many different brand names, depending on the manufacturer. These inserts are machine washable and cost less than most natural-fill inserts. New technology has made it possible to manufacture polyester fibers that have a loft and feel somewhat similar to down inserts. Quality and durability vary considerably from manufacturer to manufacturer.

Memory foam: Marketed under many different brand names, this product is dense foam that molds itself to the contours of your body and head as you sleep. It has the ability to return to its original shape every time your body weight is removed from the surface. It literally remembers its own profile. When designing for a memory foam pillow or mattress, keep in mind that they are very heavy and cumbersome.

Latex: Made from natural rubber, latex pillows are hypoallergenic, antimicrobial, mildew proof, and dust mite resistant. They provide excellent ventilation to keep you cool and dry, and they will not compress or lose their shape.

Design Considerations

There are many key concerns that you should address before finalizing your design. It is much easier to remedy problems from the outset than to retrofit them later.

Function

Personal issues: Who is using the bed? Does the bedding need to be washed frequently, as in a child's room? Does the occupant have allergies that need to be addressed? Is the height or length of the mattress a problem?

Environmental: What is the temperature range between summer and winter extremes? How can the design address these needs? Are there drafts or air circulation issues in the room? Is light control an issue? Is there traffic or street noise that must be muffled?

Use: Do the occupants watch television in the bedroom? Do they work on the computer in bed? Does the bedroom serve a dual purpose, such as a home office or sitting room?

Electrical

- Is there enough power available on the bed wall and is it conveniently located?

- Are there "hot" plugs that are wired to be controlled by a wall switch for convenience in turning on and off table or wall lamps?

- Is there power available for items such as an electric blanket, alarm clock, or laptop computer?

- Where is the phone jack? Is it located next to the bed? Does it need to be moved?

Architectural

✦ Are there wall plates, plugs, thermostats, or switches located in areas that would conflict with your design?

✦ Are there wall or floor air registers that would be covered by the bed? Is there a radiator?

✦ Are there ceiling air registers or returns that would interfere with a canopy or corona? Will they create unwanted drafts over the bed?

✦ Is there a ceiling fan? How will it affect the bedding design?

✦ Are there light fixtures on the ceiling and how will they affect your design?

✦ Does the room have crown molding or wall panels that must be taken into consideration?

Structural

✦ What is the composition of the wall and ceiling construction? Will they support the weight of any elements you are planning to add, such as coronas or canopies? Are there wall studs in the appropriate places? Will they need to be reinforced?

✦ What is the width of hallways and doors and what obstacles are present along the route into the room? Will the bed fit?

✦ What is the height of the room? Is it sufficient? Remember that a bed frame must be tipped to enter a room. If you specify a four-poster or canopy bed that is very close to the height of the room, you might not be able to maneuver it into an upright position. Give yourself a generous amount of clearance. Remember to add an allowance for flooring if you are measuring new construction.

✦ King-sized beds and mattress sets can add up to a significant amount of weight. Is the bed to be placed upstairs? Will the floor structure support it?

✦ Where is the cable outlet? Is it in the proper place for optimal viewing of the television from the bed?

Lighting

This is a critical element in bedroom design. Whether the room calls for task or ambient light, the placement of light fixtures can have a significant effect on your design. Take into account the tasks your clients perform in the room, such as reading or watching television, and plan your lighting choices accordingly.

Basic Lighting Options

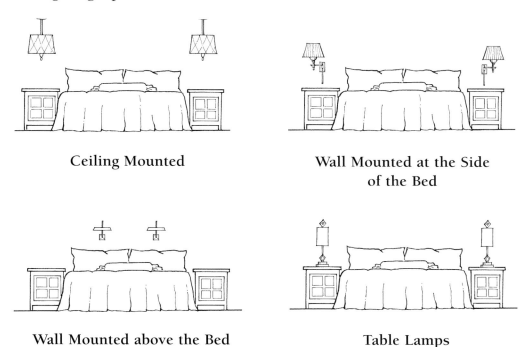

Ceiling Mounted

Wall Mounted at the Side
of the Bed

Wall Mounted above the Bed

Table Lamps

✦ Ceiling fixtures such as can, spot, or track lighting should be placed strategically to illuminate the bed or night stands.

✦ Consider installing dimmer switches for ceiling and wall fixtures to allow adjustable light levels.

✦ When designing the electrical plan for a bedroom or adding new electrical elements, consider including a "kill switch" at the side of the bed that can operate all of the lights in the room. This allows the user to turn off the lights without getting out of bed.

✦ Canopies, cornices, and large coronas can accommodate integrated lighting. This might be a good option for clients who do not want traditional light fixtures.

Key Bed Terms

Bed frame: A typical metal frame that supports the mattress and box spring independent of a headboard or footboard.

Bedposts: Decorative posts at the head or the head and foot of a bed. They may or may not support a canopy over the bed.

Bed rails: Wood or metal rails that rest on top of and between the two side rails in order to support a mattress and box spring.

Canopy: A framed rooflike structure suspended over a bed by the bed rails.

Casters: Wheels attached to a bedpost or feet.

Center supports: Structures placed underneath the bed rails for large beds to provide additional support at the center for a mattress and box spring.

Crown: The apex of a raised canopy.

Footboard: The solid or upholstered secondary focal point of a bed attached at or to the foot of the bed.

Foot: The portion of the bed at your feet. The foot is the base of the bed and usually faces out into the room.

Head: The portion of the bed that you lay your head on. It is usually the anchor of the bed and is placed against a wall or focal point.

Headboard: The solid or upholstered focal point of a bed attached at or to the head of the bed.

Platform: A boxed base for a mattress and sometimes a box spring and mattress.

Risers: Extensions made to raise a bed frame to add height to the bed.

Side rails: The support rails that anchor the headboard of a bed to the footboard.

Bed Skirts

A bed skirt is a length, or lengths, of fabric hung from the bed frame or over the box spring to the floor in order to cover the gap between the bed frame and the floor.

- The bed skirt's main function is to hide an unattractive bed frame and box spring.

- It prevents dust and debris from gathering under the bed.

- It prevents drafts under the bed.

- It hides storage space beneath the bed.

- It provides a decorative base for the mattress and bedding.

- It serves as an important element with which to introduce additional color, pattern, and style to your bedding.

- It can be used on beds with a standard metal frame or on complete or partial wood, iron, or upholstered beds.

- The bed skirt is also known as a dust ruffle, dust skirt, bed valance, or bed ruffle.

Construction Options

Each bed or mattress frame presents a different set of construction challenges that must be addressed when designing a bed skirt. Some of the key questions to be answered are the following:

✤ Is a skirt with attached decking or one with separate skirt panels the appropriate choice for your bed?

✤ What type of skirt and what design will best complement the other elements of your bedding ensemble?

✤ Will a single-layer or multiple-layer skirt be more effective?

✤ What shape is best for the hem of the skirt?

✤ What length is appropriate?

✤ What type of corner design will allow the skirt to hang properly?

✤ What style of corner will look best?

Basic Bed Skirt Components

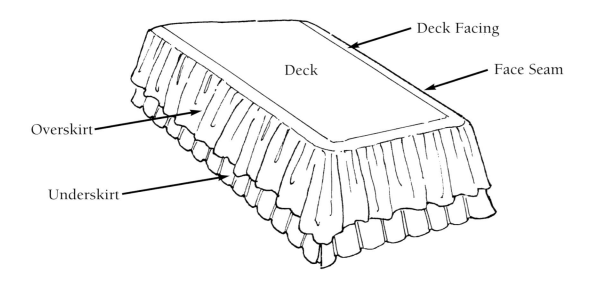

Corner Construction

Split corner with a separate flange attached beneath the face and end pieces at the corner to cover the gap

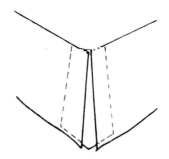

Split corner with a separate flange attached on top of the face and end pieces at the corner to cover the gap

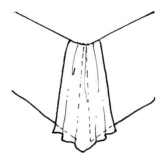

Continuous one-piece skirt with no split at the corner

Bed Skirts on Full Frame Beds

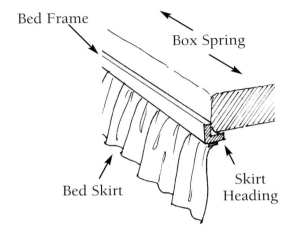

Bed Frame

Box Spring

Bed Skirt

Skirt Heading

When designing a skirt for a full frame bed, it is best to eliminate the decking and use separate panels that attach directly to the underside of the bed frame. On wood beds, the skirt can be stapled directly to the frame or attached with hook-and-loop tape. On metal beds, self-adhesive hook-and-loop tape can be used.

This method might leave a portion of the box spring exposed, and a box spring cover should be specified to coordinate with the bedding and bed skirt.

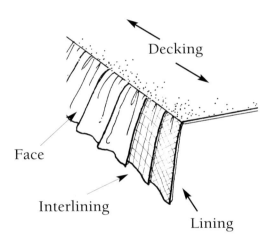

Decking

Face

Interlining

Lining

Lining: A couture-quality bed skirt should be interlined, if appropriate for the face fabric used, and lined to add body and provide a sumptuous outline to the skirt. Lining and interlining can add years of wear to a bed skirt.

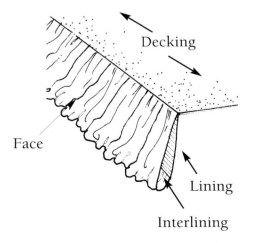

Decking

Face

Lining

Interlining

Puddled Skirts: Skirts that are meant to puddle on the floor can be sewn as a continuous loop. This allows the puddle to remain consistent and provides better wearability for the owner. Interlining should be used for silks and other lightweight fabrics.

Construction Tips for Bed Skirts

✦ To prevent slippage of the bed skirt, decking on the box spring secures it at the corners and at the foot of the box spring with iron-on hook-and-loop tape or slipcover screw pins. This will prevent the cover skirt decking from bunching or shifting while you are laying the mattress over the top of it.

✦ Consider using a complementary or contrasting fabric as lining to create a reversible bed skirt. This adds versatility and variety to your bedding options.

✦ For lightweight or sheer fabrics, specify string weight in the hem to control the hang of the skirt.

✦ Fabrics that are 100-percent polyester, and some poly-cotton linings, are conductors of static electricity. This problem might be compounded if the carpet under the bed contains polyester fibers.

✦ Side and end skirt panels can be made to attach separately with hook-and-loop tape sewn to the decking, for easy removal without having to lift the mattress. This can be useful in cases where the skirt might need to be washed frequently or the owner is not able to lift the mattress.

✦ The face fabric of the skirt should be used as a minimum 6" facing around the perimeter of the decking to avoid seeing the decking material exposed.

Important Bed Skirt Terms

Decking: A flat panel of fabric that serves as a base to which the side and end panels of a bed skirt are attached. The decking lays flat over the box spring, with the side and front panels draping over the box spring.

Easing in: Additional fullness is added to the width of a panel and then slightly and evenly gathered along the width of the heading to reduce the overall width of the panel to the appropriate size for the decking.

Memory stitch: A hand stitch that is placed at the back of a pleat to maintain its shape and position.

Overskirt: A separate or integrated skirt that is laid over the top of another skirt.

Overlay: A short separate or integrated skirt that is laid over the top of another longer skirt.

Panel: The side or end sections of a bed skirt.

Tacking in: Additional fullness is added to the width of a panel and then tacked into small pleats at strategic locations along the width of the heading to reduce the overall width of the panel to the appropriate size for the decking.

Underskirt: A separate or integrated skirt that is laid underneath another skirt.

Styles of Bed Skirts

Single Shirred Ruffle

This simple style can be made to look very sumptuous by adding interlining or a tulle underskirt for body. Increase the degree of fullness for solids, and decrease it for prints.

CD 100

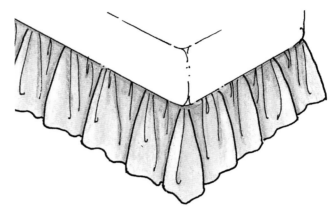

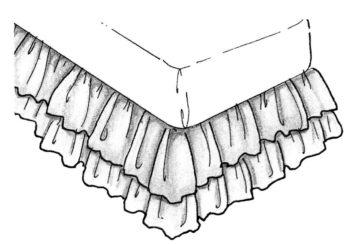

Shirred and Layered Double Ruffle

Multiple ruffles provide an opportunity to add bulk and richness to your design or to create contrast with different fabrics, colors, and patterns.

CD 101

Single Ruffle with a Border at the Hem

Use a contrasting fabric, ribbon, tape, or trim to add emphasis and dramatic effect to the edge of your skirt.

CD 102

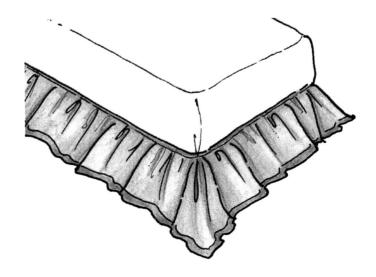

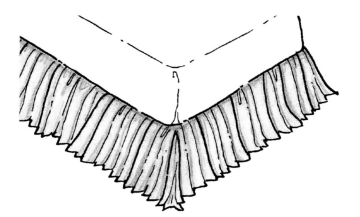

Accordion-Pleated Ruffle

These tight, crisp ruffles will set the tone for the rest of your bedding design. This look is most effective when using pre-pleated fabric or professionally ruffled yardage.
CD 103

Single Ruffle with Knotted Jabots at the Corners

Adding emphasis to the corners of the skirt can be just what a design needs to set it apart. Here, separate overlays at the corner are cinched in with a knotted sleeve to create the look of a jabot at each corner.
CD 104

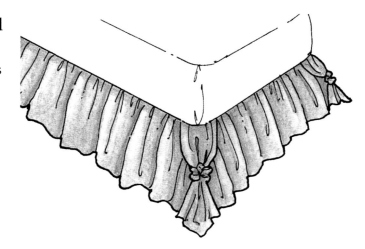

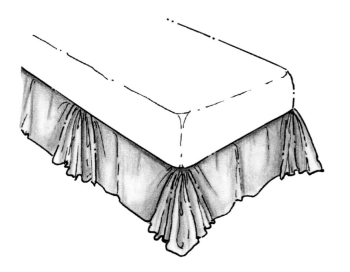

Flat Skirt with Shirred Inserts at the Side Centers and Corners

Visual interest and emphasis are created by shirring sections of fabric at the corners and center side panels of this flat-paneled skirt.
CD 105

Flat Skirt with a Boxed Corner

Flat skirts can benefit significantly from the addition of interlining or upholstery skirting to create a crisp look that will maintain its shape over time.

CD 106

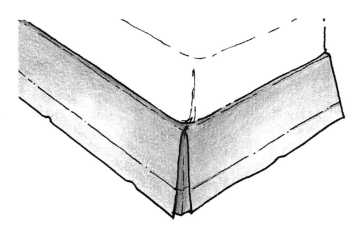

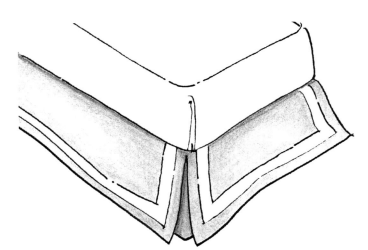

Flat Skirt with a Boxed Corner and Contrasting Border

Get creative with banding, using fabric, trim, tape, or ribbon. An infinite number of styles can be created by changing the shape, width, or number of bands.

CD 107

Wide Box-Pleated Skirt with Contrasting Trim

These wide box pleats are set off by the contrasting-stripe border. Use bullion or tassel fringe for a more formal look. Consider inserting a ruffle for a touch of whimsy.

CD 108

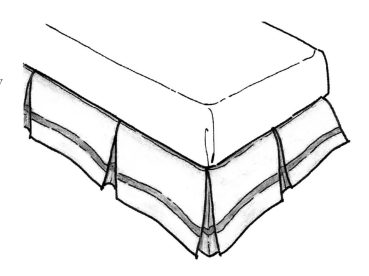

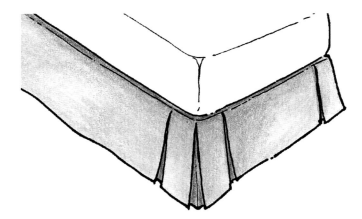

Flat Skirt with a Boxed Pleat at the Boxed Corner

Tailoring details can make a big impact in a simple design, such as on these box pleats that are placed at either side of the bed corner. This skirt would benefit from an underskirt with upholstery skirting to prevent sagging and to help maintain its crisp, sharp lines.

CD 109

Flat Skirt with an Overlay at the Corners

The hard lines of this flat skirt are softened by the addition of an overlay at each corner. Manipulating the shape and size of these overlays can dramatically change the look of this design.

CD 110

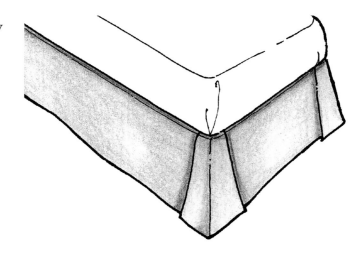

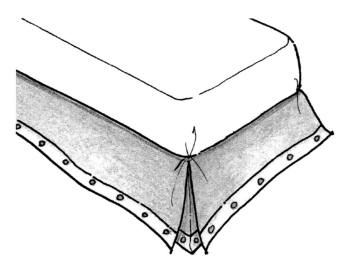

Flat Skirt with a Boxed Corner and a Contrasting Border with Button Accents

A plain flat skirt is embellished by adding a border with self-covered buttons. Try decorative buttons, silk ribbon flowers, pom-poms, pinwheels, or rosettes for a different look.

CD 111

Box-Pleated Skirt with Two Button-Down Bands at Each Pleat

Adding closures at pleats can be an effective way to add complexity to a simple skirt. For a different look try frogs, buckles, or faux-leather tabs. For alternatives to buttons consider snaps, grommets, toggles, or topstitching.

CD 112

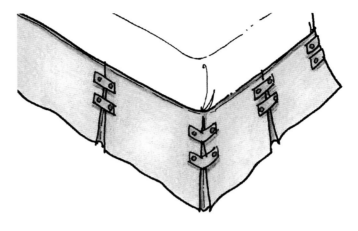

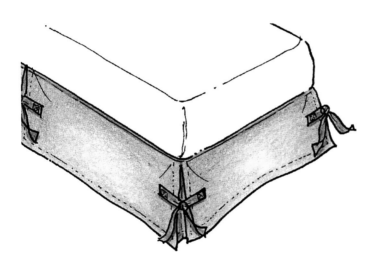

Box-Pleated Skirt with Ties at Each Pleat

The ties on this skirt are topstitched to the face, and the hem is topstitched to add interest.

CD 113

Flat Skirt with Ties Sewn into the Seam and Tied into Bows at each Boxed Corner

For a softer profile, ease an additional ¼ fullness into the panels. Embellish the corners with bows. Other options are silk flowers, rosettes, and chair-tie tassels.

CD 114

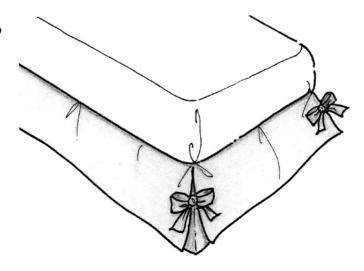

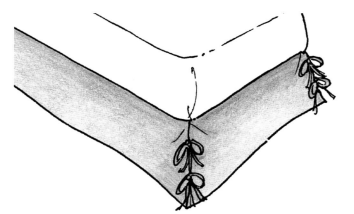

Flat Skirt with Two sets of Ties tied into Bows at Each Boxed Corner

Double ties at each pleat set off this plain skirt. Try rawhide cording, decorative braid, cotton rope, or ribbon for variety.

CD 115

Box-Pleated Skirt with Contrasting Bows at Each Pleat

Each pleat is cinched in approximately $1/4$ to $1/3$ of the way down down from the decking. Embellish with bows, knots, buttons, rosettes, or tassel ties.

CD 116

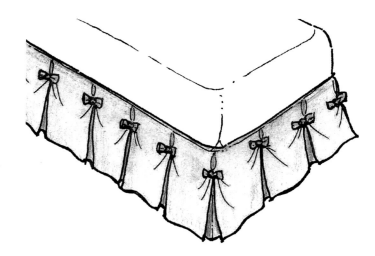

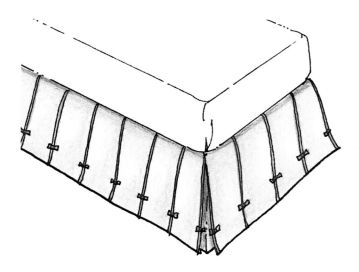

Flat Skirt with Contrasting Ribbon Applied to the Face and Embellished with Small Bows

The opportunities for appliqué on flat panels are endless. Here, thin ribbon is applied to the face in vertical stripes, and small bows are place at the hemline. Think creatively about your options.

CD 117

Flat Skirt with a Contrasting Border in a Moroccan Curved Edge

Elaborately shaped hems always command attention. This example is appliquéd at the border in a contrasting fabric. Add a contrasting underskirt for more emphasis.

CD 118

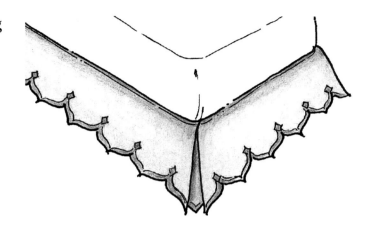

Flat Skirt with a Contrasting Scalloped Border

An appliquéd contrasting border sets off this pretty scalloped skirt. Try adding buttons or bows to the high point of each scallop for dramatic effect.

CD 119

Box-Pleated Skirt with a Small Ruffle at the Hem

A plain box-pleated skirt can be given a designer twist by the addition of a ruffle at the hem. Try small box pleats or knife pleats for a more tailored look.

CD 120

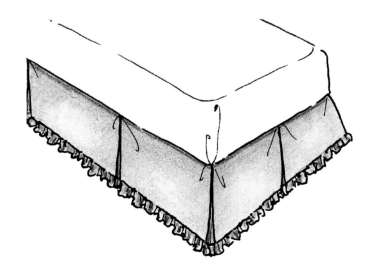

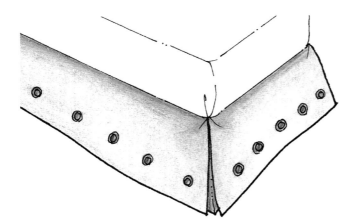

Flat Skirt with Grommets and a Contrasting Lining

Grommets—available in a large variety of shapes, colors, and sizes—are a great addition to a contemporary bed, with design possibilities.

CD 121

Flat Skirt with Grommets at Each Corner

Ribbon is laced through the grommets on each side of both pleats on this skirt and tied into a loose bow. Consider leather cording, rope, or a contrasting fabric band in place of ribbon.

CD 122

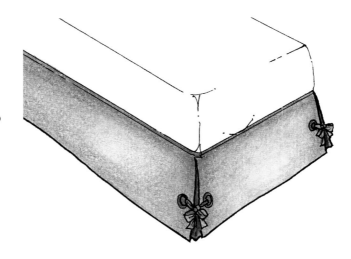

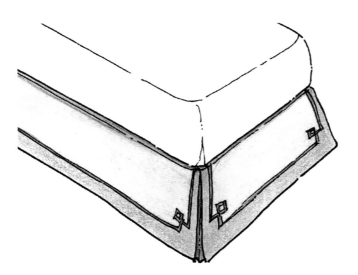

Flat Skirt with a Contrasting Border and Appliquéd Ribbon

Ribbon or decorative tapes are good options for covering the raw edges when appliquéing borders. Experiment with different shapes and patterns.

CD 123

Box-Pleated Skirt with Pleats Folded Outward

This design is created by folding the edges of large box pleats back to face flat on the face of the skirt. By adjusting the width of the portion to be folded back and the interior pleat, many different configurations can be achieved.

CD 124

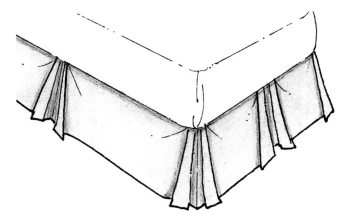

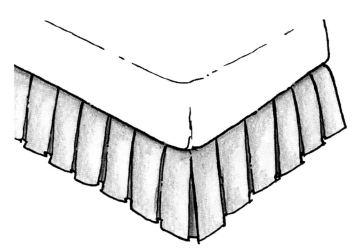

Skirt with Narrow Box Pleats

Fabric selection is a key consideration when specifying sharp pleats. Natural fibers and natural blends work best. Test your fabric by pressing a fold with a hot iron. Pleats can also be held in place using a memory stitch at the back.

CD 125

Skirt with Narrow Box Pleats and a Scalloped Hem

Consider adding a shaped hem to your boxed pleats for a new look. A softer profile can be achieved by easing in additional fullness at the decking.

CD 126

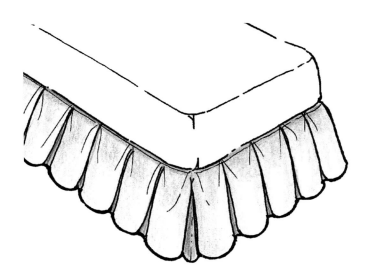

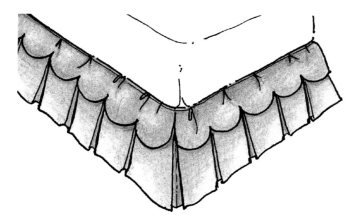

Skirt with Narrow Box Pleats and a Scalloped Overlay at the Top

A separate scalloped overlay is given additional fullness by tacking in the heading at the center of each scallop. The overlay is then joined to the box-pleated underskirt for a contrast in styles that blends nicely. **CD 127**

Flat Skirt with a Pointed Scallop Overlay at the top

Here, a flat skirt is topped with a pointed scallop overlay that has been tacked in at the heading only, at the corners and at the center of the panel. This overlay could also be eased in.

CD 128

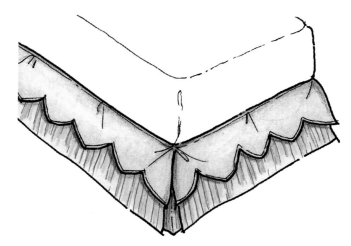

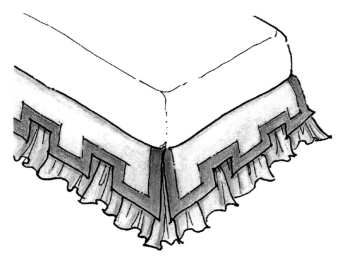

Ruffled Skirt with a Bordered Dentil-Shaped Overlay at the top

When using a flat panel over a shirred skirt, the panel should be interlined or stiffened so it maintains its shape against the fullness of the ruffle. It might be necessary to use a memory stitch at each corner to prevent the panel from flipping up.

CD 129

Ruffled Skirt with a Straight Overlay at the Top

When placing a straight, flat overlay over a ruffle, it might be necessary to ease in an additional $\frac{1}{8}$ to $\frac{1}{4}$ fullness into the overlay at the decking to prevent the ruffle from being flattened. This design is particularly suited to using a sheer overlay on top of a full ruffle.

CD 130

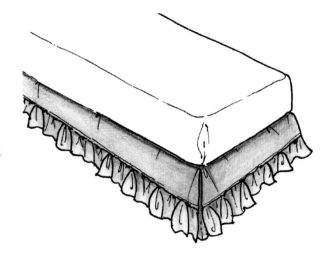

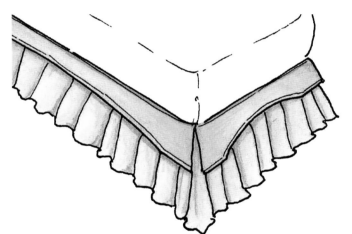

Ruffled Skirt with a Shaped Overlay at the Top

Shaped overlays are an effective way of adding detail to plain skirts. To maintain their shape, it might be necessary to interline, stiffen, or bolster with buckram.

CD 131

Ruffled Skirt with a Scroll-Shaped Overlay at the Top

The variety of edge shapes and details is limited only by your imagination. Draw inspiration for shapes from the fabrics you are using, details in a bed frame, or architectural details in the room.

CD 132

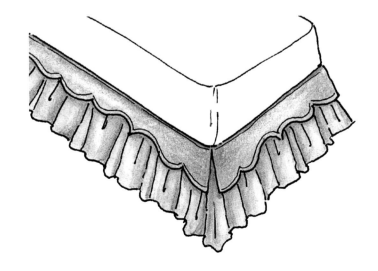

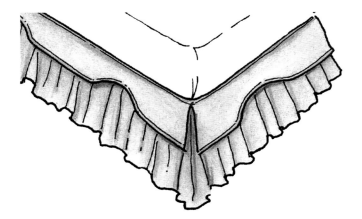

Ruffled Skirt with a Shaped Overlay at the Top

Consider adding emphasis to the edge of the overlay with decorative braid, beaded trim, or contrasting welt. Tassels or beads can be used to highlight the high or low points in your overlay pattern.

CD 133

Ruffled Skirt with a Scallop-Shaped Overlay with a Ruffled Edge

Another option to bring attention to the hemline of an overlay is to embellish the edge with ruffles, box pleats, or knife pleats.

CD 134

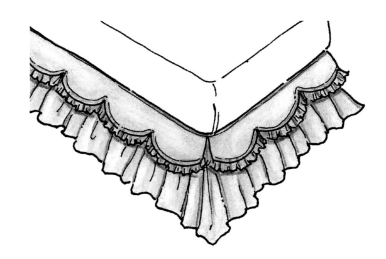

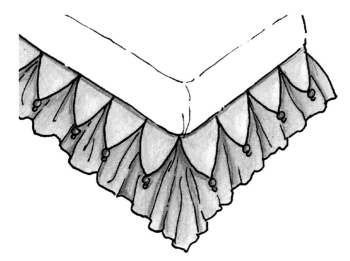

Ruffled Skirt with a Pointed Scallop Overlay Embellished with Beads

When specifying a very full ruffled skirt, the overlay might be best designed using individual pieces to construct a pattern. This allows the full ruffles to expand underneath, raising each overlay section. Here, each section is anchored with decorative beads.

CD 135

Box-Pleated Skirt with a Straight Overlay at the Top

Fabric selection is a key consideration for this tailored look. The pleats in this skirt should definitely be memory stitched to maintain their crisp lines.

CD 136

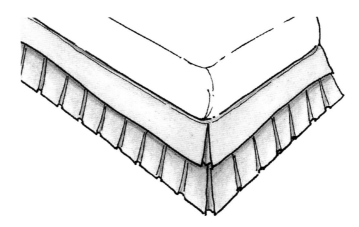

Box-Pleated Skirt with Buttons

For very long skirts, it might be desirable to sew down each pleat a few inches at the decking to avoid overspreading of the pleat. Here, a decorative button is placed at the end of the pleat closure.

CD 137

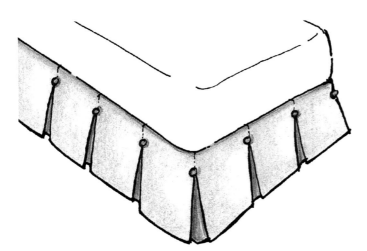

Box-Pleated Skirt with Buttons on Each Side of the Pleats

On this skirt, a button is placed on either side of each pleat. Other options: drape a chain between the buttons, tie rawhide cord in a figure eight around the buttons, or tie a ribbon around the buttons into a bow.

CD 138

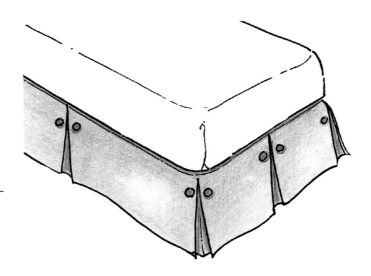

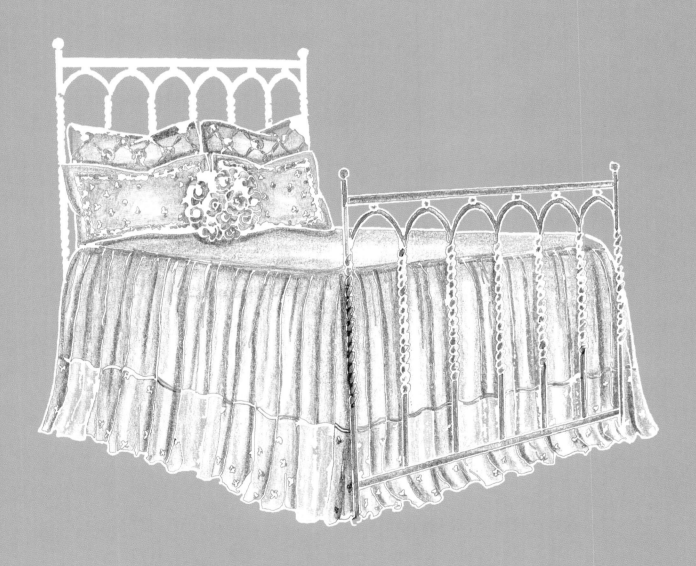

Bed Covers

Bed covers create a soft, decorative, and functional covering to disguise or hide the mattress, box spring, and functional linens on a bed.

- They provide insulation and warmth.

- They add comfort and softness to the bed.

- They serve as an important element with which to introduce additional color, pattern, and style to the bedroom.

- They add emphasis and impact to the bed and help create a focal point in the room.

- They provide an opportunity to manipulate the scale and appearance of the bed.

- They serve to protect other bedding components from wear and tear.

Choosing the Right Cover

When it comes to designing a decorative cover for the bed, there are many options available.

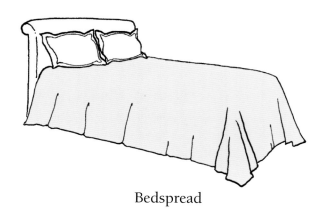

Bedspread

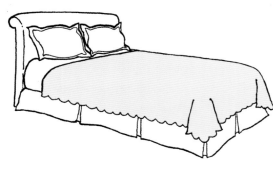

Coverlet

Duvet cover

Comforter

Quilt

Bedspread: A cover that extends the full height of the bed to the floor and does not require the use of a bed skirt. It can be thin or quilted with light to medium batting. It can be constructed in one flat piece or a face or base section with separate side panels. It can be designed to stop at the pillows or run under them with extra length so it can tuck under the front and then fold over to cover them.

Coverlet: A very lightweight cover that can sometimes include a thin layer of batting that is quilted or tacked down. Coverlets are sometimes made unlined of a single layer of fabric, such as a matte lisse or a jacquard weave. A coverlet extends just past the height of the mattress, and a bed skirt is required to finish the ensemble.

Comforter: A thick, fluffy, quilted or tacked-down cover that is filled with light- to heavy-weight batting, fiber fill, or feathers and down and sewn shut permanently. It extends just past the height of the mattress, and a bed skirt is required to finish the ensemble. A comforter is also called a duvet or duvet insert.

Duvet cover: A lightweight envelope-type cover that is designed and sized to encase a duvet or comforter. It is designed to be opened easily so the duvet can be removed and the cover can be cleaned. When the duvet is removed, the cover can still be used on the bed, much in the same way as a coverlet. A duvet covers extends just past the height of the mattress, and a bed skirt is required to finish the ensemble.

Quilt: A multipiece or one-piece cover that is filled with thin- to medium-weight batting and quilted in a specific pattern. The quilting can be done by hand or by machine, and it is the main feature of the cover. The length can vary from short to full length.

Quilting

Quilting is the method of joining together a top-face layer of fabric, a center padded layer of insulation, and a bottom layer of fabric. There are several different methods of quilting that can be used in bedding.

Traditional hand quilting: The layers of fabric and padding are sewn together by hand using needle and thread. The pattern formed by the hand stitching can be random, an overall pattern, or can follow the outline of the pattern of the face fabric. The quality of the stitching used in hand quilting can vary greatly, depending on who does the work and how small the stitches are.

Machine quilting: The layers of fabric and insulation are sewn together using a sewing machine or professional quilter. Many companies offer this service and most have a wide range of patterns available to choose from. They can also stitch to pattern, following the motifs in your fabric. The quality of the stitching is consistent in machine quilting and can be more durable than hand stitching.

Tacking: Tacking can be done by hand or by machine and consists of widely spaced small sections of stitching, usually less than 1" in diameter, that join the face, insulation, and bottom layers. The most common patterns include circles, bars, squares, or dots. This method is most commonly used for comforters with a medium-to-thick insulating layer. A pattern is created on the face of the cover by the placement of each tack.

Tufting: Tufting is usually done by hand and is done by threading through the face, insulation, and bottom layers and securing the thread with a button, bow, rosette, or other small decorative element. A pattern is created on the face of the cover by the placement of these elements.

Common Duvet Cover Closures

A duvet cover must be designed with a method for securing the opening through which the duvet is inserted. The style of closure you choose can vary greatly, from a fully concealed zipper to a wide, contrasting overlay flap with decorative bows. These details can be just as important as the design on the face of the duvet itself.

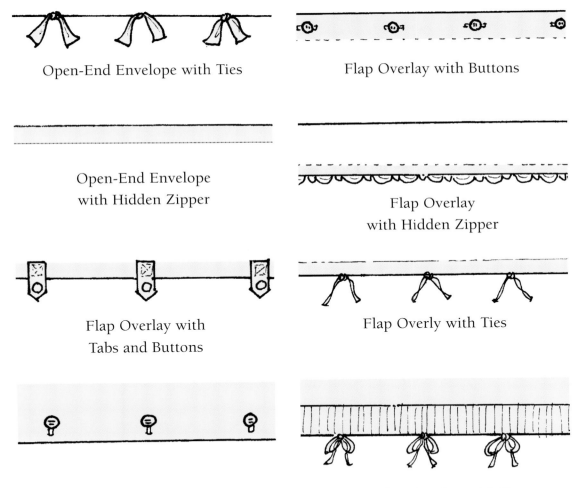

Open-End Envelope with Ties

Flap Overlay with Buttons

Open-End Envelope
with Hidden Zipper

Flap Overlay
with Hidden Zipper

Flap Overlay with
Tabs and Buttons

Flap Overly with Ties

Deep-Flap Overlay with Buttons

Deep-Flap Overlay with Bows

Calculating Yardage

When calculating the proper yardage for bed covers, several key factors must be considered:

- Pattern Repeat
- Pattern Placement
- Seam Placement
- Skirt Design and Fullness
- Hem and Seam Allowances
- Quilting Take-Up
- Pillow Tuck Allowance

There are so many variations possible that it is difficult to provide any standard yardage guidelines. The following charts give a very broad estimate of the most simple design options. It is important to calculate your yardage specifically to accommodate the requirements of your individual design.

Comforter, Coverlet, Duvet Cover Yardage Requirements (One Side Only)

MATTRESS	TWIN 39" x 75"	DOUBLE OR FULL 54" x 75"	QUEEN 60" x 80"	KING 76" x 80"
Bedspread Sizes	69" x 90"	84" x 90"	90" x 95"	106" x 95"
Fabric	6 yds	6 yds	7 yds	10½ yds

- Yardage quoted is based on 54" fabric with no pattern repeat. 15" side drop
- Double the yardage required for self lining or contrast lining

Bedspread with Pillow Tuck Yardage Requirements

MATTRESS	TWIN 39" x 75"	DOUBLE OR FULL 54" x 75"	QUEEN 60" x 80"	KING 76" x 80"
Bedspread Sizes	69" x 117"	84" x 117"	90" x 122"	106" x 122"
Fabric	7 ½ yds	7 ½ yds	8 yds	12 yds

- Yardage quoted is based on 54" fabric with no pattern repeat. 15" side drop
- Double the yardage required for self lining or contrast lining

Common Bed Cover Designs

✦ Flat Covers

✦ Pleated Covers

✦ Shirred Covers

✦ Boxed Covers

The individual bed cover designs in this chapter are drawn as short coverlets with a length that ends just a few inches below the mattress. Most can be modified as comforters, quilts, duvet covers, and full-length bedspreads.

There are many other bed cover designs shown on the illustrations of different types of beds throughout other chapters of this book.

Flat Bed Covers

Flat bed covers are constructed of one or several sections of fabric that are pieced together all on the same flat face. The finished cover is a flat rectangle that lies over the bed with the excess fabric draping over the sides of the mattress.

✦ A flat cover is versatile and can be used on many different beds. It is flexible and conforms to fit the contours of whatever bed it is placed on.

✦ Flat covers can be left draped over the bed or tucked under the mattress for a different look.

✦ They can easily be constructed to be reversible by using a contrasting or complementary fabric on the underside. This is also an advantage when folding the cover back on the bed, exposing the coordinating fabric.

✦ Flat covers are very versatile and can be quilted, tufted, or left to lie flat over the bed.

✦ They are easily ironed and lie flat when folded and stored.

Flat Bed Covers

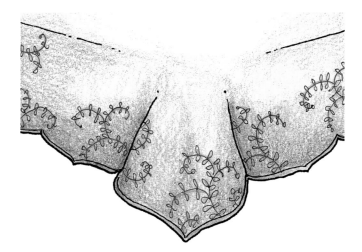

This pointed-scallop hem
has a contrasting banding.
CD 201

Large-scallop border with
complementary banding.
CD 202

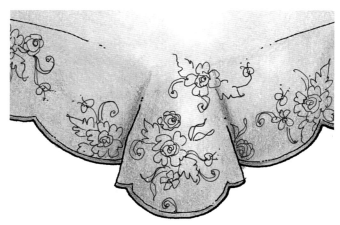

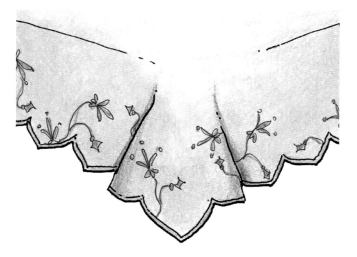

Zigzag border with welting.
CD 203

Waved edge with a
contrasting welt.
CD 204

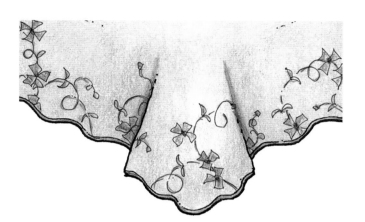

Straight edge tied into a
pleat with a ribbon at each
corner.
CD 205

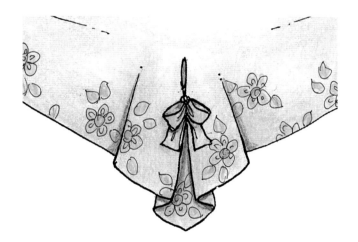

Straight edge with a wide
contrasting banding.
CD 206

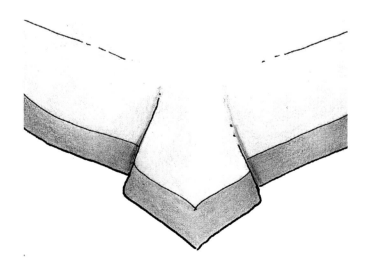

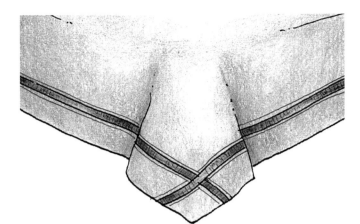

Straight edge with a ribbon border crisscrossed at each corner of the foot of the cover.
CD 207

Straight edge with a contrasting banding topped with decorative tape. This cover also has a band of tape at the mattress edge highlighted by a single tassel at each corner.
CD 208

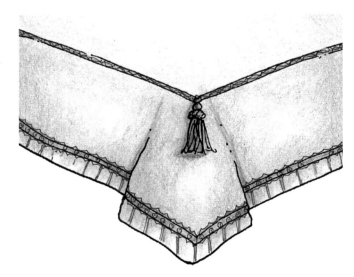

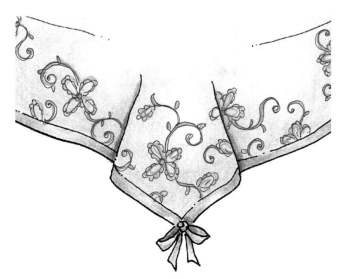

Straight edge with ribbon banding tied into bows at each corner.
CD 209

Straight edge with a contrasting band highlighted by a ribbon threaded through it and tied into a bow at each corner.
CD 210

Scalloped edge banded in a contrasting fabric that has also been scalloped to match the edge. Contrast banding sets the scalloped band apart from the face of the cover.
CD 211

A straight edge slightly rounded at the corners has a scalloped band separated by contrasting welt.
CD 212

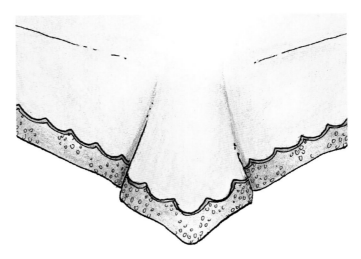

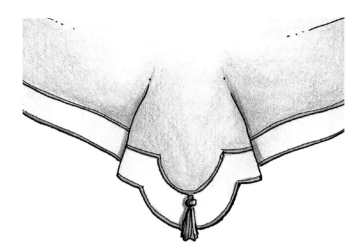

Straight edge leading into a deep scallop at each corner. The edge has a deep banding bordered in contrasting welt and highlighted with a tassel at the center of the scallop.
CD 213

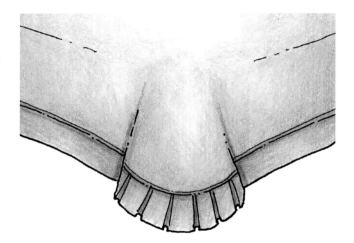

Straight edge with a contrasting band and welt leads into box pleats at each rounded corner.
CD 214

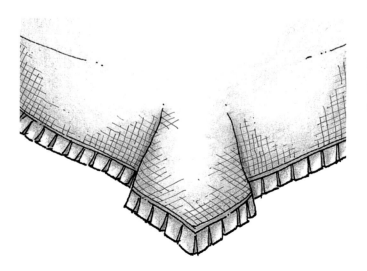

Straight edge has a box-pleated ruffle and welting.
CD 215

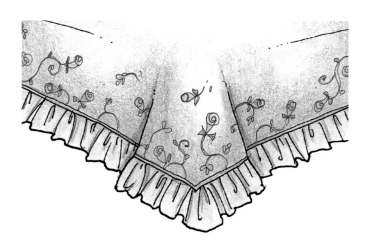

Straight edge with a gathered ruffle and contrasting welt.
CD 216

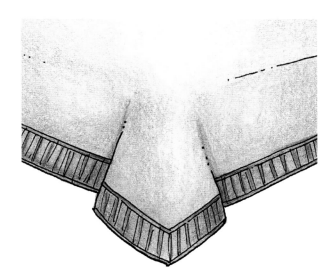

Straight edge with a contrasting band that has been box pleated and edged with welting on both edges.
CD 217

The corners of this flat cover are pleated together with buttons.
CD 218

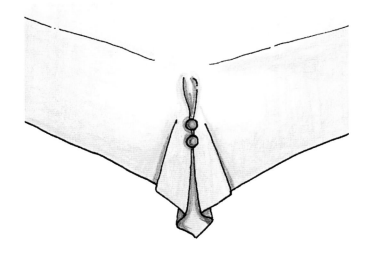

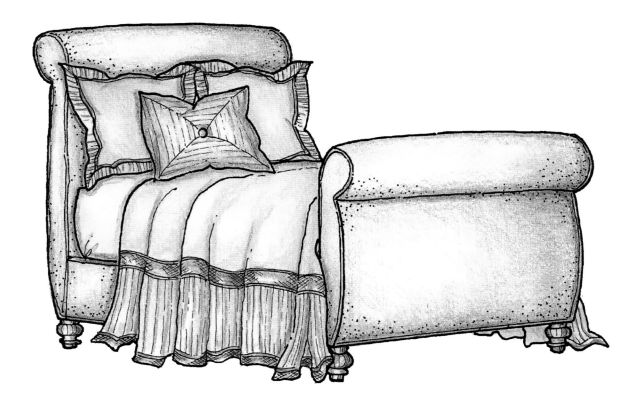

This fully upholstered bed is draped with a flat cover that is bordered on the two sides with a wide band of striped fabric banded at the top and the bottom with a contrasting fabric. Welting, tape, or cording is used to separate the different sections of fabric. The cover is made to be identical on the reverse side so it can be folded back and still retain its same appearance.

CD 219

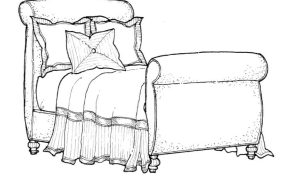

Wide bias-cut banding borders this flat cover. To accentuate these bias-cut folds, the face of the cover is cut with a zigzag edge and trimmed with decorative tape. The high and low points are highlighted with rosettes to further accentuate the lines of the zigzag. Lining for the border must also be cut on the bias to achieve this look.

CD 220

This simple flat cover is given its great look by applying ribbon to the face in a crisscross pattern. Ribbon pom-poms are placed at the intersections of the ribbons, and ribbon fringe is used as trim at the hem. This style can be left flat as a coverlet, duvet cover, or bedspread or used with batting to create lush quilted sections in between the ribbon squares.

CD 221

Borders, trims, and welting can be used to produce countless variations for bed covers. Use trims and tapes of varying textures and sizes to break up single or multiple borders. This design has an interior band of contrasting fabric bordered by a wide decorative tape at the bottom edge and a smaller gimp trim at the top edge. Braided cording finishes the edge of the cover.

CD 222

Striped fabric makes for particularly effective banding. It can be laid flat or can be shirred to create texture. It is best to plot banding that will fall on the face of the bed to stop a few inches inside the mattress edge. If it is too close to the full size of the bed face, it will be difficult to make the bed and get the border lined up perfectly at the edge.

CD 223

A plain duvet cover or comforter might be all you need when it is made of vibrant and colorful fabric. In this design, the pillows are the focal points and the duvet acts as a backdrop.

CD 224

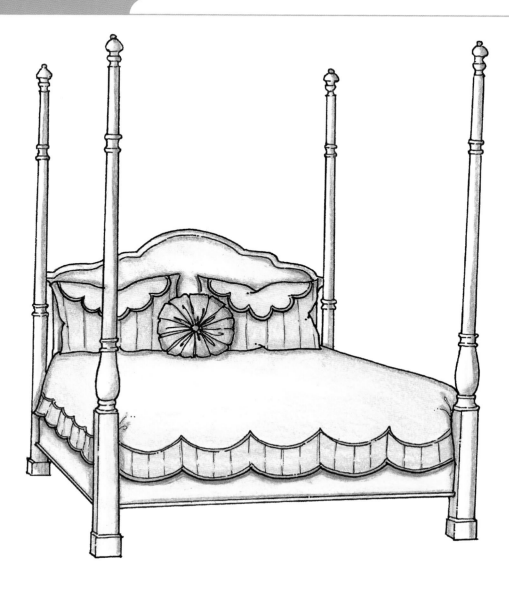

A double-scalloped border creates drama within this plain ensemble. Using a striped fabric adds direction and height to the bed. The double scallop is repeated in the pillow shams, with the fabrics reversed to finish the design.

CD 225

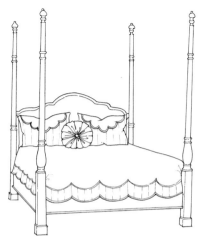

This type of simple coverlet is best for quilting or tufting. In designs using multiple fabrics, it is nice to have the option of making it reversible by using another fabric for the underside. Measuring is critical with this type of cover to ensure that it will have enough length to cover the mattress well below the box spring so the gap does not show.

CD 226

A deep-pleated ruffle edges this full-length bedspread. A smaller scalloped trim separates the pleated ruffle from the body of the cover. The informal throw repeats the box-pleated edging in a smaller scale while also integrating other trim used on the pillows.

CD 227

Classic simplicity of crisp linens and contrasting line motifs is always in vogue. Here, the banding is a bit more exotic than the norm, forming florets and fleurs-de-lis at corners and centers of duvet and pillows. Use your imagination to design your own unique motifs. Just remember that if you choose a design that has rounded, sinuous lines, you must use tape that is cut on the bias or flexible gimp or cording that is capable of bending to achieve the look of your design.

CD 228

Center panels and borders do not have to have straight lines. Almost any reasonable shape can be achieved. Here, a Moroccan look is achieved by using scallops and pointed corners on the cover and pillows. Experiment with different shapes and motifs to create new and unique designs.

CD 229

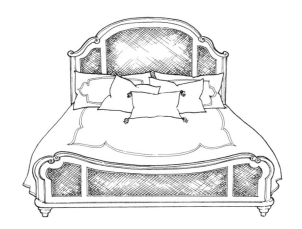

A flat cover can be fitted at the end of the mattress by cinching in the corners. In this design, large square grommets are strategically placed at the corners and cinched with a ribbon tied through them. The grommets are repeated in the large pillow for impact.

CD 230

Pleated Bed Covers

A pleated bed cover is a fitted cover constructed of multiple sections of fabric that are pleated to create volume or to tailor the sides and foot of the skirt.

✦ A pleated bed cover has a top, or face, section that lies flat on top of the mattress.

✦ A pleated bed cover has three separate pieces that make up the two sides and foot of the skirt. These sections may or may not be pleated along their length, but there is always a pleat at the two corners at the foot of the skirt.

✦ It is critical that the face section fit the top of the bed perfectly. You must take exact measurements with the bed linens in place to ensure an accurate fit.

✦ A pleated cover will generally only fit the bed it is made for or another one that has identical dimensions.

✦ Most pleated covers cannot be constructed to be reversible.

✦ For a very tailored design, consider using a memory stitch at the back or top of each pleat to keep a crisp profile and prevent the pleats from falling out.

✦ Buckram, interfacing, or upholstery skirting can be used in the side panels to add stability and maintain a flat surface.

✦ For a finished professional look, micro welt or trim should be used at the seams where the face panel and the side panels are joined.

Pleated Bed Covers

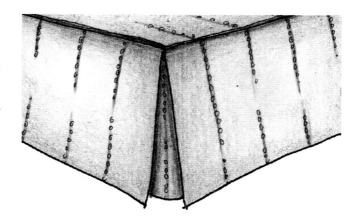

Separate side panels are given the appearance of being pleated by inserting a smaller corner panel at the gap.
CD 231

Wide banding at the face and bottom edge of this cover emphasize the square lines of this design.
CD 232

Fabric straps held in place with decorative buttons are laced over the gap at each corner of this rustic look. Topstitching is added in lieu of trim.
CD 233

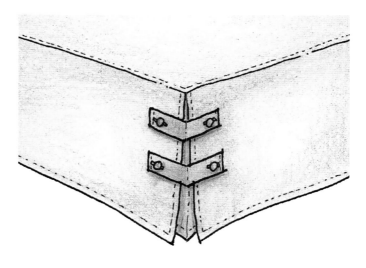

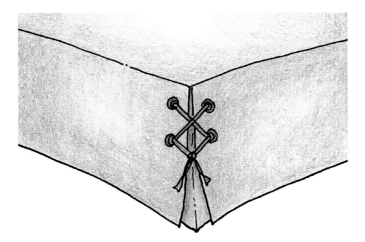

These side panels are laced up by using small grommets and a faux suede tie. This design would be a strong candidate for using upholstery skirting as a stiffener in the skirt to maintain its crisp lines.
CD 234

Tailored box pleats make up the skirt of this design.
CD 235

The box pleats in the skirt of this cover are shaped to create a scallop at each pleated panel.
CD 236

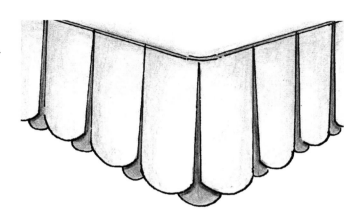

Two layers of individual scalloped panels in contrasting colors are overlaid to create the appearance of a double-scalloped box pleat. This design can also be achieved by pleating one panel of a single fabric or piecing the panel together with sections of contrasting fabric.

CD 237

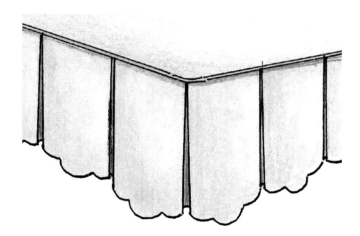

The bottom of these box pleats is cut in a clover-leaf scallop to achieve a unique finish to the hem of this cover.

CD 238

Long pleats are topped with contrasting buttons to create a tailored look.

CD 239

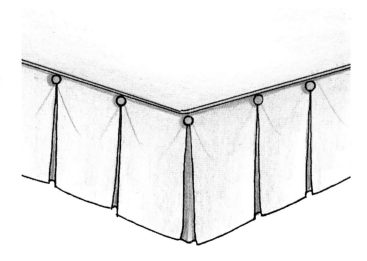

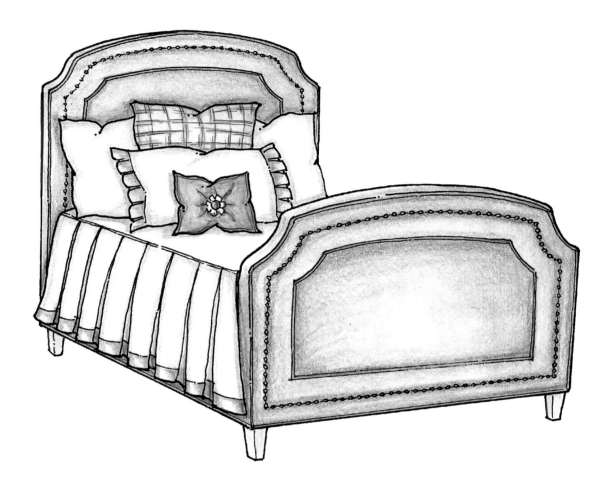

When designing a cover for a full bed frame, it is important to take the frame into consideration. With this design, there are two long side skirts with a shorter nonpleated end skirt section. The long sides can hang freely over the bed frame and the shorter, flat end skirt tucks easily between the mattress and the footboard.

CD 240

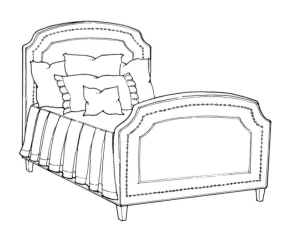

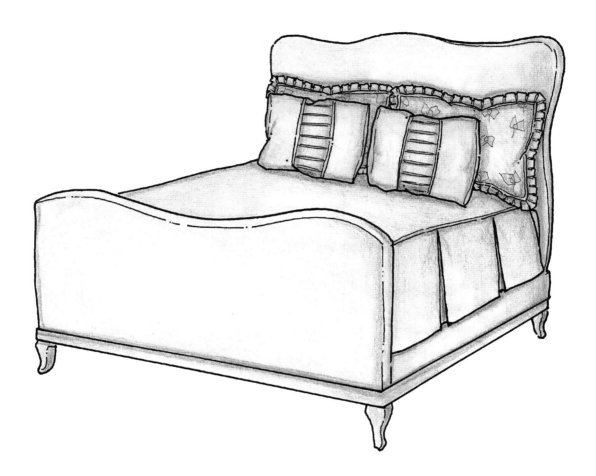

Extra-wide pleats in the skirt of this tailored cover are given emphasis with a contrasting tint fabric at the inside of the pleat. Large pleats benefit from the use of a memory stitch at the back of each pleat to prevent them from sagging or opening. A pleated insert is used in the pillow shams to reinforce the lines created by the bed cover.

CD 241

In this design, sharp knife pleats are each topped with a scalloped pelmet that adds a touch of whimsy to an otherwise tailored look. Contrasting welt or braid is used to trim the top of the skirt.

CD 242

The face of this cover is tufted in a checkerboard pattern and highlighted with self-covered buttons. Large knife pleats are faced toward the head of the bed, drawing the eye's attention to the headboard and pillows. The square bolster at the foot of the bed is channel tufted to correspond to the checkerboard pattern on the face of the cover and the bed.

CD 243

A simple flat coverlet for this contemporary bed is pleated at each corner and embellished with a contrasting border and straps sewn over the top of each pleat and decorated with buttons. In this type of cover, it is best to tack down or topstitch the decorative straps securely at the corners to prevent them from flapping up or being torn off.

CD 244

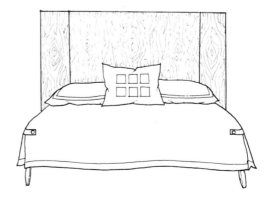

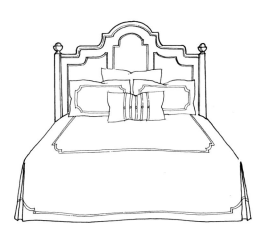

Crisp banding reinforces the strong lines of the headboard in this full-length bedspread that is pleated at each corner. Notice how the banding is continued on the interior of the pleat to correspond to the banding on the outside of the skirt.

CD 245

Shirred Bed Covers

A shirred bed cover is a fitted cover constructed of multiple sections of fabric that are shirred, or gathered, to create volume in the sides and foot of the skirt.

* A shirred cover has a top, or face, section that lies flat on top of the mattress.

* It has three separate pieces or one continuous piece making up the two sides and foot of the skirt. These sections are gathered along their length and can be split at the two corners at the foot of the skirt.

* It is critical that the face section fit the top of the bed perfectly. You must take exact measurements with the bed linens in place to ensure an accurate fit.

* A shirred cover will generally only fit the bed it is made for or another one that has identical dimensions.

* Most shirred covers cannot be constructed to be reversible.

* Interlining and lining can add volume and richness to the skirted panels of the cover.

* Micro welt or trim should be used at the seams where the face panel and the side panels are joined for a finished, professional look.

Shirred Bed Covers

Single-ruffle skirt with welting.
CD 246

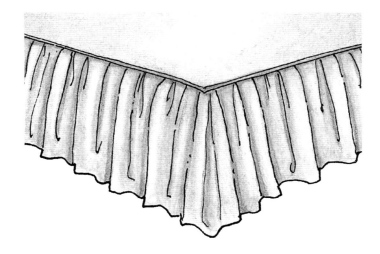

Scalloped panels with gathered inserts spaced evenly around the skirt.
CD 247

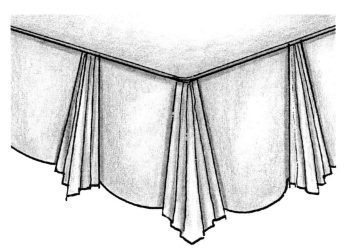

Single ruffle with a decorative ruffle at the hem.
CD 248

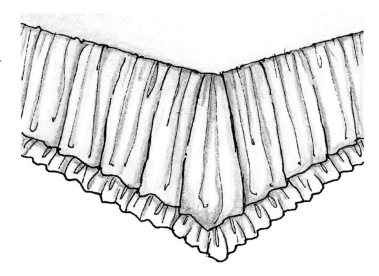

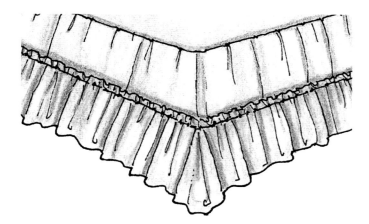

Slightly gathered skirt base with a single ruffle top-stitched to it.
CD 249

Triple graduating ruffle descending in fullness toward the hem of the skirt.
CD 250

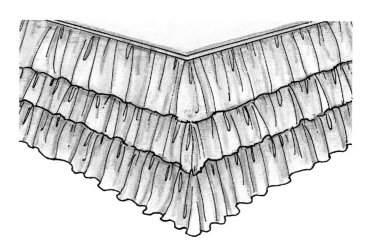

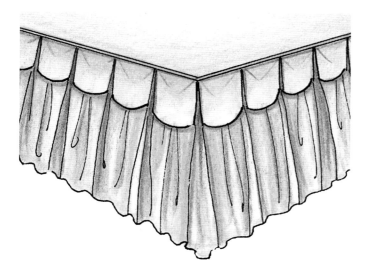

Single-ruffle skirt with long scallops bordering at the top.
CD 251

Light batting is tufted in place with ribbon ties on the face of this shirred bedspread. This design is very effective when using a sheer overskirt over an opaque underskirt. The skirt should be lined so the bulk is compatible with the fullness of the padded face.

CD 252

The shirred folds on the panels of this cover are held in place by a flat underskirt to which they are attached at the bottom. Welting and a decorative ruffle trim the hem. This design allows the perception of the volume of a gathered skirt while providing the sleek lines of a flat skirt.

CD 253

When designing for children, it is important to address the fact that the bedding might need frequent washing. To avoid having to remove the bed skirt, this cover is constructed to achieve the look of multiple pieces of bedding, but they are all attached as one piece. The faux coverlet with pointed-scallop edging is attached via an underskirt to the double-ruffle skirting. With this design, the entire bed clothes come off in one piece and can be laundered and easily replaced.

CD 254

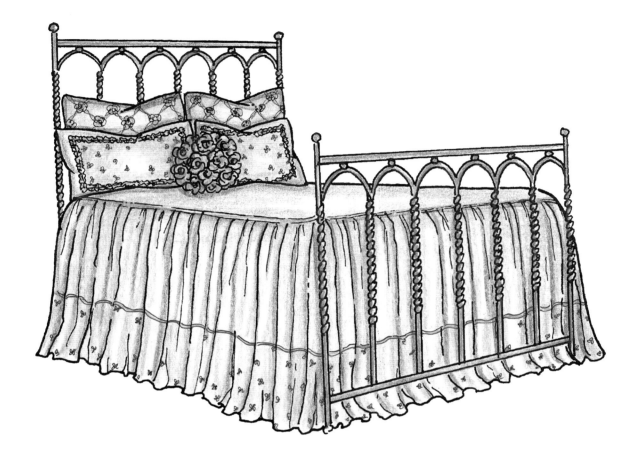

A wide band of contrasting fabric hems this long, flowing, gathered cover. Another band caps off the top of the skirt at the face. This design is suitable for sheer fabrics laid over an opaque underskirt. When using sheers, a string-weighted hem or lingerie hem works best.

CD 255

For clients who do not want to wrestle with a full cover, a half cover might be appropriate. It is exactly as described, a half-length cover that extends from the foot of the bed to approximately half of the length of the bed. This type of cover keeps the feet warm while leaving the upper part of the bedding light and free. It can easily be folded down to cover even less of the bed, if needed.
CD 256

A double ruffle makes up the skirt of this cover that is split at the bedpost. A decorative tie of contrasting fabric allows the corners to be secured around the post after the cover is put in place. The finished top edge of the ruffled skirt is exposed at the face to add texture and interest.

CD 257

Boxed Bed Covers

A boxed bed cover is a fitted cover constructed of multiple sections of fabric that are boxed together to cover the entire face and side surfaces of the mattress, tightly cinching underneath the mattress itself for a closer fit.

✦ A boxed cover has a top or face section that lies flat on top of the mattress.

✦ It has three or sometimes four separate pieces, or one continuous piece, that make up the two sides and foot and sometimes the head of the skirt. These sections are gathered or pleated along their length or at the corners to create a snug-fitting cover.

✦ It is critical that the face section and the sides fit the bed perfectly. You must take exact measurements with the bed linens in place to ensure an accurate fit.

✦ A boxed cover will generally only fit the bed it is made for or another one that has identical dimensions.

✦ Most boxed covers cannot be constructed to be reversible.

✦ Micro welt or trim should be used at the seams where the face panel and the side panels are joined for a finished, professional appearance.

✦ An underskirt fitted with an elastic edge similar to a fitted sheet can be integrated into the cover to allow it to hug the mattress tightly.

Boxed Bed Covers

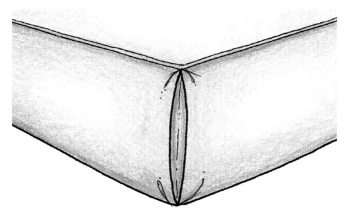

Fitted box single pleat at each corner and welting at the face.
CD 258

Fitted box cover with a three-piece overskirt to give the appearance of a traditional pleated bedcover.
CD 259

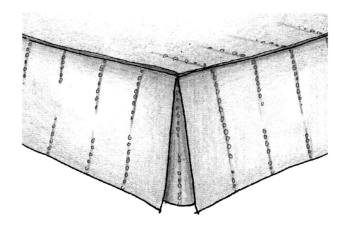

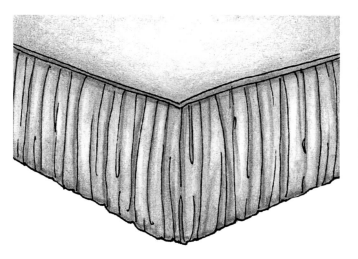

Fabric tightly shirred on the face of a flat boxed under-skirt adds interest to the sides.
CD 260

Boxed cover with a separate pleated panel inserted over the skirt. Fusing the pleats in place at the back of the panel will help maintain this clean look, as these pleats will sag and open with time.
CD 261

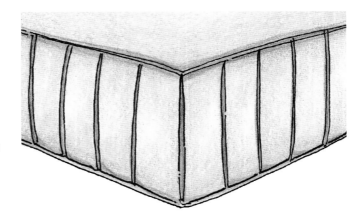

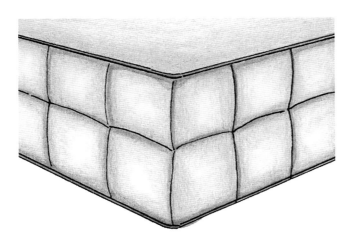

Side panels quilted in a checkerboard pattern and bordered with self-welting at the edges.
CD 262

Diagonal and horizontal quilting lines create a pattern that is given emphasis by the contrasting buttons applied at the intersecting lines.
CD 263

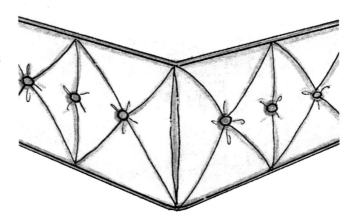

Shirred bands of contrasting fabric
are inserted into this cover and
trimmed out with ribbon and
gimp. The lines of the banding
correspond to the lines in the
footboard. A similar band is used
on the neck roll to reinforce the
theme.

CD 264

The simplest of bed covers is the single panel fitted with elastic at the selvage edges, head, and foot. It works in the same way as a fitted sheet, draping over the bed and cinching in underneath the mattress. Keep in mind that you will have significant bunching at the corners if they are not darted correctly.

CD 265

When using large inserts on the face of a fitted cover, piece the sides and foot and join them in a 45-degree angle at the corners of the face piece. This looks superior to running seams straight down the edge of the face panel. Making the cover four-sided to enclose the entire mattress will be helpful when trying to position the face panel correctly. With four sides, it will always fall in the correct spot.
CD 266

Pillowcases

A pillowcase is a functional, easily removable cover for a bed pillow. It protects the pillow from body oils and soiling while providing a smooth, comfortable surface for the user's face and head.

- Pillowcases are constructed with one end to remain open for easy insertion and removal of the pillow from the interior.

- They should be constructed using durable washable fabric, such as cotton or a cotton blend.

- If trim or other embellishments are used, they should also be washable.

- Fabric and trim should be prewashed before construction to avoid shrinking after they are sewn together.

- Pillowcases are meant to come in contact with the face and skin of the user. Fabrics and trims should be chosen with this use in mind. Do not use embellishments that can scratch the skin or get caught in hair.

- A close-fitting pillow cover made of microfiber fabric can be used to cover the pillow before it is inserted into the pillowcase. This will prolong the life of the pillow. It can also prevent quills from poking through feather/down pillow inserts and reduce the presence of dust mites.

Typical Bed Pillow Sizes

PILLOW TYPE	PILLOW SIZE	CASE SIZE	YARDAGE
Euro	27" x 27"	28" x 28"	2 yds
King	36" x 20"	40" x 21"	2 1/8 yds
Queen	30" x 20"	40" x 21"	2 1/8 yds
Twin	26" x 20"	30" x 21"	1 1/5 yds

*The yardage quoted is for a plain double folded hem pillow case.

Pillowcase Construction

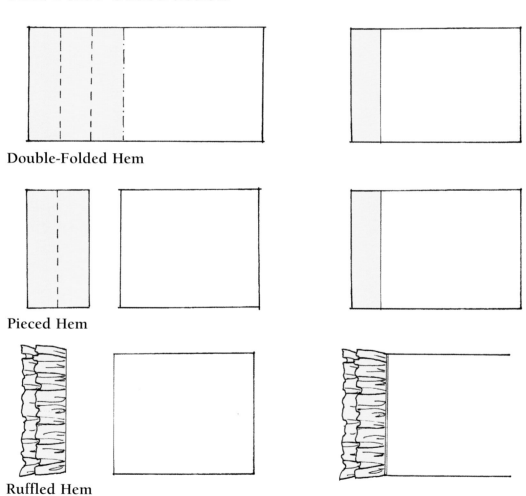

Double-Folded Hem

Pieced Hem

Ruffled Hem

Ruffled Pillowcases

Single ruffle with welting at the hem seam.
CD 300

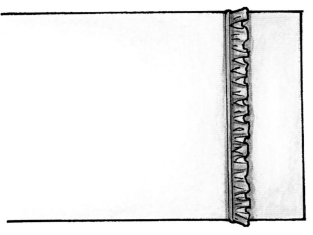

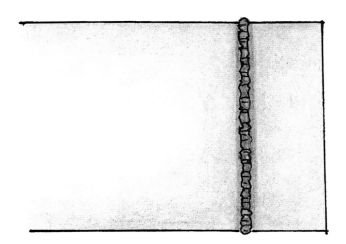

Single shirred ruffle at the hem seam.
CD 301

Flat ruffle shirred in the center applied to the face at the hem seam.
CD 302

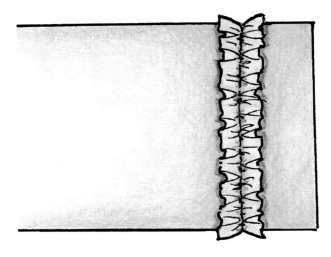

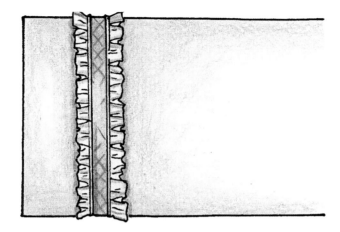

Decorative tape with micro welt and a small ruffle at each edge.
CD 303

Single long ruffle with a ruffled edge bordered with micro welt at the seam.
CD 304

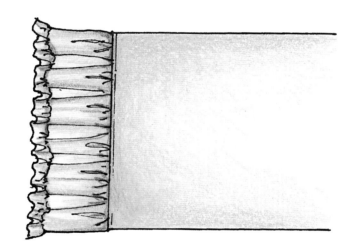

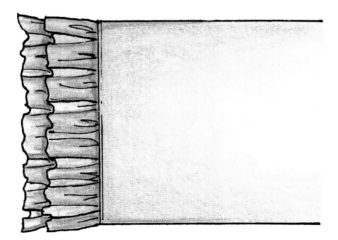

Double ruffle bordered with micro welt at the seam.
CD 305

Extra-long accordion-
pleated ruffle with welting
at the seam.
CD 306

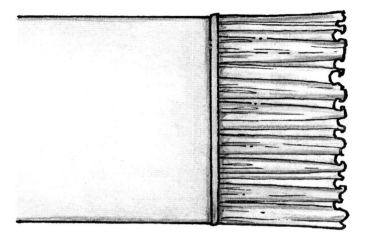

Extra-long ruffle sewn to
a scallop-shaped case bordered with welting.
CD 307

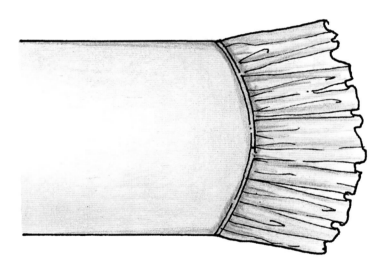

Balloon ruffle with welting
at the seam.
CD 308

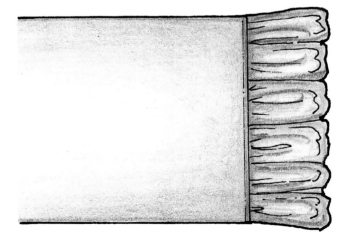

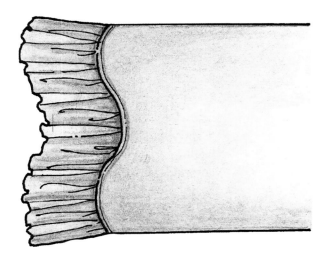

Single ruffle sewn to a wave-shaped face and bordered with welting.
CD 309

Scallop-shaped ruffle sewn to a straight face bordered with welting.
CD 310

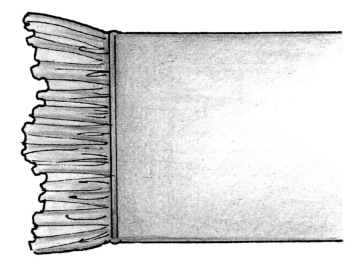

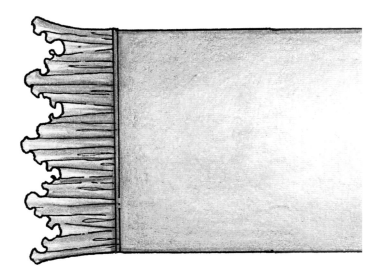

Zigzag-edged ruffle sewn to a straight face bordered with welting.
CD 311

Double-sided ruffle sewn on top of a straight face. Decorative cording covers the topstitching.
CD 312

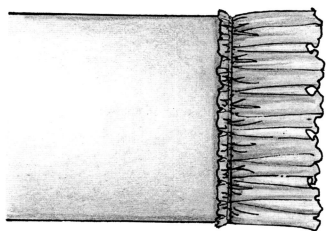

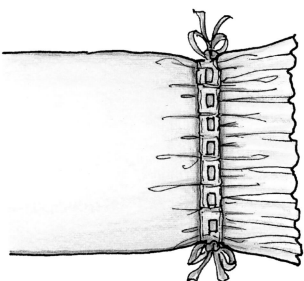

Button holes sewn into a band of contrasting fabric through which a ribbon is threaded. This band is sewn between the face and the ruffle. When the ribbon is pulled tight, the case is cinched in at the end around the pillow. Premade eyelet trim can also be used.
CD 313

A pointed-scallop border placed over a single ruffle of contrasting fabric at the face. Welting creates a break at the face seam.
CD 314

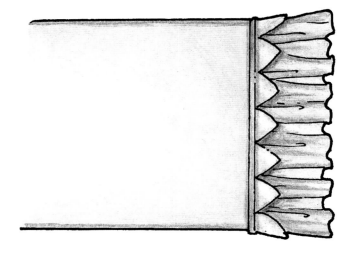

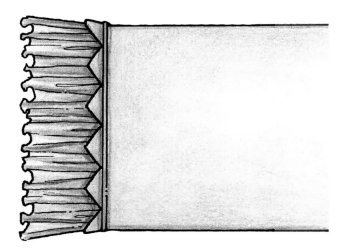

Accordion-pleated ruffle topped with a narrow zigzag band bordered with contrasting welt.

CD 315

The unique shape of this face edge is made graceful with an added ruffle. A bow is attached at the center for added drama.

CD 316

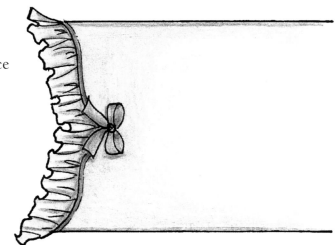

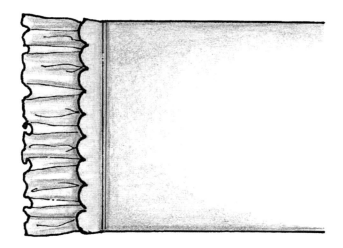

Deep scalloped banding in a contrasting fabric tops a single ruffle sewn to a straight face.

CD 317

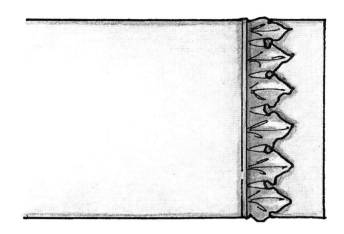

A wide zigzag band is pleated into a fancy ruffle and attached at the hem seam underneath a fold of fabric.

CD 318

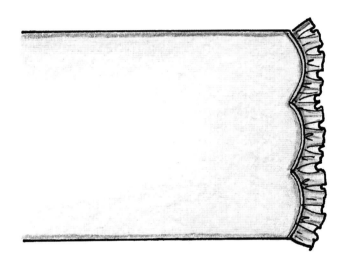

The scalloped edge of the face is a base for a short ruffle.

CD 319

A ruffled section of fabric is added to the center of this contrasting hem band to create volume and interest.

CD 320

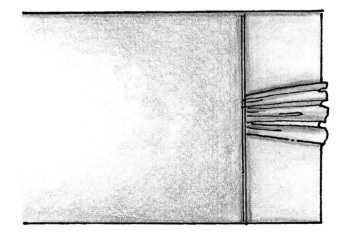

Pleated Pillowcases

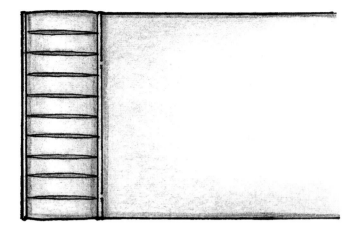

Box-pleated banding is sewn over the hem section of this case. Welting finishes the two edges.
CD 321

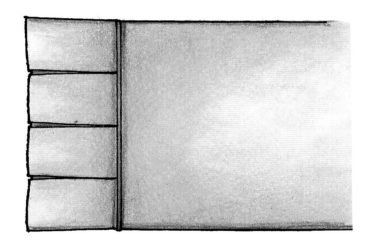

Wide box pleats with contrasting welting edge this case.
CD 322

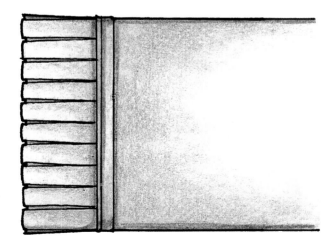

Long, thin box pleats are separated from the face by a folded contrasting fabric band and welting.
CD 323

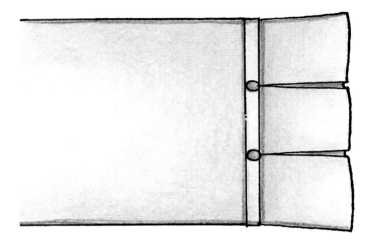

Three large box pleats topped with a contrasting band of fabric are high-lighted by fabric-covered buttons at each pleat.
CD 324

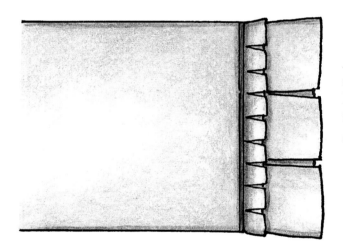

A row of small box pleats tops a layer of larger ones. The ratio here is 3:1—three small pleats to one large pleat.
CD 325

Scalloped pleats give this border a whole new look.
CD 326

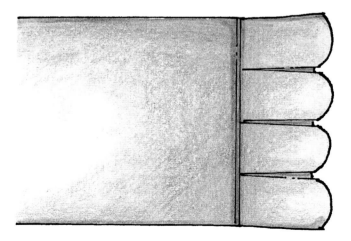

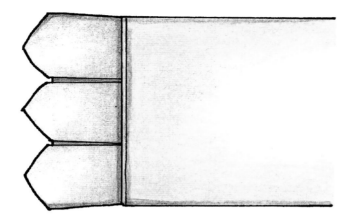

Pleats folded at the bottom give this edge a zigzag flair.
CD 327

A layered look is achieved by sewing the pleated ruffle to a facing and allowing the scalloped face to fold over the pleats.
CD 328

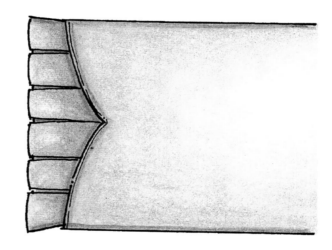

The pleats on this case run perpendicular to the face rather than vertical. To achieve the flair at the sides, cut the panel in a Christmas tree shape, as you would a swag.
CD 329

Shirred Pillowcases

Shirred fabric is secured over a facing of the hem section.
CD 330

For a cinched shir, add half the width of the case in additional fabric to the end of the scallop-shaped face. Sew a casing at each side and thread a tie through it so it can be cinched up.
CD 331

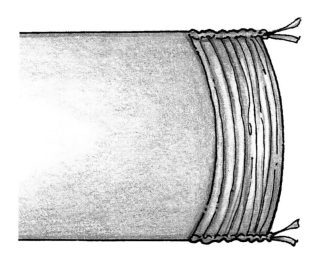

The hem on this case resembles a balloon shade. The ribbons are decorative and are held in place by the buttons and tacked in place at the edge so they can be tied into bows.
CD 332

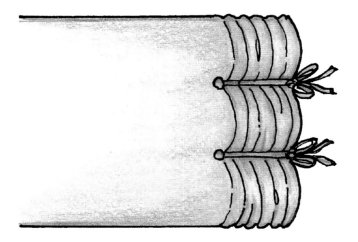

Straight-Edge Pillowcases

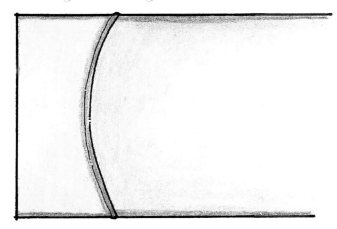

The curved shape of this case occurs at the hem seam, where contrasting welt separates the face from the straight hem.
CD 333

Scallops separate this face from the straight edge of the hem. Topstitch it in place along the scallop edge or in a straight line down the hem seam.
CD 334

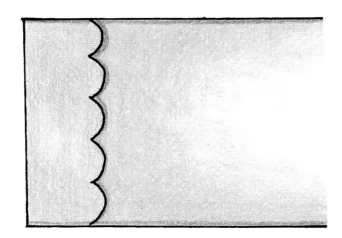

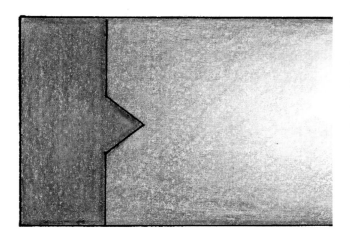

A chevron-shaped inner hem is the focal point of this design.
CD 335

Pointed scallops top a contrasting facing at the hem.
CD 336

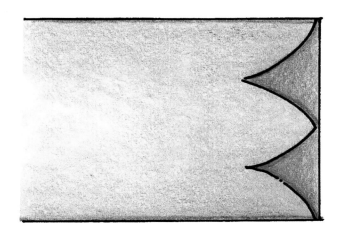

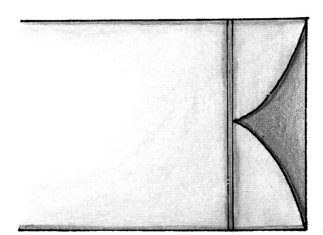

A deep point exposes the contrasting facing of the hem, which is delineated by contrasting welting.
CD 337

This hem is made with a contrasting facing that is exposed by the deep scoop to the face.
CD 338

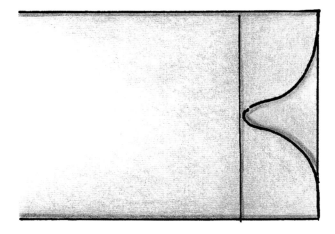

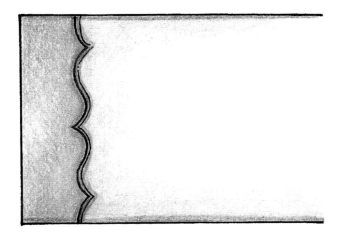

Contrasting trim forms an in-and-out scallop-shaped border between the face and hem.
CD 339

The center point of this contrasting hem creates a southwestern motif.
CD 340

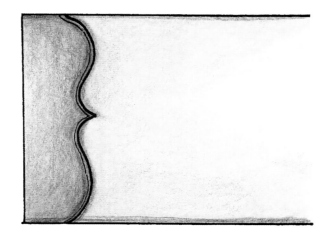

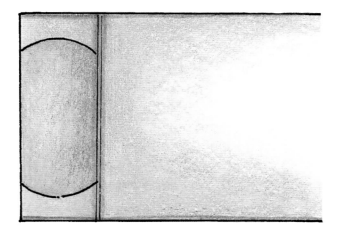

A contrasting insert with rounded ends is sewn into the hem section. Consider scalloping the ends inward for a completely different look.
CD 341

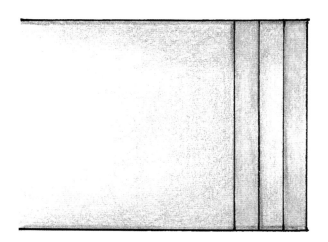

Constructing the hem portion of the case using three straight bands of contrasting colors is a simple detail that will really stand out.
CD 342

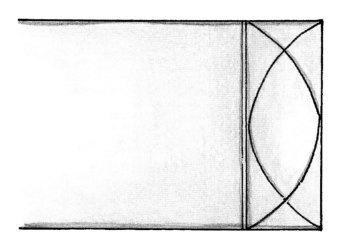

This hem design can be achieved by piecing contrasting fabrics together or by simply appliquéing trim in this shape.
CD 343

When this design is pieced together using contrasting fabrics, it takes on a three-dimensional look.
CD 344

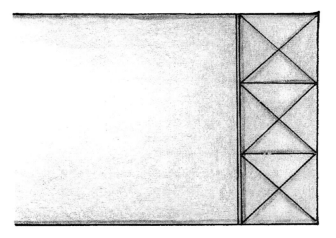

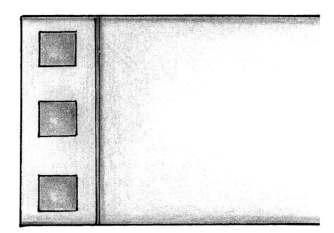

Square inserts in the hem portion add color and detail to a simple design.
CD 345

A single square insert in a contrasting fabric can be very dramatic.
CD 346

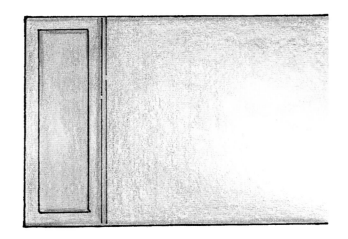

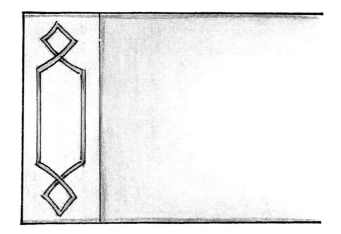

Bias tape or flexible trim can allow you to achieve almost any shape you can think of to embellish your cases.
CD 347

This harlequin design at the hem of this case can be subtle or dramatic, depending on the degree of contrast in the fabrics used.
CD 348

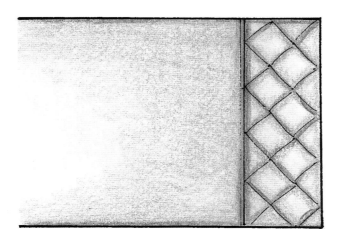

Quilting the hem section of your case is a nice way to add subtle texture.
CD 349

A contrasting facing is exposed between the overlapping scallops at the front of the hem.
CD 350

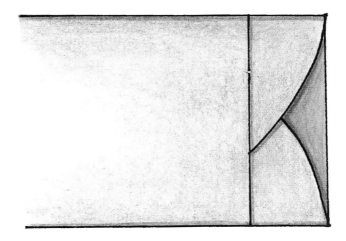

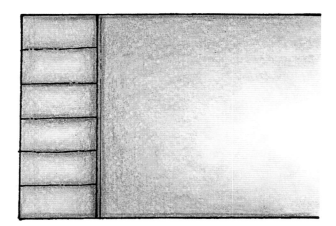

Channel-quilted stripes add a soft touch to the hem.
CD 351

Ribbon can be used to embellish the hem and create a number of patterns, as long as they are straight lines.
CD 352

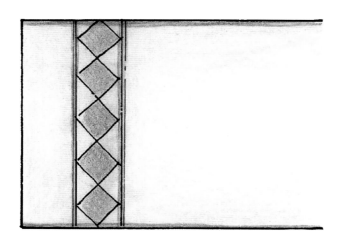

A checkerboard insert is sewn between the face and hem and bordered by contrasting welt.
CD 353

Two layers of triangles are juxtaposed over each other to create a stacked zigzag border.
CD 354

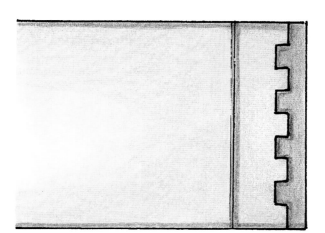

A dentil detail is created with a contrasting facing under the shaped hem.
CD 355

Curved diamonds are linked together in an appliqué to separate the hem and face of this case.
CD 356

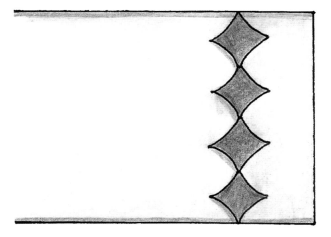

Shaped-Edge Pillowcases

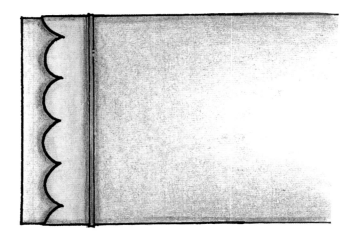

A wide band with shallow scallops highlights the hemline.
CD 357

The scalloped hem is repeated at the face seam.
CD 358

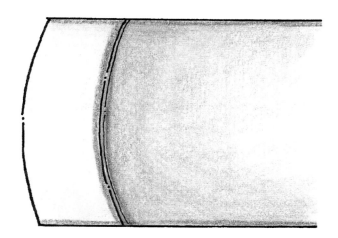

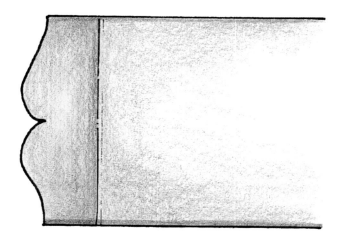

Interfacing in the hem is sometimes necessary when it has an elaborate shape.
CD 359

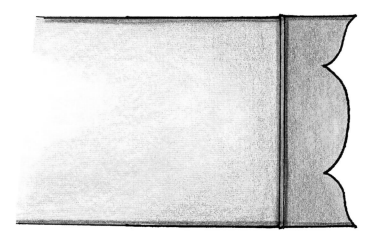

Micro welt at the edge
will help to maintain the
shape of this hem.
CD 360

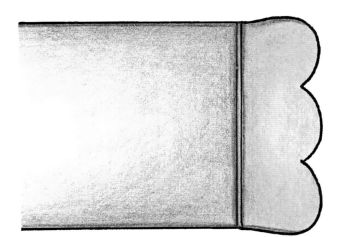

This scalloped hem has a flare
at both ends to accentuate the
curve of the design.
CD 361

A plain flat case is given
new dimension when this
slanted, rounded insert is
applied at the hem.
CD 362

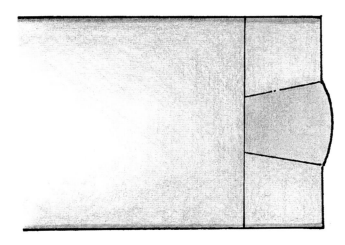

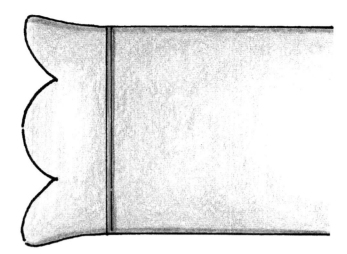

A wide flare added to this scalloped hem gives it additional width at the end.
CD 363

A simple scalloped hemline is separated from the face by a fold of the face fabric.
CD 364

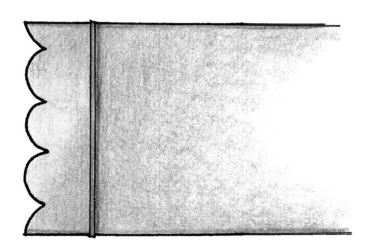

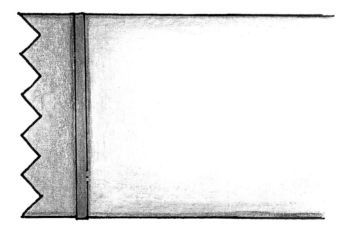

Dramatic banding at the face seam shows off the zigzag hem edge.
CD 365

A facing applied to the interior of the hem is exposed through the angled slit in the face side of the hem. Be sure to plan for the case to be extra long so the pillow cannot be seen through the cutout.

CD 366

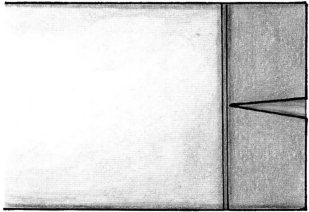

Buttoned Pillowcases

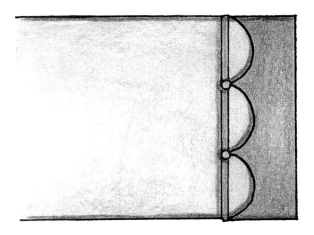

A contrasting border is topped with three scallops at the hemline held in place by a contrasting band and embellished with small buttons.

CD 367

An extra-long hem with a reversed scallop border and contrasting banding at the face seam is folded out onto itself to expose its contrasting facing. It is tacked in place with fabric-covered buttons.

CD 368

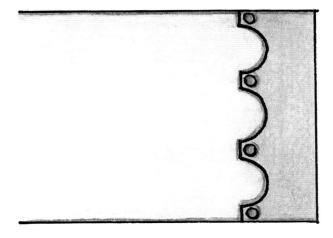

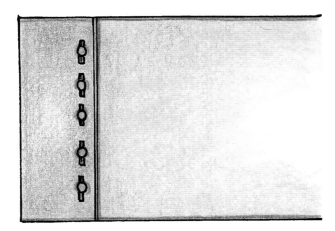

The hem section of this case is folded back and held in place with buttonholes and contrasting buttons.
CD 369

The deep, pointed scallops of this hem border give the design a touch of whimsy. Buttons emphasize each point at the face.
CD 370

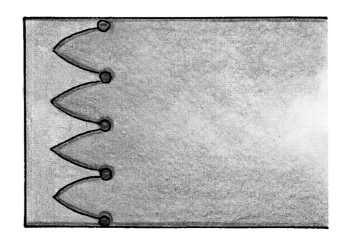

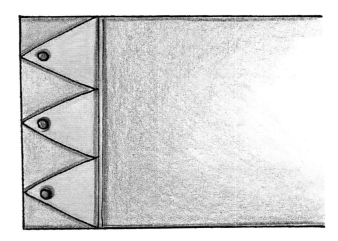

Flags in a contrasting fabric are inserted into the face seam, pointing out to the hem's edge. They are secured in place by decorative buttons.
CD 371

The wave shape of the face is highlighted by contrasting welt and buttons.
CD 372

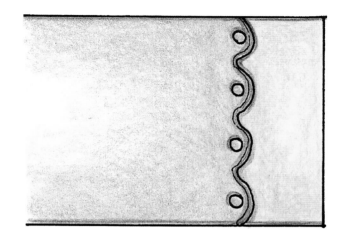

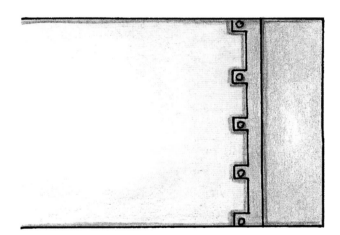

Banding with tabs is sewn into the face seam, folded back, and secured in place with small buttons.
CD 373

Tabs constructed of the banding fabric are integrated into the face seam of this case and are folded back and held in place with buttons.
CD 374

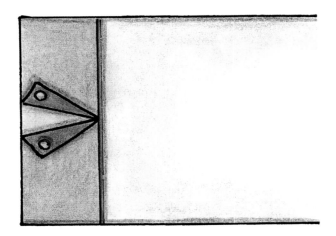

A tuxedo opening at the center of the hem is buttoned back to expose a contrasting facing.
CD 375

This hem is split and overlapped to create a flange opening. It is embellished with buttons and loops as closures. Topstitching adds the finishing detail.
CD 376

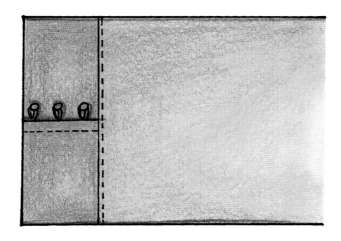

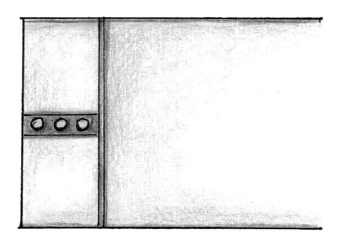

A faux flange is created by sewing a band perpendicular to the face seam and finishing it with buttons.
CD 377

Quilted squares in the padded hem of this case are tufted at the center with buttons.
CD 378

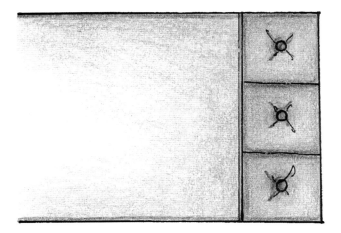

Contrasting tabs are sewn into the face seam, pointing out to the edge of the hem. They are folded back and secured with buttons.
CD 379

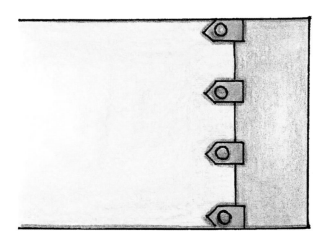

A shallow zigzag border is sewn into the face seam and tacked down with buttons.
CD 380

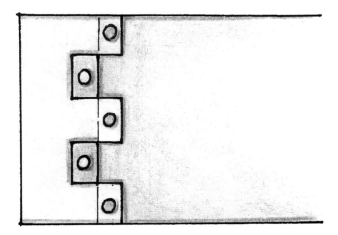

Wide tabs on this case are separate pieces sewn into the face seam. They are folded in alternating directions and secured in place with buttons.
CD 381

Two slanted V-shaped cutouts in this hem are tacked together with fabric tabs that are cross-stitched on either side of the cutout.
CD 382

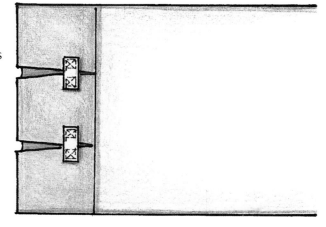

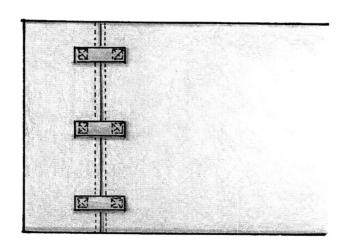

A simple case with double topstitching detail at the face seam is embellished with fabric tabs that are cross-stitched at each end.
CD 383

Tied Pillowcases

Braided frogs are sewn in place over a faux opening created by inserting a contrasting band at the center of the hem. Sew frogs closed to prevent them from being damaged during washing.
CD 384

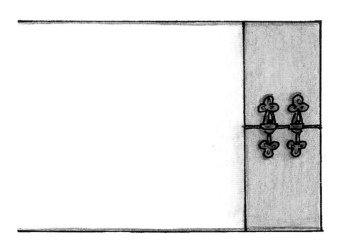

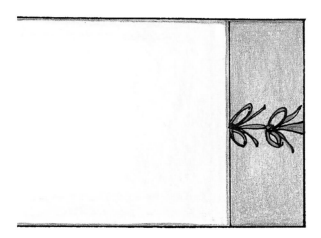

A V-shaped slit in the center of the hem on this case is held together with matching bows.
CD 385

Deep scallops are highlighted by contrasting bows. Interface this hem for stability.
CD 386

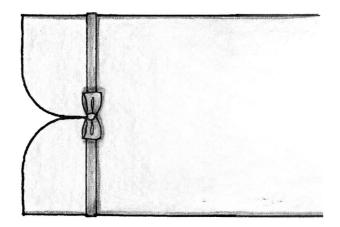

This hem is split in the center on both sides of the case and curved outward to create a feminine look. Contrasting banding and a centered bow finish the design.
CD 387

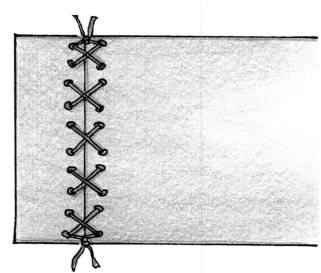

A simple case is fitted with grommets on either side of the face seam. Contrasting cording is laced through and tied at both ends.
CD 388

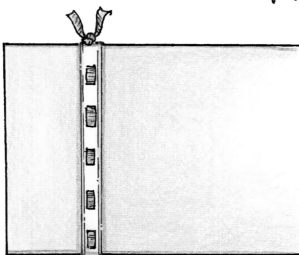

Laced banding is inserted between the hem and face of this case. The ribbon lacing is pulled free at one end and tied in a knot.
CD 389

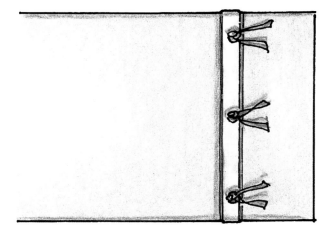

A contrasting flange between the face and hem is tied down by ribbon pulled through buttonholes and tied in knots.
CD 390

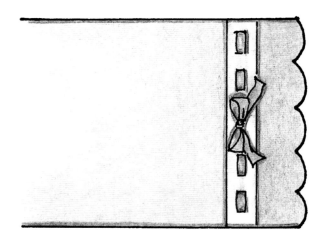

The scalloped hem is bordered by a laced insert. The ribbon is pulled through at the center and tied in a bow.
CD 391

V-shaped cutouts in the hem have been filled with circle-cut inserts, which add volume and a frilly touch to this flat case. Small bows at each insert finish the design.
CD 392

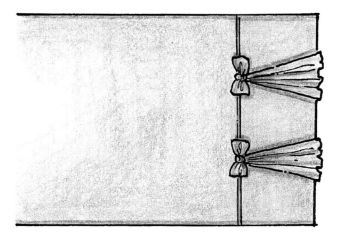

Bordered Pillowcases

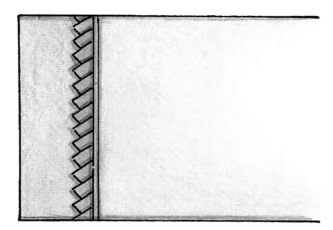

Overlapping triangles and contrasting welt make up this fun border detail at the face seam.
CD 393

A simple lace overlay can dress up the face seam of any ready-made case.
CD 394

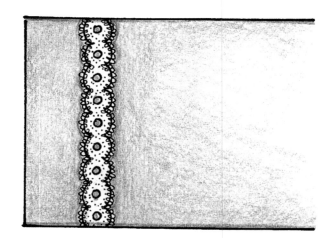

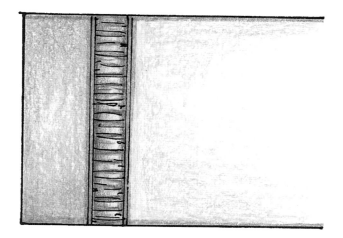

Shirred banding is bordered on each side by contrasting welt and inserted between the hem and face of this case.
CD 395

A continuous circle appliqué cut from felt dresses up this plain design.
CD 396

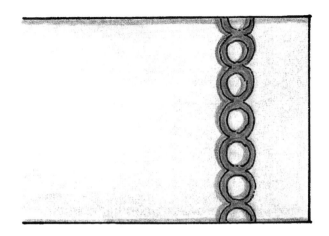

Box pleats make up this simple border with contrasting welt.
CD 397

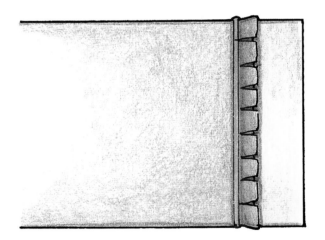

A border of wide shallow scallops in a contrasting fabric are trimmed with welting and placed between the hem and face.
CD 398

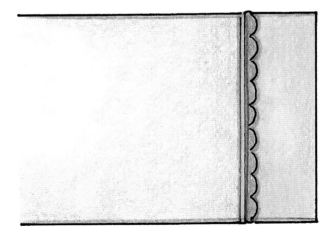

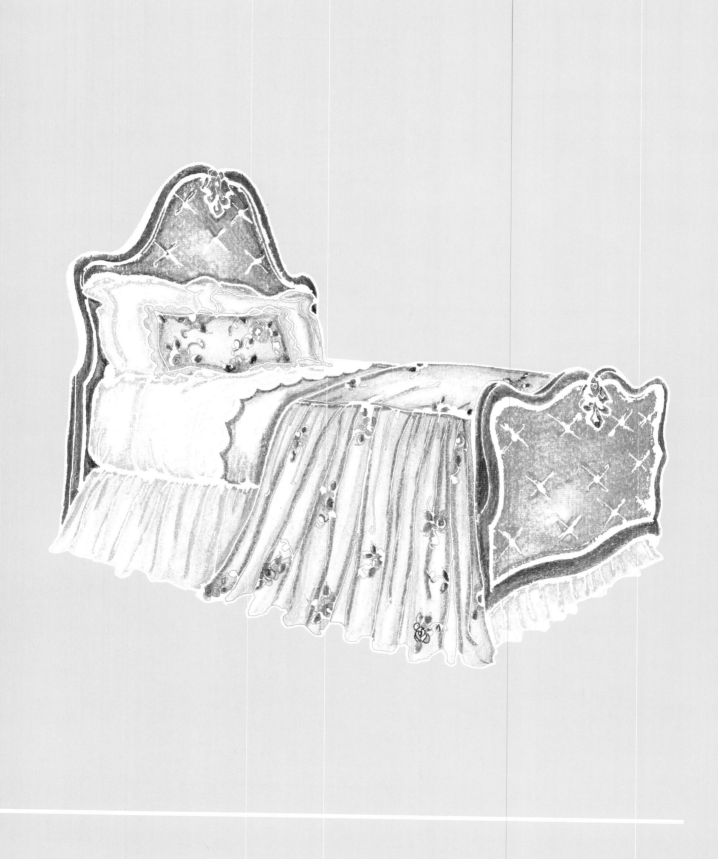

Pillow Shams

A pillow sham is a decorative pillow cover that is enclosed on all four sides and has a closeable opening in the back or side to insert a pillow form.

- Shams can be decorative or functional. Functional shams are meant to touch one's face daily, and decorative shams are meant for show only and are removed from the bed before it is used.

- Pillow shams are more secure than pillowcases, as they hold the pillow form tighter within their interior. There is less slippage of the insert.

- Functional shams that will be used every day should be constructed of durable, washable fabric such as cotton or a cotton blend. If trim or other embellishments are used, they should also be washable. Fabric and trim should be prewashed before construction to avoid shrinking.

- Decorative shams can be made of more delicate, dry-cleanable fabrics and trims, as they do not experience the same amount of wear and tear as functional shams do.

- A close-fitting pillow cover made of microfiber fabric can be used to cover the pillow before it is inserted into the pillow sham. This will prolong the life of the sham and the pillow. It can also prevent quills from poking through feather/down pillow inserts.

- Be sure to plot the placement of the pattern of your fabric carefully on the face and back of the sham.

Pillow Sham Construction

Pillow shams can be very simple or quite elaborate in design and construction. The designs shown in this chapter focus on edge or border details. Many of the hundreds of designs shown in the Decorative Pillows section of this book can also be constructed as pillow shams.

Pillow shams can have a simple welted edge or can be embellished with an exterior flange, ruffles, pleats, trimmings, or a combination thereof.

Special attention should be paid to the type and style of closure used at the back of the pillow.

Parts of a Pillow Sham

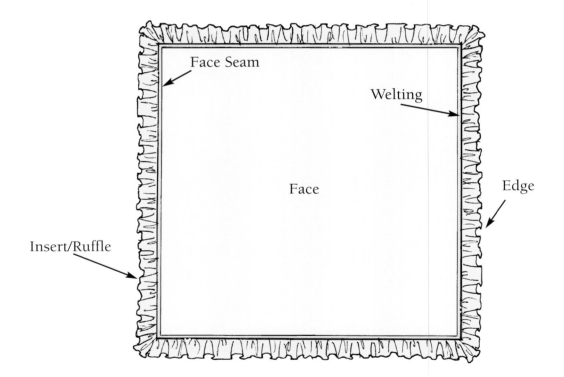

Face Seam

Welting

Face

Edge

Insert/Ruffle

Yardage Requirements

PILLOW SHAMS	STANDARD—QUEEN—KING—EURO
Knife Edge	1½ yds
Corded	body 1½ yds; cord ½ yd
Shirred Cord	body 1½ yds; cord 1½ yds
Ruffled	body 1½ yds; ruffle 1½ yds
Double Ruffled	body 1½ yds; 1st ruffle 1½ yds; 2nd ruffle 2 yds
Flat Flange	2 yds
Flat Contrasting Flange	body 2 yds; contrast flange 1 yard
Jumbo Knotted Corners	body 1½ yds; cord 1½ yds

Common Methods of Closure

The back side of the pillow sham should look as good as the face. Choosing the appropriate method of closure can add detail and style to your design.

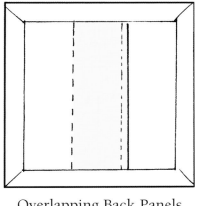

Overlapping Back Panels

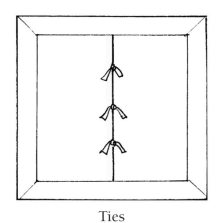

Ties

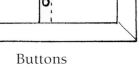

Buttons

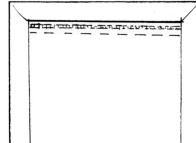

Hidden Zipper

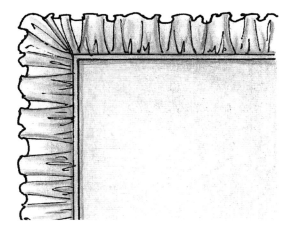

This sham has a single ruffle with welting.
CD 400

Flange border topped with a double-sided ruffle attached to the face at the border seam.
CD 401

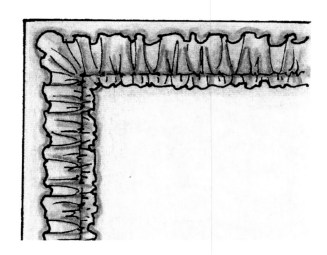

Two ruffles of staggered lengths make up this double border.
CD 402

A short crisp ruffle border.
CD 403

The flange border of this sham is embellished with a short ruffle and welting.
CD 404

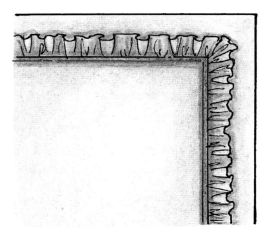

Pleated triangles are lined up to create this interesting border.
CD 405

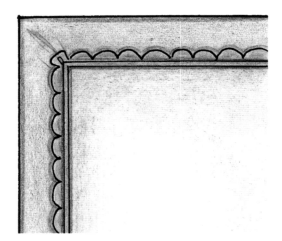

Borders should be tacked in at the corner, such as with this short scalloped trim.
CD 406

This zigzag border is broken at the corner to maintain its straight lines.
CD 407

Short box pleats are tacked in at the corner.
CD 408

Scallops generally grow in length at the corner.
CD 409

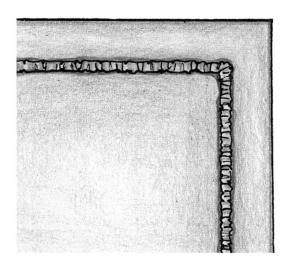

A ruched banding is inserted at the border seam of this flanged sham.
CD 410

Cord with lip separates this flanged border that is edged with welting.
CD 411

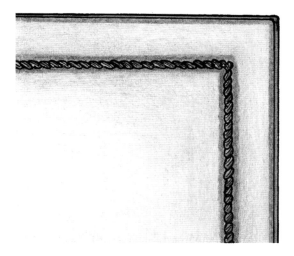

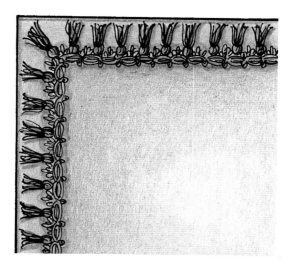

The border seam is covered by tassel fringe.
CD 412

Decorative braid can be used to cover the border seam and to form decorative shapes, such as this fleur-de-lis.
CD 413

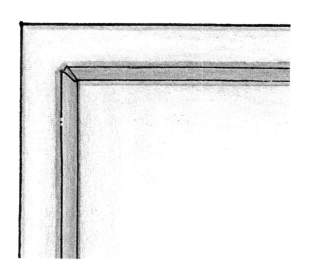

A small, thin knife-edge welt is inserted between the face and flange border of this sham.
CD 414

A padded flange border with contrasting micro welt at the edge and a larger welt at the face seam create a classic look.
CD 415

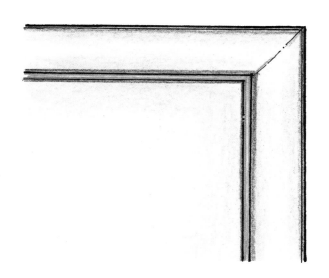

A double, staggered flange borders this colorful sham.
CD 416

A flat flange border is gathered tightly at each corner into a flourish of ruffles.
CD 417

The face is edged with a contrast banding set apart from the flange border by welting and a bow at each corner.
CD 418

A contrast facing is exposed at each corner of the flange border and set off by a bow.
CD 419

Frogs highlight the corner seam of this flange border. Be sure to sew them closed.
CD 420

Cross-stitched topstitching holds the fabric tabs in place at each corner of this sham. The topstitching is repeated at the face seam for continuity.
CD 421

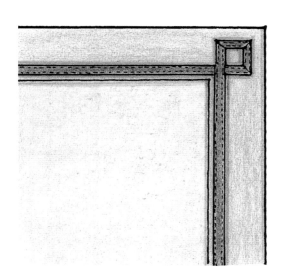

Crisp banding forms a square pattern at each corner of the flange.
CD 422

Bias-cut fabric tape is used to make the loop motif at the corners of this flanged sham.
CD 423

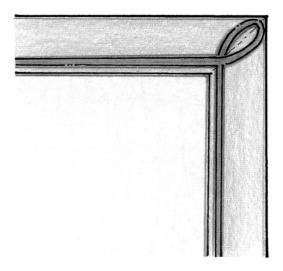

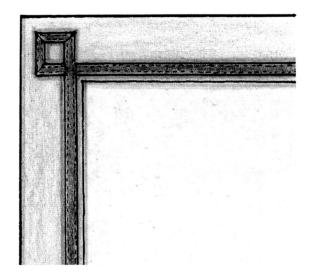

Grosgrain ribbon is top-stitched to the face of this flange border for additional style.
CD 424

A fancy quilting stitch adds depth to this quilted flange.
CD 425

Sewing quilt lines perpendicular to the face seam creates this square-border motif.
CD 426

This flange is quilted in a diamond pattern.
CD 427

Small pleats are sewn into the face of this flange to achieve a square pattern.
CD 428

The interior pattern on this flange is appliquéd to the face of the border.
CD 429

Soutache cord can be used to create any number of decorative motifs.
CD 430

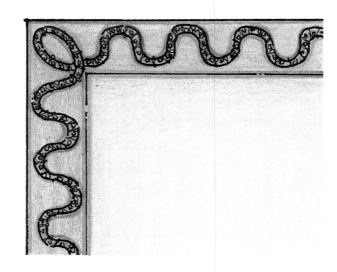

Flexible fabric tape or gimp can also be used to make sinuous designs such as this one.
CD 431

Scallops intersect at the corner of this sham to form a loop.
CD 432

Buttonholes are sewn into the face of this flange, and ribbon is threaded through and tied into a bow at each corner.
CD 433

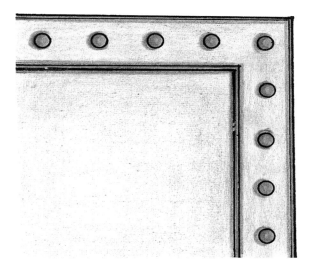

Decorative buttons are evenly spaced around this flange.
CD 434

Grommets make a great decorative addition to this sham.
CD 435

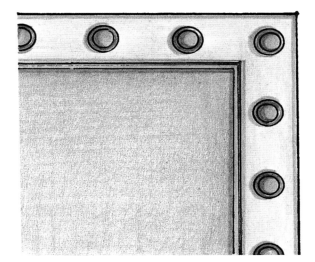

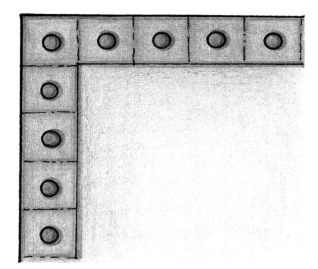

This quilted flange is decorated with buttons at the center of each square.
CD 436

Knotted double ties dot this flange.
CD 437

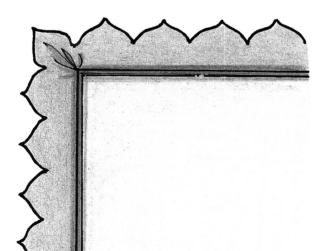

The edge of a flanged sham does not have to be straight. Here, it is shown in a pointed scallop.
CD 438

Decorative Pillows

Decorative pillows—or throw pillows, as they are sometimes called—are possibly the single most effective element for adding color, pattern, texture, and style to an interior. They are incredibly versatile and can be constructed in an endless number of shapes and styles.

- Pillows can be strictly decorative or they can serve vital functions, such as neck, arm, or lumbar support.

- Choose a pillow insert that will provide the appropriate look and support for each pillow.

  - Down and feather inserts are comfortable and luxurious and can be shaped to a desired form. They will compress with use and must be fluffed to bring them back to their original shape.

  - Polyester fiber inserts are firm and will retain their original shape without fluffing. They are less malleable than feather-down inserts and may compact and lose volume over time.

- All pillow inserts will eventually compact over time and lose some of their volume. Over-stuffing pillows at the outset can ensure that they remain plump longer and help avoid loose, saggy-looking covers.

- Pillow inserts should be removed and cleaned once a year. This will help maintain their shape and prolong the life of the pillow.

- Pillow covers should always be constructed with a hidden zipper or other type of professional closure unless there is a specific reason not to include it.

- Adding a bit of loose fill or batting in the corners of your pillows, in addition to a pillow form, will produce sharp, plump corners.

- Many pillow insert manufacturers and suppliers offer custom sizes and shapes. You do not have to settle for standard options.

Common Pillow Shapes and Sizes

Square, Rectangle, Circle

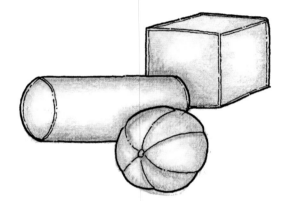

Cube, Basketball, Neck Roll

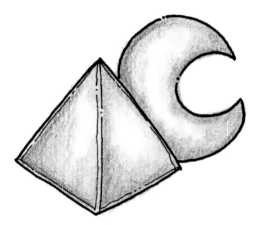

Triangle, Crescent

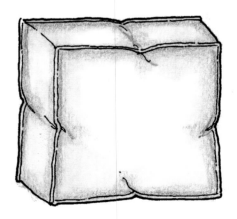

Boxed

Welting

Welting is an important finishing detail that signifies quality in bedding design. It is an extra added touch that sets custom bedding apart from ready-made. Welting is used to separate, define, or contain components of the design. It is particularly important in the construction of pillows.

Cord Welting

A narrow continuous length of fabric that has been folded in half and into which a length of cording has been inserted.

The fabric should be cut on the bias for optimal performance; however, fabric cut with the grain can be used if the pattern demands it.

Flat Welting

A narrow continuous length of fabric that has been folded in half and then folded, pleated, or gathered into a decorative trim.

Knife Edge Welt

String Welt 1.8 mm

Double Knife Edge Welt

Cord Welt
$^4/_{32}"$, $^6/_{32}"$, $^{10}/_{32}"$,
$^{12}/_{32}"$, $^{16}/_{32}"$, $^{22}/_{32}"$

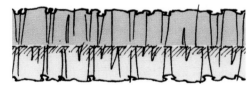

Ruffled Welt

Jumbo Welt 1', $1^1/_2"$, 2"

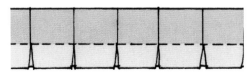

Box Pleated Welt

Ruched Cord Welt

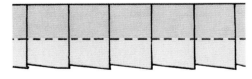

Knife Pleat Welt

Color Blocked Pillows

One of the simplest ways to add detail to a pillow is to use sections of contrasting fabric to create a pattern on the pillow face.

- Color or pattern blocking can be done by joining sections of fabric together to create the pillow face or by appliquéing contrasting sections or shapes of fabric onto the fabric face.

- Appliquéd sections of fabric must be finished at the raw edges with a satin stitch or by covering the raw edge with trim.

- If the pillow is to be washed, be sure to prewash the fabrics before construction in order to prevent shrinking and color bleed when washing the finished product.

- Avoid topstitching unless it is an integral part of your design. It can cause puckering and bunching, especially on curved edges.

- When overlapping sections of fabric, be aware of color bleed that might occur when placing dark colors under light ones.

Creating Directional Pattern

Manipulating the direction and placement of striped fabrics or sections of contrasting fabric can be a creative way to add impact to your designs. From bed covers to pillow shams, these patterns can be used to great effect. Here are a few possible combinations, from the very simple to the complex.

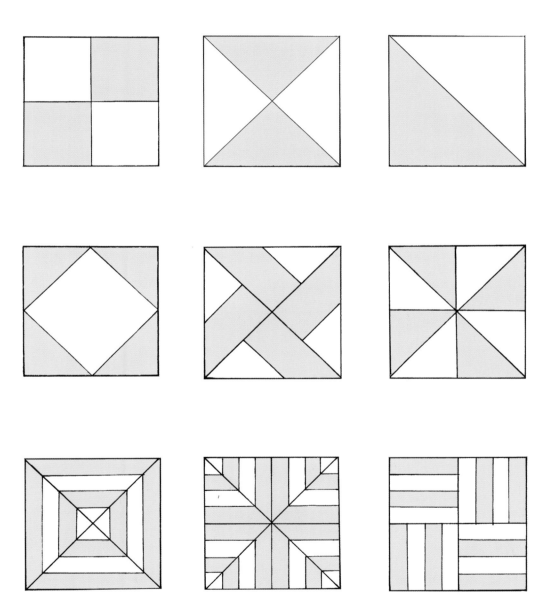

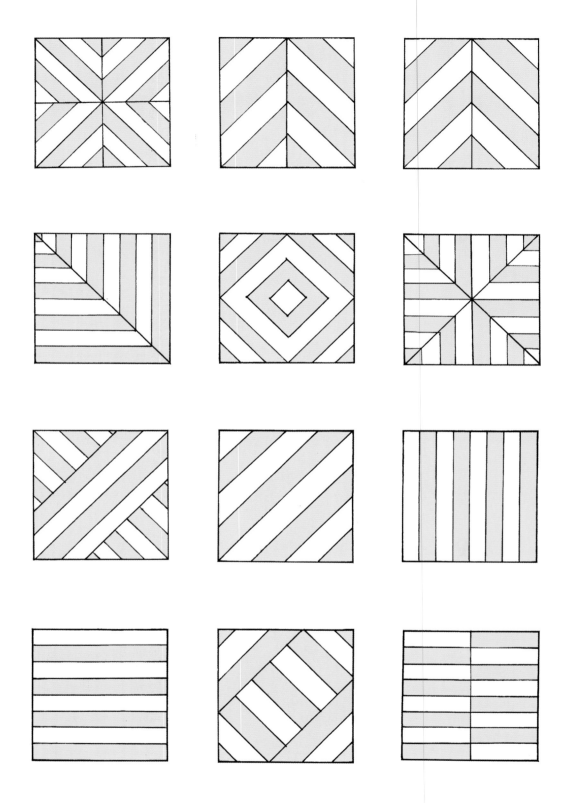

Color Blocked Pillows

Diagonal Banding
CD 441

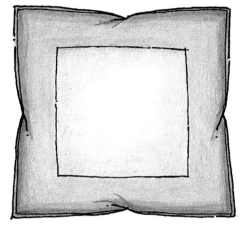

Square Center
CD 442

Diamond Center
CD 443

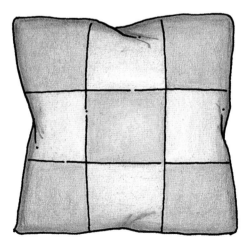

Checkerboard
CD 444

Asymmetrical Blocks
CD 445

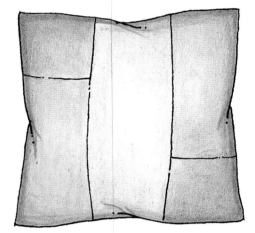

Asymmetrical Blocks
CD 446

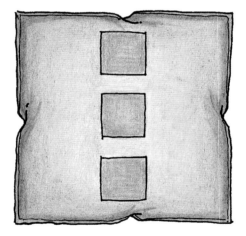

Centered Blocks
CD 447

Stacking Squares
CD 448

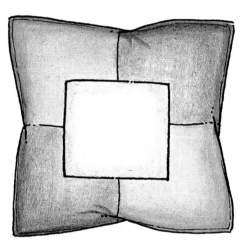

Quarters with
a Center Square
CD 450

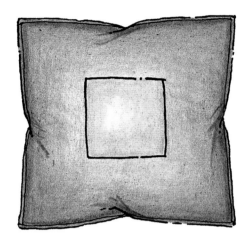

Center Square
CD 449

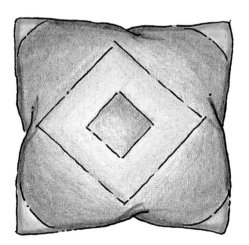

Rounded Corners with
Stacked Diamonds
CD 452

Stacked Diamonds
CD 451

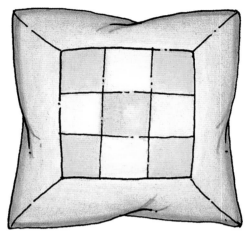

Checkerboard Center
CD 453

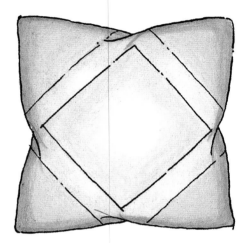

Bordered Diamond
CD 454

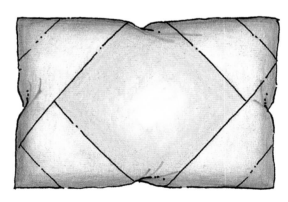

Overlapped Borders
CD 455

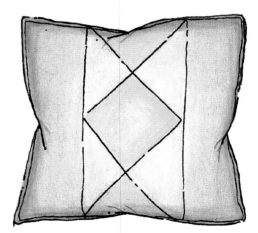

Harlequin Banding
CD 456

Rounded Square
CD 457

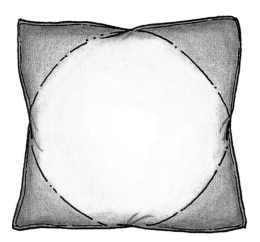

Centered Circle
CD 458

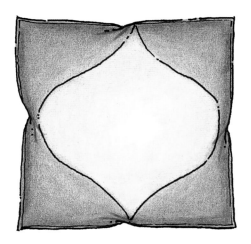

Pointed Circle
CD 459

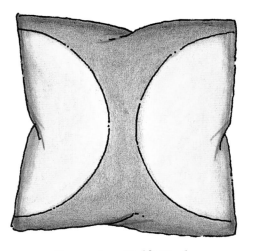

Opposing Half-Circles
CD 460

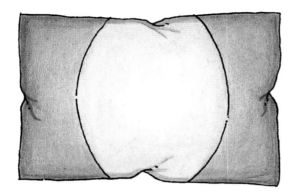

Rounded Center
CD 461

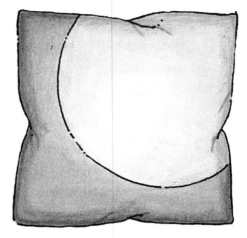

Cropped Circle
CD 462

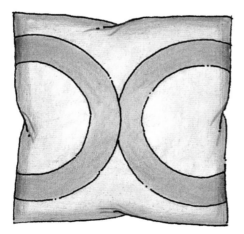

Opposite Rings
CD 463

Open Cloverleaf
CD 464

Fancy Square
CD 465

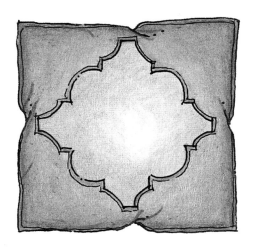

Fancy Diamond
CD 466

Fancy Square
CD 467

Fancy Circle
CD 468

Pillows with Ribbon

Ribbon, gimp, gallon, or decorative tape can be used to create specific effects on any pillow face.

✤ Use it to define specific areas of the pillow face.

✤ Use it to create intricate patterns and designs.

✤ Use it to cover seams where different sections of fabrics overlap or are joined together.

✤ Use it as the unifying element on a pillow with several different fabrics.

✤ Ribbon can be attached to the face of the pillow with fusible tape, double-stick fabric-bonding tape, or trim adhesive.

✤ It may be necessary to stitch the ribbon in place, even when using other adhesive methods, to prevent it from coming loose over time.

✤ When using heat-transfer tape, be sure to pretest your fabric and trim for heat tolerance with your iron set on high. Many fabrics and trims will shrink when exposed to heat.

Pillows with Ribbon

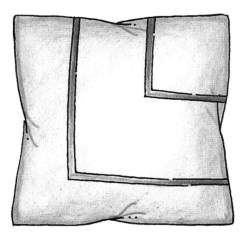

Right Angles
CD 473

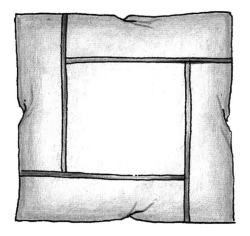

Rotating Lines
CD 474

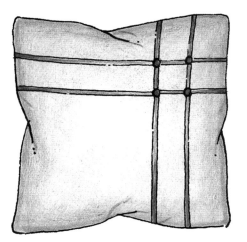

Double Corner Crossover
CD 475

Multiple Right Angles
CD 476

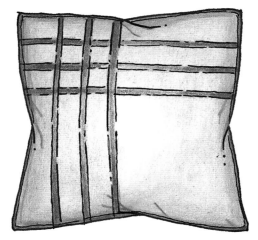

Corner Crossover
CD 477

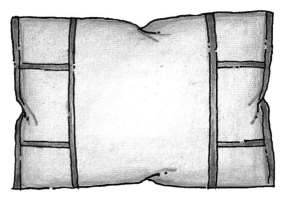

Squares at the Sides
CD 478

Diagonal Diamonds
CD 479

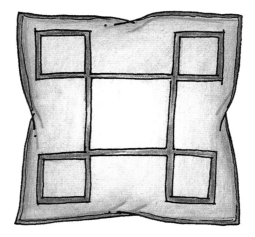

Five Squares
CD 480

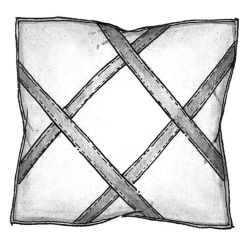

Crisscrossed Diamonds
CD 482

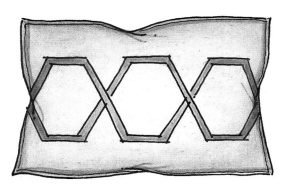

Triple Hexagon
CD 481

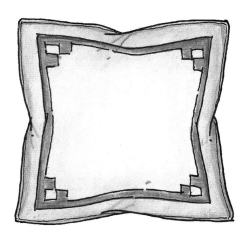

Fancy Border
CD 484

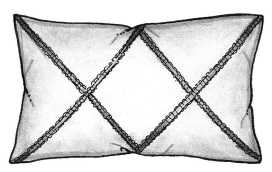

Crisscrossed Diamonds
CD 483

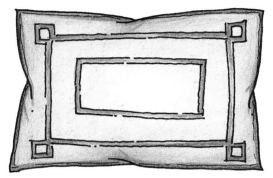

Rectangles Inside Rectangles
CD 485

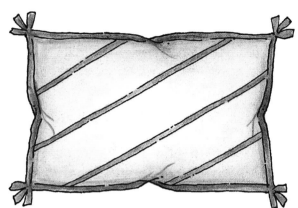

Diagonal Lines
CD 486

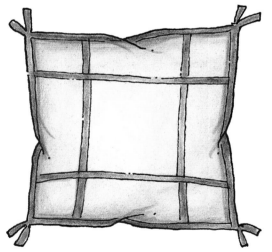

Crisscrossed Corners
CD 487

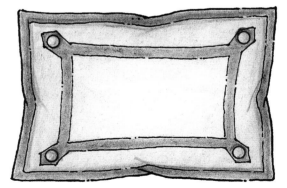

Buttoned-Down Border
CD 488

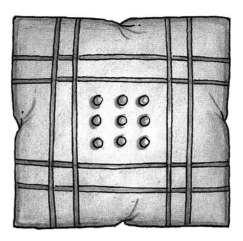

Double Crisscrossed Corners
with a Square of Buttons
CD 489

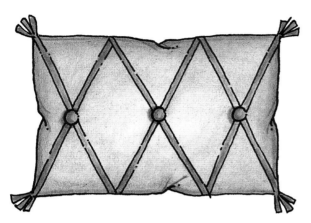

Diamonds with Buttons
and Ribbon Tabs
CD 490

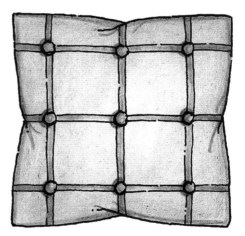

Checkerboard with Buttons
CD 491

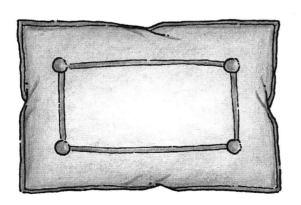

Center Rectangle with Buttons
CD 492

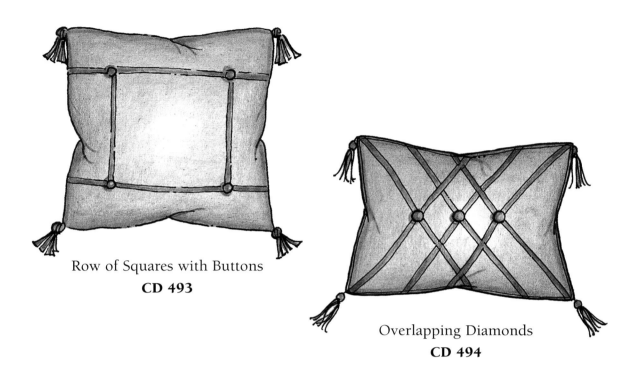

Row of Squares with Buttons
CD 493

Overlapping Diamonds
CD 494

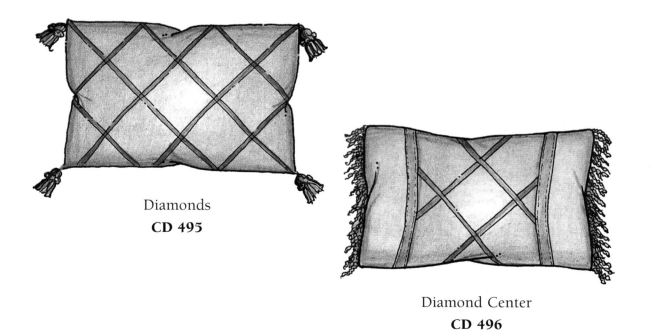

Diamonds
CD 495

Diamond Center
CD 496

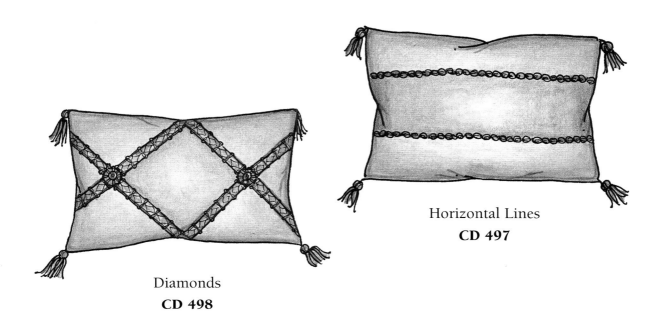

Diamonds
CD 498

Horizontal Lines
CD 497

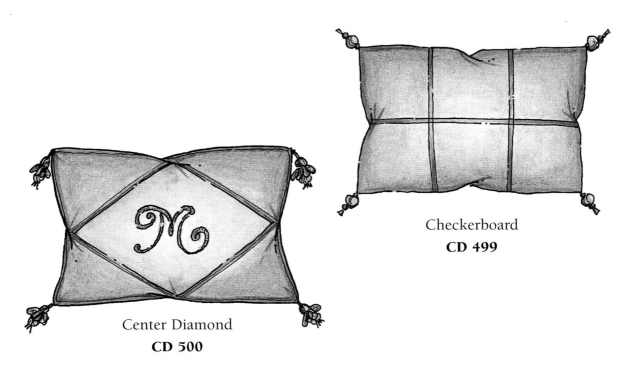

Center Diamond
CD 500

Checkerboard
CD 499

Crisscrossed Corner with
Ribbon Rosette

CD 505

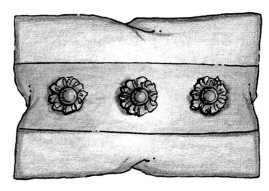

Horizontal Band with Triple Rosettes

CD 506

Crisscrossed Center with Rosette
and Ribbon Tabs

CD 507

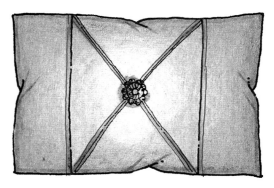

Crisscrossed Center Panel
with Rosette

CD 508

Pillows with Buttons and Closures

Buttons and other fastening elements, such as buckles, toggles, and frogs, can add detail and texture to any pillow.

Types of Closures

+ Decorative Buttons
+ Fabric-Covered Buttons
+ Decorative Snaps
+ Frogs
+ Buckles
+ Toggles

+ Buttons can be functional when paired with buttonholes or loops, or they can be purely decorative.

+ When using buttons on pillows that will be placed in a high-traffic area, specify padded self-covered buttons that won't scratch or irritate the user.

+ Make sure the buttons are sewn on with heavy-duty button twist thread that has been knotted several times during sewing. This might prevent the button from coming loose or falling off.

+ Always provide an extra button or two with the pillow for replacement purposes.

+ Decorative buttons should be removed before cleaning the pillow cover.

+ Use a fabric-marking pen that has disappearing ink to mark the placement for your buttons. If a button does fall off, there will be no obvious mark present on the pillow.

Pillows with Buttons and Closures

Four triangle-shaped flaps are attached at the sides of this pillow. They fold over the face and are held in place at the center with a contrasting button.

CD 509

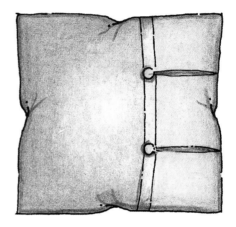

Two inverted box pleats run perpendicular to a contrasting band and are highlighted by fabric-covered buttons.

CD 510

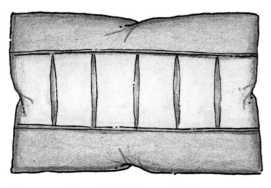

A center band of pleated fabric runs the length of this pillow. It is separated from the side bands with welting.

CD 511

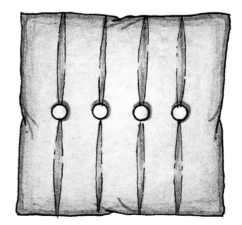

A series of inverted pleats with contrasting inserts are cinched in at the center with contrasting buttons.

CD 512

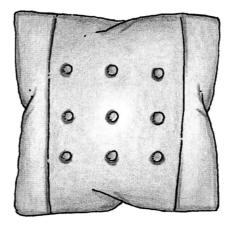

A slipcover sleeve is attached to the face of the pillow with a series of contrasting buttons.

CD 513

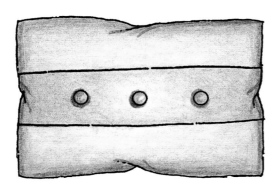

A band of contrasting fabric is attached at both ends of the pillow and tacked to the face with three contrasting buttons.

CD 514

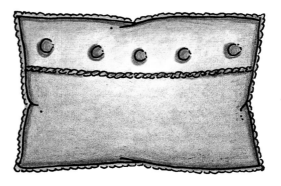

The top contrasting section of this pillow is separated with decorative braid and highlighted by five buttons.

CD 515

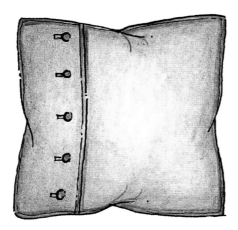

Nonfunctional buttonholes and buttons run down the face of a contrasting side panel, giving it the illusion of being a separate flap.

CD 516

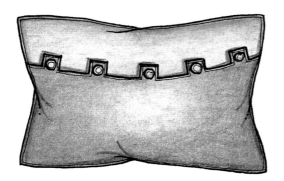

The tabbed bottom section of this pillow overlays a contrasting panel and is held in place by buttons.
CD 517

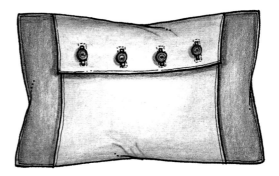

A separate panel of fabric is wrapped around this pillow and buttoned together at the front.
CD 518

The face of this pillow is split to reveal a contrasting facing. Decorative frogs hold the panels together at the center.
CD 519

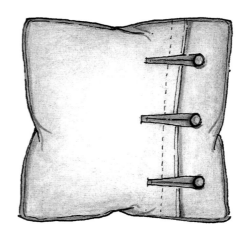

An overlaid panel covers all but the end of this pillow. Fabric loops attached to the panel wrap around contrasting buttons.
CD 520

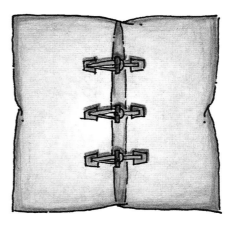

Leather-and-wood toggles hold closed a split at the center of that exposes a contrasting facing.
CD 521

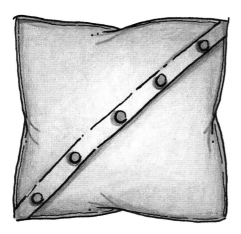

A wide tuck running diagonally across the face of this pillow is held down with contrasting buttons.
CD 522

An overlay with tabs running on the diagonal is laid over the top of this pillow and held in place with a button at each tab.
CD 523

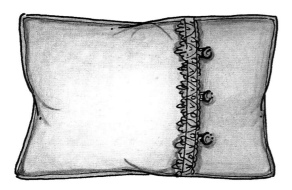

A band made of two decorative trims runs down the face of this pillow. Loops are fastened with buttons, giving the illusion of a functional opening.
CD 524

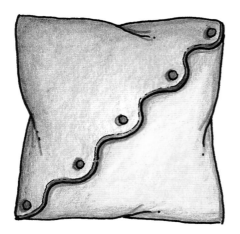

A scalloped edge on this overlaid, buttoned-down panel adds a fun twist to the design.
CD 525

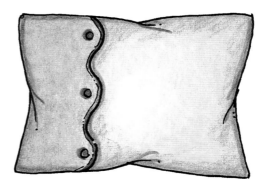

An overlaid buttoned-down panel runs down the face of this pillow.
CD 526

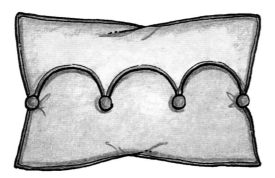

The overlaid panel at the top of this pillow has three inverted scallops coming to sharp points at the edge. Each point is held in place with a large button.
CD 527

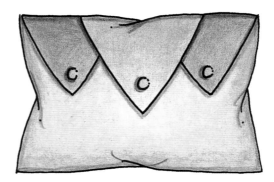

One large triangular flap is folded over two smaller flaps at the top of this pillow. They are held in place with buttons.
CD 528

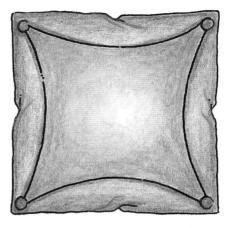

A separate contrasting panel of fabric with scooped-in sides is held in place on the face of the pillow, with buttons at each corner point.

CD 529

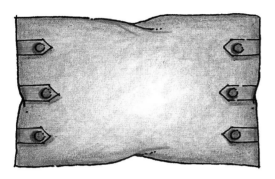

Decorative tabs with pointed ends are sewn into the side seams. They are folded over the face of the pillow and buttoned in place.

CD 530

Decorative tabs are sewn into the seams at the four corners. They are folded over the face of the pillow and buttoned in place.

CD 531

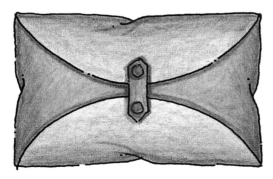

Two scalloped panels are sewn into the top and bottom seams. They are folded to the center of the face and held in place with a buttoned-down decorative band.

CD 532

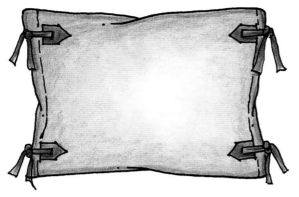

Fabric ties with decorative anchors are attached at the four corners of the center contrasting panel on the front and back of this pillow. They are tied in knots at both sides.
CD 533

Decorative purse buckles are used to embellish the face of this pillow.
CD 534

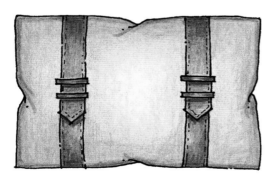

Long fabric ties wrap around this pillow and are secured by being threaded through fabric loops.
CD 535

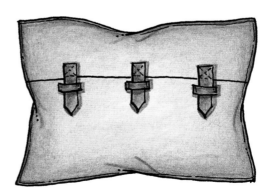

Small pointed tabs are cut from leather strapping to create these mini belt closures.
CD 536

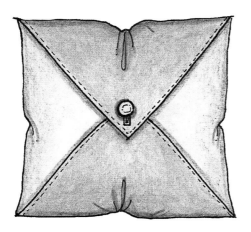

Two triangular flaps are sewn into the seams at the top and bottom. The flaps overlap at the center and are held in place with a functional button.
CD 538

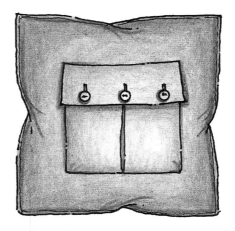

A pleated pocket is centered on the face of this pillow. The pocket flap is buttoned down with functional buttons.
CD 537

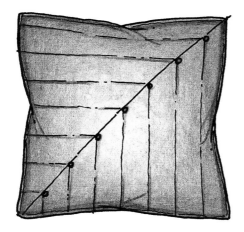

Small tucks are sewn into the two sections of the pillow face in opposing directions. When the pieces are sewn together, the tucks form a pattern that is emphasized by small buttons at each intersection.
CD 540

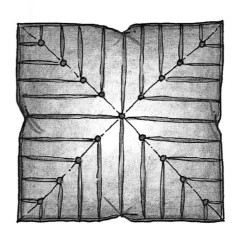

The triangular sections of this pillow face are pleated so that when they are joined together, the pleats form a pattern. Small buttons are placed at the intersecting pleat lines.
CD 539

Pillows with Bows and Ties

Bows and ties can be a versatile and creative addition to your pillow designs.

+ They can be decorative additions to the design or can serve a functional purpose.

+ They can be constructed of fabric and should be lined and turned so there are no raw edges.

+ When using ribbon, be sure to seal the cut end with a liquid sealer such as Fray Check to prevent it from unraveling.

+ Decorative tape and gimp can be sealed at the end to prevent raveling by sewing a stay stitch across the end and then applying Fray Check.

+ After securing bows and ties into tight knots, stay-stitch them in place to prevent them from untying. Tack down the underside of bows to prevent them from folding over on themselves or becoming misshapen.

Pillows with Bows and Ties

A faux slipcover sleeve is scooped in at the sides and attached at the top and bottom of the pillow. Gathered ties are looped into bows at each side.
CD 542

A separate slipcover sleeve covers the pillow and long ties are looped into bows at each side, holding the cover in place.
CD 541

Four triangle-shaped flaps are attached at the sides of the pillow. They fold over the face and are tied in place with a decorative cord attached to each triangle point.
CD 544

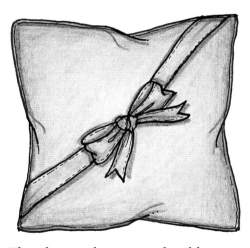

This design shows a wide ribbon on the diagonal, with a bow at the center.
CD 543

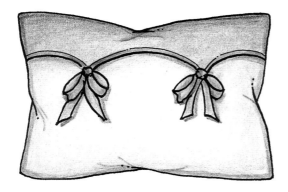

The points of the contrasting overlay at the top of this pillow are tied down with decorative bows.
CD 545

A diagonal slit in the pillow face exposes a contrasting fabric. It is held closed with a series of small decorative bows.
CD 546

Envelope flaps overlap at the center of this bordered pillow. A decorative bow holds them together.
CD 547

This pillow is given the illusion of being slipcovered by the addition of a contrasting border at each side that is embellished with ties and bows.
CD 548

Ribbon is attached to the face and back of this pillow, and bows are sewn to the top to create the illusion of a single length of ribbon tied into a bow.
CD 550

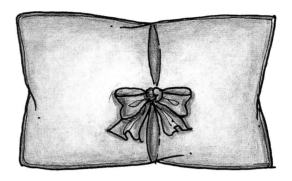

A slit at the center is held closed with a wide bow.
CD 549

A band of ribbon circles the top half of the pillow, while long ribbons are sewn beneath the band at the back and wrapped under the bottom and up over the face. Shorter lengths of ribbon are sewn under the front band and the two sections are tied into bows.
CD 552

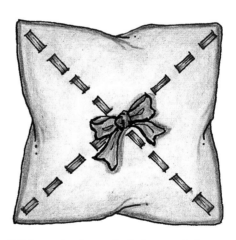

Ribbon is threaded through buttonholes on the face of this pillow. A large bow marks the center.
CD 551

Four independent border sections are folded over the face of the pillow and tie together into bows at each corner.

CD 553

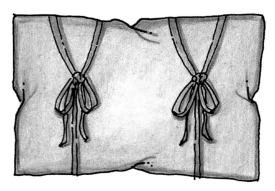

V-shaped intersecting ribbons lead to a single ribbon extending beneath a decorative bow.

CD 554

Ribbon is laced through small shoe hooks attached to the face of this pillow in a diagonal pattern. It is tied into bows at each end.

CD 555

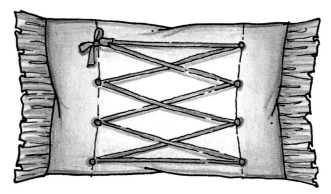

The center panel of this pillow is laced with ribbon threaded through grommets at each side. A small bow at one corner is a whimsical finishing touch.

CD 556

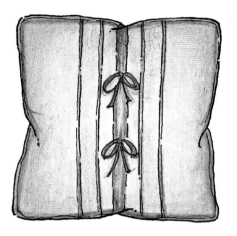

A series of tucks and a slit opening with bows at the center are the focal point of this pillow.
CD 557

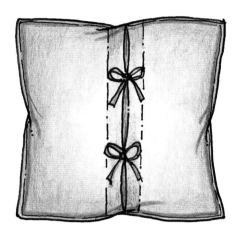

The slit opening is bordered with contrasting fabric that matches the facing.
CD 558

Pleats at the bottom of this pillow are topped with a flap that is held down with decorative bows.
CD 559

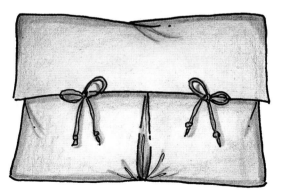

This flap-top pillow has a central pleat and two long bows tied into knots at the ends.
CD 560

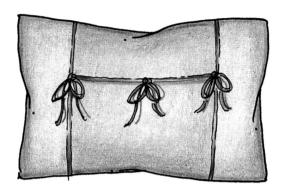

Ribbon and bows separate the different sections of fabric on this pillow.
CD 561

A double ribbon border is embellished with two staggered bows.
CD 562

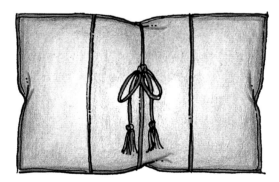

Decorative cord with lip borders the center section of this pillow, while the same cord without lip is used to cinch in the center. Tied into a bow, the cord is knotted at the end and unwound into a tassel.
CD 563

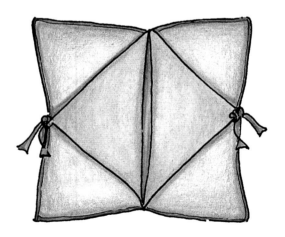

Two large triangular panels fold out at the center of the pillow, exposing a contrasting facing. They are tied down at each side.
CD 564

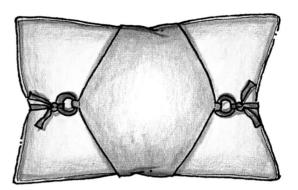

The contrasting sleeve that covers this pillow is tied on with ribbon knotted to plastic rings that are attached to each end with fabric loops.

CD 565

Diagonal stripes of ribbon criss-cross at the center of this pillow, which is embellished with a double knot with ties.

CD 566

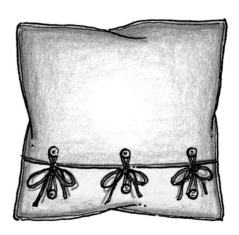

A continuous loop of ribbon is wound tightly around the opposing buttons at the bottom border of this pillow. A bow is tied around the loop at its center.

CD 567

This pillow is tied up like a present with intersecting ribbons and a long bow.

CD 568

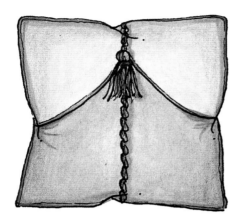

A peaked border is given a focal point by a line of decorative braid, with a large tassel at the peak.
CD 569

A faux sleeve is created by bordering the center section of the pillow with braid and attaching matching ties at each end.
CD 570

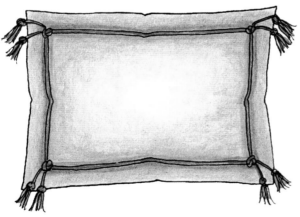

A border is created with cording that is tied into knots at each corner and finishes in a double tie with knotted and tasseled ends.
CD 571

Decorative braid separates the two sections of fabric on this pillow face. Key tassels with braided medallions embellish the side border.
CD 572

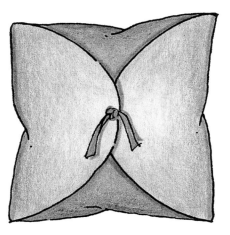

Half-circle envelope flaps cover the face of this pillow. They are held together with a knotted tie.
CD 573

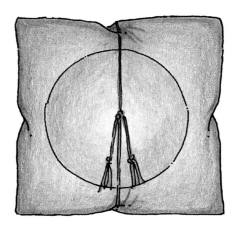

A large circle appliquéd to the face of this pillow is topped with a cord and knotted ties for an Asian look.
CD 574

These envelope flaps are shirred at the center to create volume. A loop of braid and key tassels hide the shirring seams.
CD 575

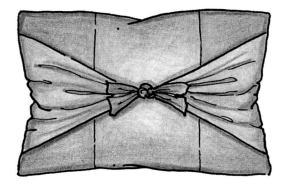

Sheer rectangular flaps are sewn into the sides of this pillow. They are brought to the front and tied together at the center.
CD 576

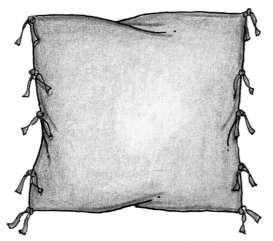

Knotted ties run down the sides of this simple pillow.
CD 577

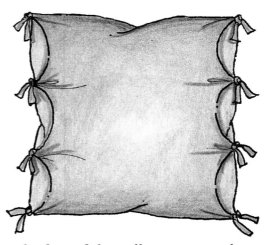

The face of this pillow is covered with a scalloped overlay that is tied to the side seams at each point.
CD 578

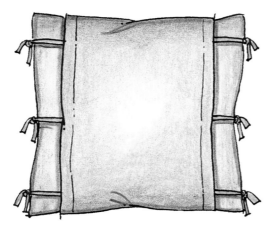

A straight sleeve is attached to this pillow with three ties on each side. Always sew ties and bows in place to prevent sagging.
CD 579

Decorative tape forms a diamond on the face of this pillow. The points of the diamonds are accentuated by knotted ties.
CD 580

A square plastic hoop is attached to the end of this tent flap with a fabric loop and tie.
CD 581

The corners of the pocket sewn to this pillow face are pleated to create volume. The pillow flap is embellished with a knotted tie.
CD 582

A scalloped overlay is topped with silk rosettes. A contrasting facing shows through the scalloped cutouts.
CD 583

Clam-shaped cutouts in the face expose a contrasting facing. Silk rosettes are placed at the ends of the cutouts.
CD 584

Dog ears are added to each corner and embellished with a knotted tie.
CD 585

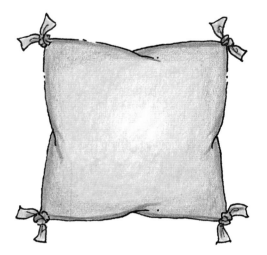

Knotted ties are sewn to each corner of this pillow.
CD 586

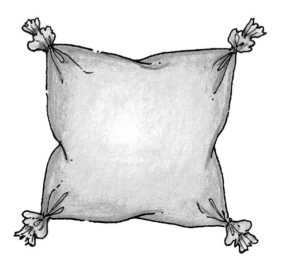

The open dog ears at the corners of this pillow are cinched in at the corner and just below the end to create this interesting shape.
CD 587

Open, gathered dog ears are added to the corners of this pillow. They are tied with long bows.
CD 588

Welted Pillows

Jumbo welt cord covered in fabric can
be used to create some dramatic designs.

CD 590

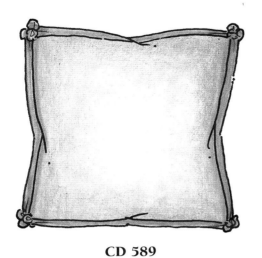

CD 589

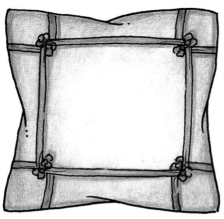

CD 591

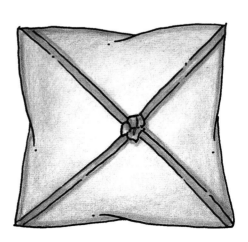

CD 592

Pillows with Grommets

Grommets have recently gone from purely functional devices to popular decorative elements. They provide an effective means to embellish contemporary designs.

- Grommets are two-sided metal frames that snap into place over the face and back side of fabric to provide a sealed opening.

- Grommets are now available in a large variety of shapes, sizes, and finishes.

- They can be used as purely decorative elements or they can serve a specific function.

- Most grommets require the use of a commercial machine for proper application.

- Grommets can be difficult to use with loosely woven, very heavyweight, or very sheer fabrics.

- Fabric fitted with grommets should not be washed in a washing machine. Specify dry-cleaning only.

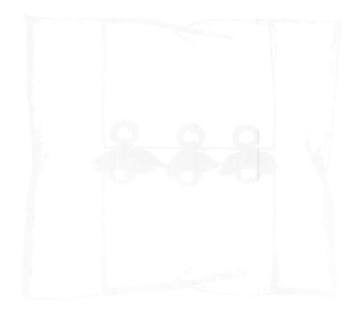

Pillows with Grommets

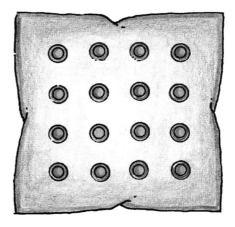

The face of this pillow is covered with carefully placed grommets that form a large square. Contrasting fabric is seen through the grommet openings.
CD 593

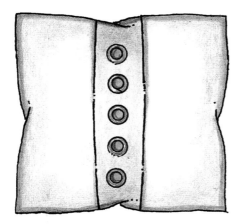

A thin contrasting sleeve fitted with a row of grommets is centered over the face of this pillow, allowing the face fabric to show through.
CD 594

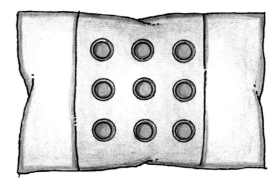

This pillow has a faux sleeve with extra-large grommets showing off a contrasting facing.
CD 595

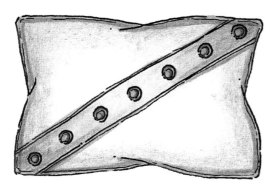

Grommets follow the line of a diagonal band that is sewn over the face fabric, allowing it to show through.
CD 596

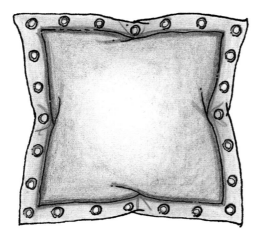

Medium-sized grommets decorate a flange border.

CD 597

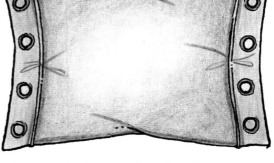

Two wide flanges fitted with grommets flank the sides of this pillow.

CD 598

The four corners of this pillow are fitted with grommets that are highlighted with pointed ties knotted through the grommet.

CD 599

Two extra-large grommets are placed at kitty-corner on two of the four squares that make up the front of this pillow. A contrasting facing shows through, and a wide tie is threaded through them and knotted at the front.

CD 600

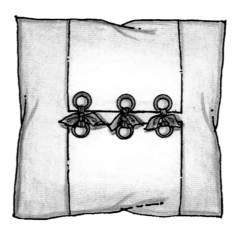

An open sleeve fitted with grommets at each end is laced together with knotted ties at the center of the pillow face.
CD 601

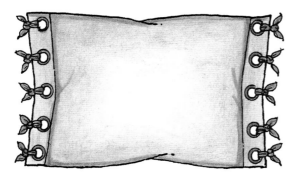

Flanges at each end of this pillow are fitted with grommets that are decorated with small knotted ties.
CD 602

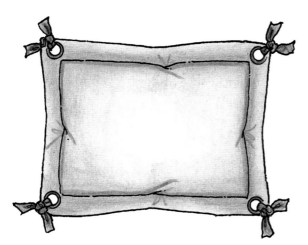

The four corners of this flanged pillow are fitted with grommets and knotted ties.
CD 604

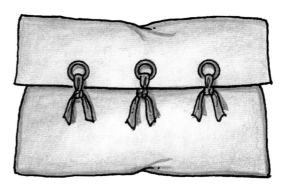

Long knotted ties are threaded through grommets at the edge of this tent-flap pillow.
CD 603

Tent-Flap Pillows

A tent-flap pillow is the perfect design to place at the front of the pillow stack on any bed. Its unique design creates a focused point that brings the eye down to the bed covers.

✤ "Tent flap" is the term used to describe a separate flap of fabric that is attached at the top of the pillow and folds down over the face.

✤ The tent flap can be left loose or can be tacked down to the face of the pillow.

✤ The tent flap should be lined with self-lining or a contrasting fabric.

✤ Loose tent flaps hang best when weighted with a decorative element such as a tassel or beads.

✤ Tacking down elements such as tassels or bows will prevent them from losing shape or tearing free with wear.

✤ A faux tent flap has the appearance of a loose flap but is actually created with a change in fabric on the pillow face or a border that delineates the shape of a tent flap.

Tent-Flap Pillows

A contrasting center panel serves as a backdrop for the flap point and decorative tassel.
CD 605

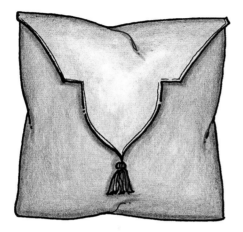

The distinctive shape of the tent flap is the focal point of this pillow.
CD 606

This flap is bordered in a contrasting color, and a matching bow hangs from the point.
CD 607

A simple flap is embellished with a stone hoop and knotted tie on this pillow.
CD 608

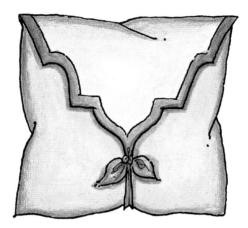

The bordered edge of this tent flap ends in a knotted tie that is anchored to a matching ribbon running under the flap. This gives the impression that the flap is tied down.
CD 609

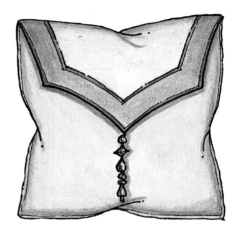

Beads are an effective method of highlighting the point of a flap. Use a variety of shapes and sizes for the most impact.
CD 610

A faux flap is created on the face of this pillow by a V-shaped border placed at the top half of the pillow. A vertical strip of contrasting fabric runs down from the point, creating a backdrop for the key tassel.
CD 611

Beaded trim edges this tent flap, which is weighted with a beaded tassel at the point.
CD 612

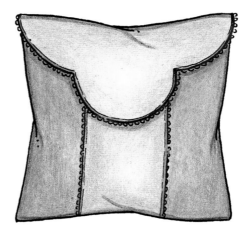

The end of this tent flap is rounded off rather than ending in the typical point.
CD 613

A faux tent flap is created by the asymmetrical placement of the chevron-shaped top panel and the tassel at the point.
CD 614

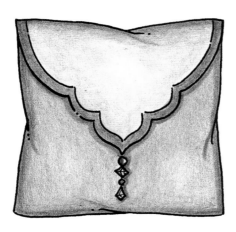

Scallops border the edges of this tent flap, which culminates in a sharp point that is weighted with chandelier crystals.
CD 616

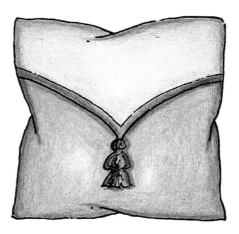

This tent flap is a separate piece, but it is sewn into the top and side hems of the pillow, leaving only the bottom edge hanging free.
CD 615

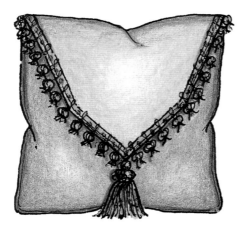

The sharp angles of this extra-long tent flap are trimmed with onion fringe and a tassel at the point.
CD 617

Bullion fringe adds length and detail to this rounded tent flap.
CD 618

The end of this rounded tent flap is cut in a circle to accentuate the large ribbon flourish that tacks it down to the pillow face.
CD 619

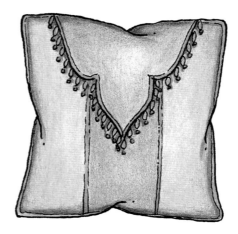

This mini tent flap is mounted at the center of the top of the pillow, leaving the corners uncovered.
CD 620

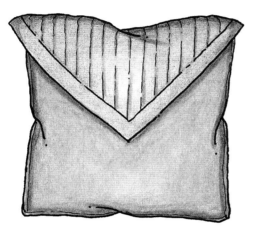

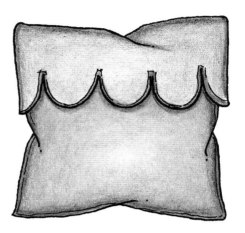

A series of deep scallops form the edge of this tent flap.
CD 621

The top corners of this tent flap angle in sharply, creating the impression that the flap extends beyond the side of the pillow.
CD 622

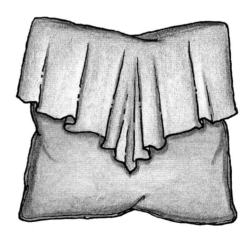

This informal flounced tent flap is created by cutting the flap in a circular shape.
CD 623

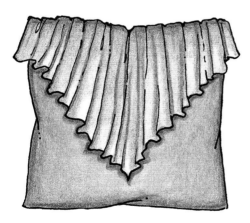

This V-shaped tent flap is pleated at the top, creating a waterfall effect.
CD 624

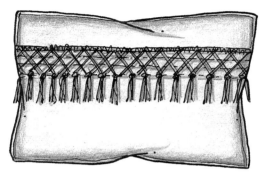

Long hand-tied fringe can give the illusion of a tent flap when placed on the top half of the pillow.
CD 625

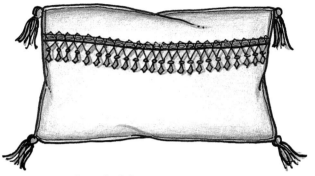

Long beaded fringe can also make a pillow look like it has a tent flap.
CD 626

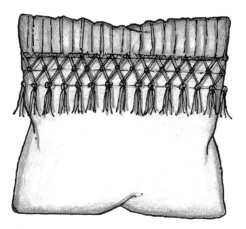

The top panel of this pillow is shirred above a row of hand-tied fringe.
CD 627

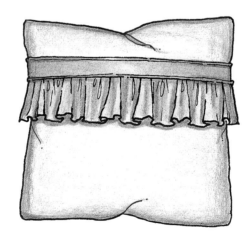

A contrasting band of fabric is bordered by welting and dressed up with a long ruffle.
CD 628

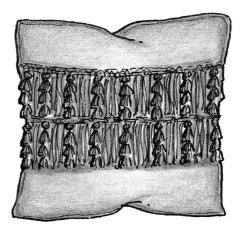

A double row of triple tassel and bullion fringe has the look of a double tent flap.
CD 629

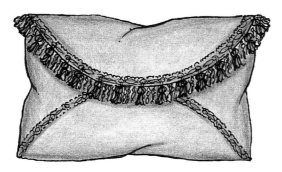

A faux tent flap is created by overlapping half circles of trim.
CD 630

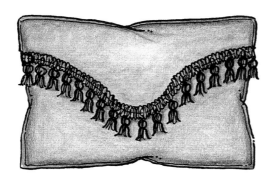

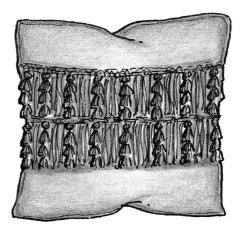

Long bullion fringe can be draped in almost any shape to create a faux flap.
CD 631

Try running trim in interesting shapes to create unusual effects.
CD 632

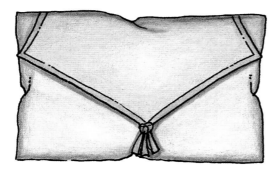

This tent flap is angled in at the top corners, creating a sharp point at either side.
CD 633

The sides of this flap angle out slightly at the top and then go back into a point that is fitted with a grommet and a knotted bow.
CD 634

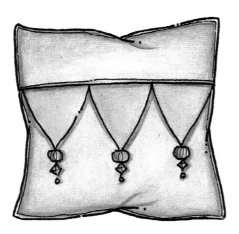

Three pennants weighted with beads hang from the top panel of this pillow.
CD 635

Three separate sections bordered with trim make up the tent flap on this pillow.
CD 636

Ruffled Pillows

Ruffles are not just for the edges of the pillow. They make wonderful decorative additions to the face as well.

✦ Ruffles can be sewn between sections of fabric on the pillow face or they can be sewn directly onto the face itself.

✦ Ruffles should be double folded to avoid a hem or should have a finished edge accomplished with the following methods:

- Double-Turned Hem
- Lingerie Hem
- Rolled Hem
- Napkin Hem

Types of Ruffles

✦ Shirred
✦ Pleated
✦ Accordion Pleated
✦ Smocked

Ruffled Pillows

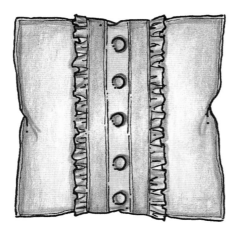

The ruffles and buttons on the face of this pillow resemble a shirt front.
CD 637

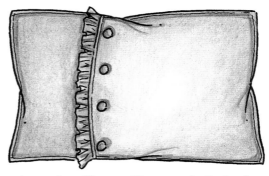

A single offset ruffle is embellished with buttons.
CD 638

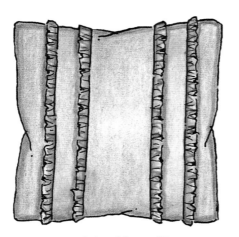

Two rows of double ruffles create strong vertical lines on this design.
CD 639

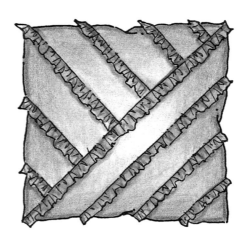

Rows of ribbon set on the diagonal run perpendicular to each other on this pillow face.
CD 640

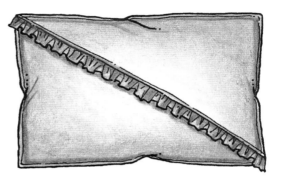

A single diagonal ruffle lays across the face of this pillow.

CD 641

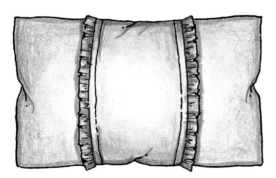

This pillow has two tucks at the edge of the center panel, under which a ruffle is mounted.

CD 642

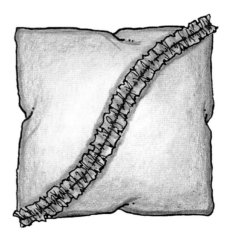

A double-edged ruffle is shirred along the center line and sewn to the face in a sinuous line.

CD 643

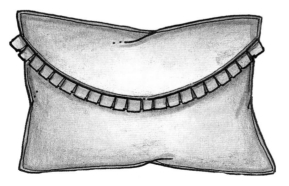

A short, crisply pleated ruffle runs in a large scallop across this pillow face.

CD 644

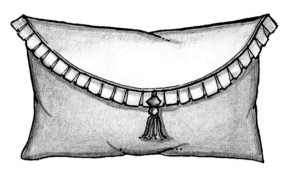

A pleated ruffle trims the edge of this rounded tent-flap pillow.
CD 645

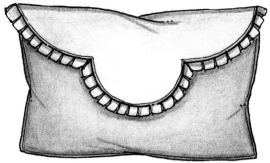

A triple-scalloped tent flap is finished with a pleated ruffle.
CD 646

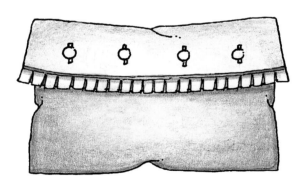

This ruffled tent flap is buttoned down with functional fabric-covered buttons.
CD 647

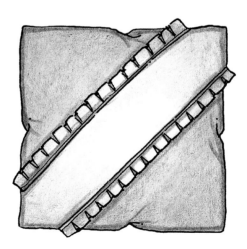

Pleated ruffles on the diagonal each face out from the center.
CD 648

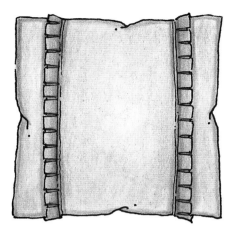

Two rows of short pleated ruffles run vertically across this pillow face.
CD 649

A half-circle tent flap with a scalloped border tops this pillow.
CD 650

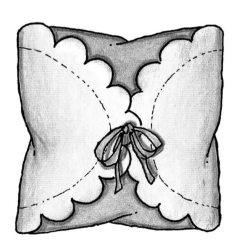

Two scallop-edged flaps cross over one another at the center of this pillow, where they are held in place with a long bow.
CD 652

The scalloped circle cutout at the center of this pillow lays over a contrasting face fabric that calls attention to the scalloped border.
CD 651

A pleated zigzag ruffle tops a recessed, contrasting center panel on this pillow. The ruffle points inward toward the center and lies underneath the triangular corner panels.
CD 653

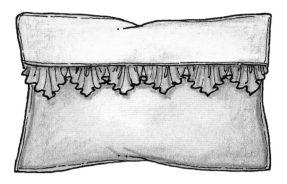

This pillow is banded with a zigzag-edged ruffle.
CD 654

This pleated zigzag ruffle is topped with a center panel and topstitched so the ruffle lays flat.
CD 655

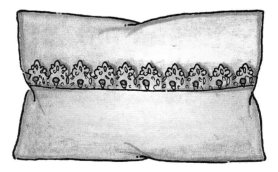

A lace ruffle banding is topped with elastic loops and pearl buttons for a very feminine design.
CD 656

Shirred Pillows

Inserting panels of shirred fabric in your pillows adds depth and texture to what typically would be a flat surface.

✦ Shirring is accomplished by gathering both sides of the fabric so it is condensed in length, adding volume.

✦ Shirring looks best when using solid-colored or small-print fabrics. It is not suitable for large patterns.

✦ Sections of shirred fabric that are very wide can blouse out and lose their tight gathers. Tacking the gathers in place at the center on a large section can prevent this.

✦ It is best to apply the gathering stitches at both sides of your piece of fabric going in the same direction. They should also be gathered up in the same direction. This prevents the gathers on the opposite sides from fighting each other and produces a tight shirred effect that will lay flat.

Shirred Pillows

A fabric panel shirred on the diagonal is placed opposite a flat panel.

CD 667

A shirred band is laid under face panels that appear to be split on the diagonal.

CD 668

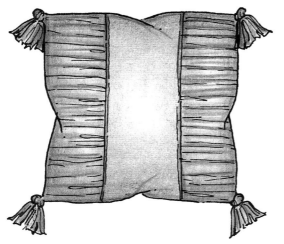

Alternating bands of shirred and flat fabric add texture and richness to this pillow.

CD 669

The border of this pillow is made of flat corner sections centered with shirred bands. Decorative tape separates the different sections from one another.

CD 670

This border is shirred and surrounds a middle panel that is tufted in the center.
CD 672

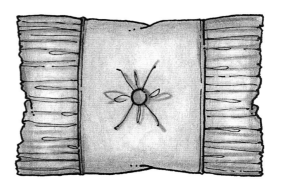

Shirred side panels flank the center panel, which is tufted at the center with a button.
CD 671

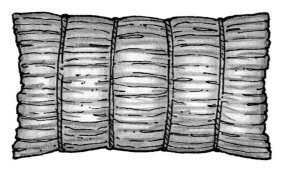

Decorative braid separates five sections of shirred fabric on this pillow.
CD 674

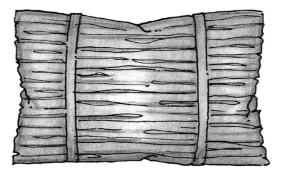

Three separate sections of shirred fabric make up the face of this pillow.
CD 673

Two sections of shirring are placed at the center of this pillow.
CD 675

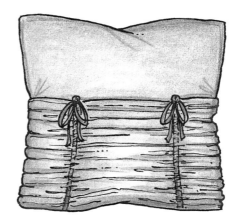

A separate shirred sleeve open at only one end covers the bottom portion of this pillow. Casings sewn into the front of the sleeve are threaded with ties that are pulled up and end in bows at the top.
CD 676

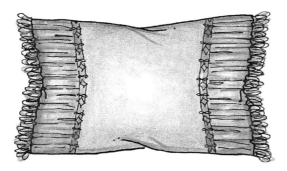

This pillow is covered with closed-end shirred sleeves on both ends. Fabric tape runs along the width of the pillow in two bands that are embellished at the end of the sleeve with long bows.
CD 677

Shirred panels at both ends are embellished with decorative tape and loop fringe.
CD 678

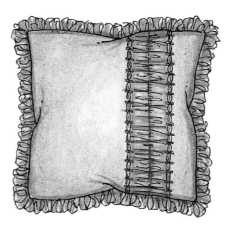

An offset shirred band is gathered at the center as well as at the sides for a unique look.
CD 679

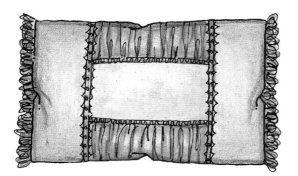

Small inserts of shirred fabric can add texture and richness to any combination.
CD 680

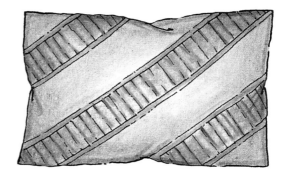

Pleated bands of contrasting fabric are run on the diagonal across the pillow face. Flat banding separates the alternating bands.
CD 681

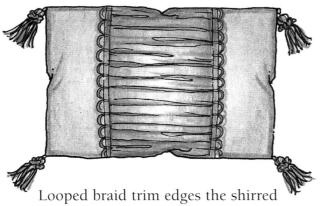

Looped braid trim edges the shirred center panel of this pillow.
CD 682

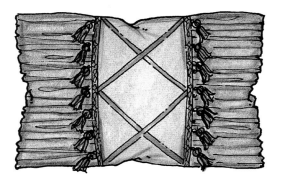

The shirred ends of this pillow flank a flat center panel that is decorated with crisscrossed tape and tassel fringe.

CD 683

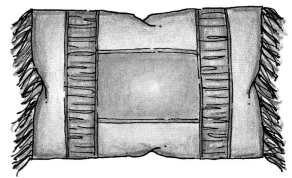

Narrow shirred bands serve as borders in the combination of this face.

CD 684

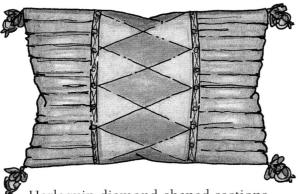

Harlequin diamond-shaped sections of this center panel are flanked by shirred ends.

CD 685

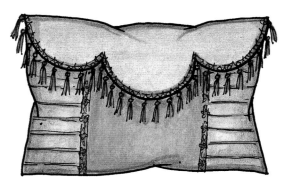

Pleated end panels are topped with a triple-scalloped tent flap embellished with tassel fringe.

CD 686

Intersecting shirred banners on the face of this pillow are knotted at the center.
CD 688

Shirred banners meet in the top corner of this pillow, where they are embellished with a silk rosette.
CD 687

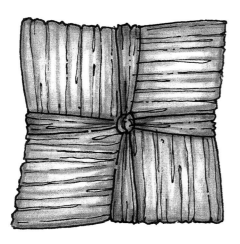

Shirred quarter sections are juxtaposed in different positions on the face of this pillow. Contrasting shirred banners cover the seams on the face.
CD 690

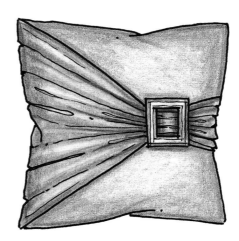

An extra-wide shirred banner spans the full height of this pillow at one end. It is cinched in at the other end with a decorative buckle that is sewn in place.
CD 689

This pillow features a shirred banner that is knotted off center.
CD 691

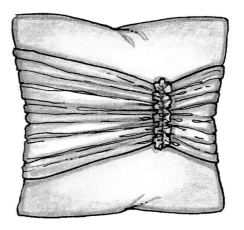

The ends of this shirred banner are joined together at the front of the pillow, leaving a short double ruffle off center.
CD 692

Shirred banners radiating from the center to the corners are embellished with a rosette at the center.
CD 693

A large button highlighted with a ruffle centers the shirred banners on this pillow.
CD 694

A wide, shirred, two-piece banner is placed at the center of the face and cinched in with a pointed knot tie.
CD 695

A shirred two-piece banner that covers the full height of the pillow is cinched in at the center and embellished with a knotted tie.
CD 696

An extra-large knot decorates the center of this banner pillow.
CD 697

A separate extra-long tie is placed at the junction of two shirred banners.
CD 698

This specialty pillow is made with shirred sections of fabric that extend beyond the ends of the pillow and are folded back over the corner to produce this unique design.
CD 699

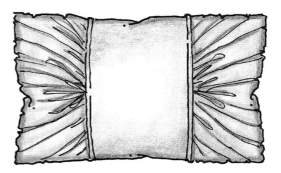

To produce the unique shirred panels at each end of this pillow requires a special pattern that is wider at the inner edge than at the outside edge.
CD 700

Corner panels are curved at the inside edge and shirred up the center to produce this look.
CD 701

Triangular panels are shirred on all three sides to create this design.
CD 702

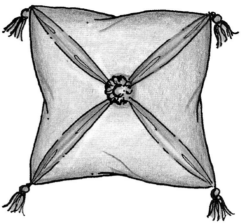

Narrow banners are cinched in at the ends and centered with a ribbon rosette.
CD 703

The fully shirred face of this pillow is tufted in the center and embellished with a looped rosette.
CD 704

Shirred triangular flaps fold over the face of this pillow. They are held in place with a center rosette.
CD 706

Multiple intersecting shirred banners crisscross over the face of this pillow.
CD 705

Trimmed Pillows

Decorative trim such as braid, gimp, tape, gallon, fringe, and bullion have long been traditional elements used to embellish pillows and bedding.

✤ Most decorative trim is not washable and must be dry-cleaned.

✤ Trim can shrink after it is removed from the card or bolt. Allow it to rest overnight before applying it to the pillow.

✤ Trim on the face of a pillow should be stitched in place even if you have used fusible tape, as the flexibility of the pillow and wear and tear can loosen fusible tape over time. Stitching will keep it in place.

✤ Trim will shrink considerably when used with iron-on tape. Do not cut your trim until you have ironed the tape onto the back side and preshrunk the trim.

✤ When attaching tassels at the corners of a pillow, don't rely on the tassel loop to hold it securely at the corner seam. Stitch the head of the tassel in place with loops of heavy-duty upholstery thread. This will prevent the tassel from being easily torn off.

Trimmed Pillows

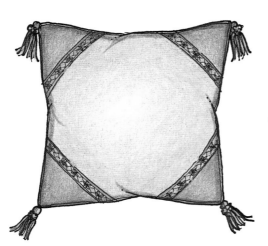

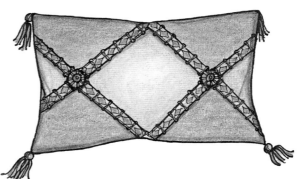

When overlapping trim, using a button or medallion at the intersections will emphasize the pattern created.
CD 707

The contrasting corner sections of this pillow and the decorative tape frame the center panel.
CD 708

When using a four-piece border, be sure to cut your corners on the diagonal.
CD 709

Small sections of contrasting fabrics can be unified by using a single trim to border them.
CD 710

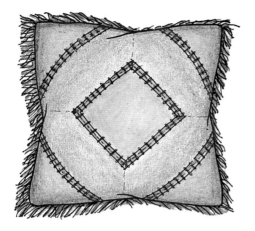

If your design contains exposed seams, be sure to plan where they fall. The middle border of this pillow contains seams that fall in line with the corners of the center diamond.
CD 711

Ribbon rosettes mark the four corners of the center diamond in this design.
CD 712

An intricately pieced center panel is trimmed with a small lace tape and set on the diagonal.
CD 713

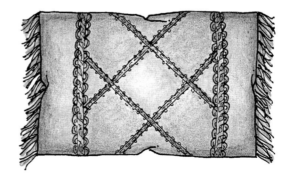

While this pillow has only two fabrics, the trim pattern on the center panel makes it appear much more intricate in design.
CD 714

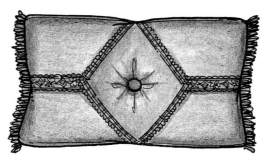

Wide decorative tape runs outward from the side points of a center diamond that is button tufted.
CD 715

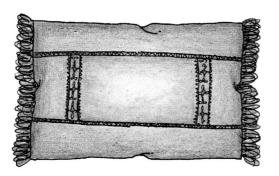

The width of this pillow is accentuated by the horizontal lines of trim.
CD 716

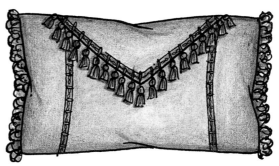

A V-shaped panel at the top of the pillow is embellished with tassel fringe, forming a faux tent flap.
CD 717

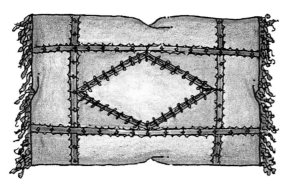

A wide diamond-shaped center panel is surrounded by vertical and horizontal lines of trim.
CD 718

Crisscrossed ribbon creates a diamond pattern at the center of this pillow. Bullion fringe trims the perimeter.
CD 719

An assortment of trims and fringes decorate the face of this pillow, creating an eclectic design.
CD 720

When using fringe or trim that has a direction to its design, be aware of its position on the pillow and how its direction affects the design.
CD 721

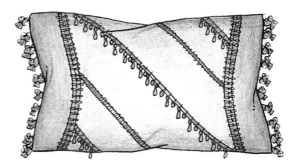

Alternating rows of tape and beaded trim are placed on the diagonal at the center of this pillow.
CD 722

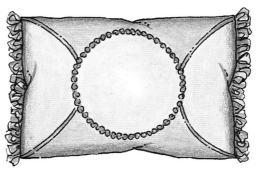

When specifying trim for curved or circular shapes, make sure it is flexible enough to achieve the desired effect.
CD 723

Lace trims and medallions are available in a huge variety of shapes and sizes and are perfectly suited for use on pillows.
CD 724

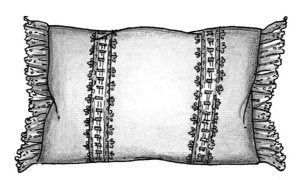

In many cases, a combination of trims is needed to produce the desired size and profile. Here, an eyelet tape threaded with ribbon is flanked by cloverleaf tape on each side, creating a multilayered effect.
CD 725

Tufted Pillows

A tufted pillow is cinched together through its layers of fabric and filled with buttons and thread or decorative stitching.

✦ A pillow can be tufted using stitching or buttons.

✦ It can be tufted on the surface only or it can be tufted through and through from front to back.

✦ Surface tufting is achieved by adding a layer of flat batting to the face section of the pillow and threading buttons or stitching through the face fabric and batting only.

✦ Use self-covered or smooth-surface buttons to avoid scratching or irritating the user.

✦ Consider how the chosen buttons will look on the back of the pillow as well as on the face. It might be necessary to use an alternative or a more subtle button choice for the back.

✦ Consider including an extra button or two with the pillow for easy replacement.

Tufted Pillows

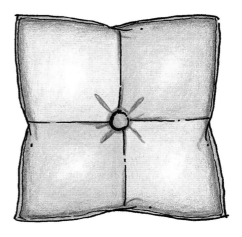

This pillow face is separated into four quarters and tufted at the center with a button.
CD 726

Diagonal quarters meet in the center of this button-tufted pillow.
CD 727

This pillow face is separated into 45-degree-angle diagonal eighths.
CD 728

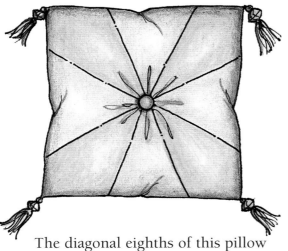

The diagonal eighths of this pillow face are offset and the lines fall at either side of the corner points rather than at the points.
CD 729

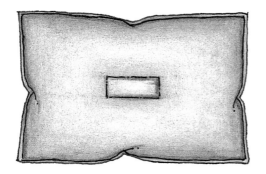

This pillow is tufted at the center by a rectangular section of topstitching.
CD 730

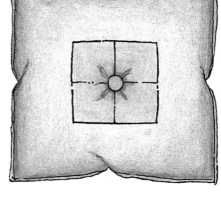

A small quartered square panel is the base for the tufting button on this pillow.
CD 731

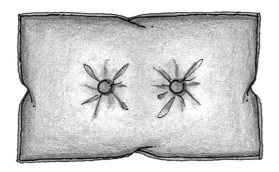

Two-button tufting.
CD 732

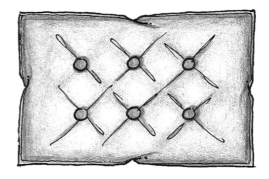

Six-button tufting.
CD 733

Concentric borders surround the center tufting button on this pillow face.
CD 734

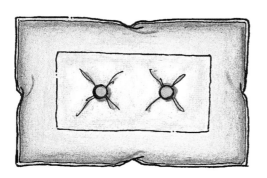

A wide border surrounds double buttons.
CD 735

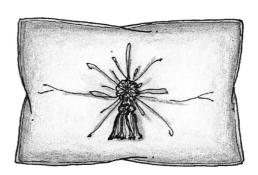

A tassel takes the place of a button on this tufted pillow front.
CD 736

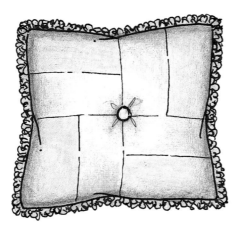

This pillow front is constructed with four quarters that are each split into two sections. The direction of the two bands in each quarter is rotated as they are placed around the face, creating a directional pattern.
CD 737

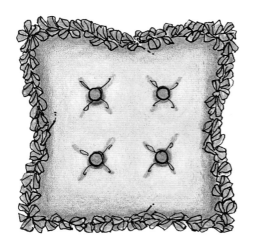

Four-button tufting.
CD 738

This pillow is channel tufted to create deep indentations between sections.
CD 739

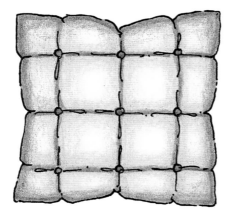

This pillow has sixteen separate tufted sections.
CD 740

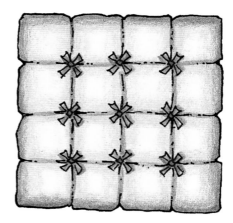

The tufts of this pillow are highlighted with small double-knotted ties.
CD 741

Silk rosettes are used to tuft this pillow.
CD 742

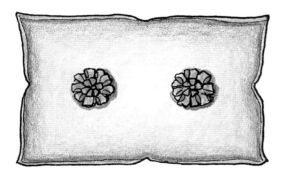

Ribbon rosettes with large decorative buttons are used to tuft this pillow.
CD 743

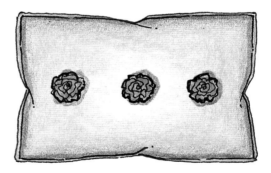

This pillow is tufted using handmade fabric roses.
CD 744

Silk or velvet leaves can add size and dramatic impact to any rosette.
CD 745

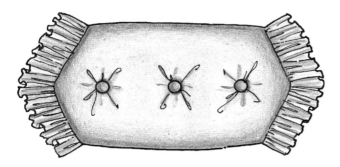

The unusual shape is the focal point
of this triple-tufted pillow.
CD 746

This small pillow is framed by a
very long shirred ruffle.
CD 747

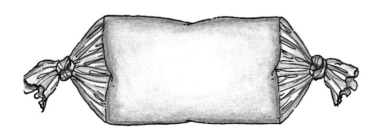

The ends of this tufted pillow are
fitted with long gathered ruffles
that are cinched in with a separate
faux knot.
CD 748

Neck Rolls and Bolsters

A **neck roll** is a cylindrical pillow that can support the neck of the user or be used for purely decorative applications.

✤ Neck rolls use the same type of natural or man-made inserts as other decorative pillows. They are sized and shaped specifically for that purpose.

✤ Neck rolls typically do not have an opening element such as a zipper or hook-and-loop tape. They are usually sewn closed, although some designs have an integrated opening at the ends.

A **bolster** is a long firm pillow that is used for back or arm support or for decorative application. It can be made in any shape but is almost always longer than it is wide.

✤ Bolsters are usually not a standard size and are sized and shaped for a specific purpose.

✤ A bolster most often requires a custom insert, or it can be stuffed with loose polyfill.

✤ For additional support, a foam insert wrapped with batting might be necessary.

✤ Bolsters commonly have a zipper or hook-and-loop enclosure.

The ends of the neck roll or bolster are just as important to the design as the face.

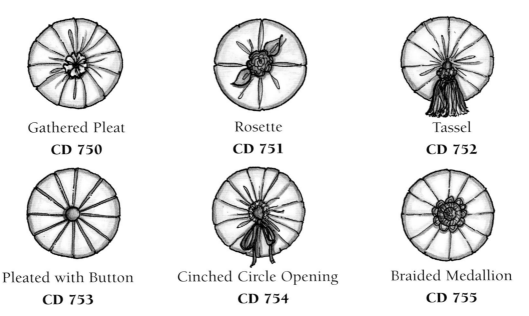

Gathered Pleat
CD 750

Rosette
CD 751

Tassel
CD 752

Pleated with Button
CD 753

Cinched Circle Opening
CD 754

Braided Medallion
CD 755

Neck Rolls and Bolsters

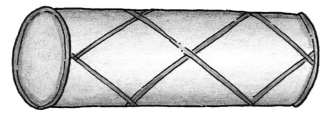

Ribbons are crossed over one another diagonally to form a diamond pattern on this neck roll.

CD 756

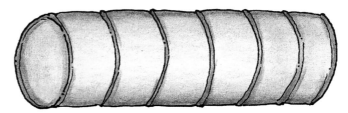

Evenly spaced rows of welting cover this neck roll.

CD 757

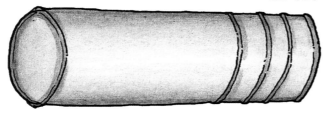

Three bands of contrasting fabric at one end of this neck roll are highlighted by welting.

CD 758

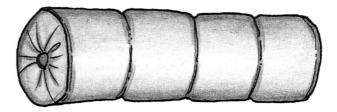

This neck roll is given a tufted look by cinching in lengths of cord around the circumference of the pillow.

CD 759

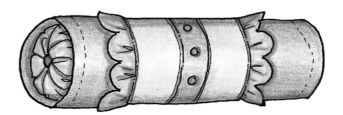

Recessed ends are covered by a sharp flange at each end of the pillow. The center is decorated with scalloped ruffles and a contrasting band with buttons.
CD 760

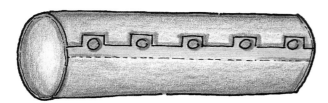

A line of tabs with fabric-covered buttons runs the length of this pillow.
CD 761

A false opening edge created with contrasting bands running along the length of this neck roll is tied with long bows.
CD 762

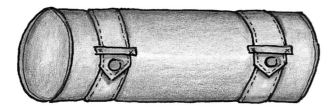

Belts and closures are made with faux suede fabric and held closed with buttons at each end of this design.
CD 763

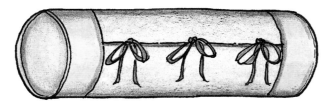

Long bows decorate a center panel on this neck roll.

CD 764

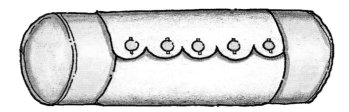

A contrasting sleeve with a scalloped edge is buttoned in place over the face of this neck roll.

CD 765

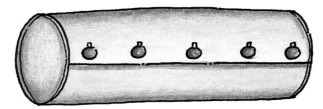

A buttoned-down opening runs the length of this neck roll pillow.

CD 766

Contrasting bands of fabric circle the ends of this pillow. They are cinched in at the appropriate point, and a separate bow is applied to simulate the look of a single ribbon wrapped around the pillow and tied in a bow.

CD 767

A false opening runs on the diagonal across the face of this pillow. It is held closed by leather toggles.

CD 768

An independent sleeve with a zigzag border at each end is fitted with grommets and tied together with knotted ribbon.

CD 769

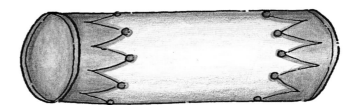

The ends of this pillow are trimmed with a long zigzag border that is embellished with buttons at the points.

CD 770

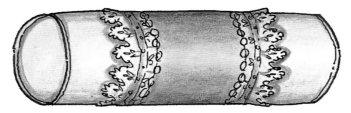

Multiple lace trims are pieced together to create wide bands at each end of the pillow.

CD 771

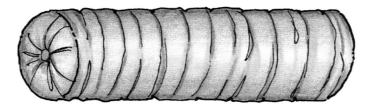

The face of this neck roll is shirred
vertically along its full length.
CD 772

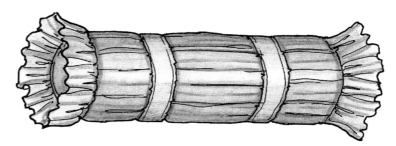

This pillow is shirred horizontally across the
face. Two contrasting bands wrap around
the pillow, and ruffles decorate each end.
CD 773

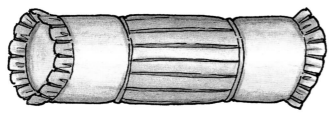

The center panel of this pillow is pleated
horizontally and edged in welting. Short
pleated ruffles encircle each end.
CD 774

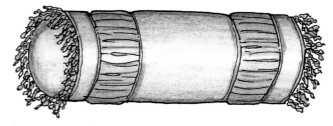

Two shirred bands decorate this neck roll
with bullion fringe at each end.
CD 775

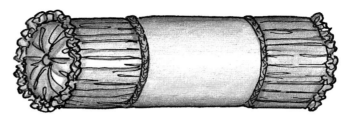

Shirred panels at each end of this pillow are separated from the center panel by decorative braid, and the end caps are trimmed with ruched welting.
CD 776

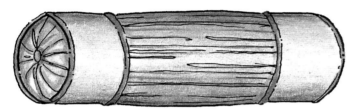

A horizontally shirred center panel is trimmed with welting.
CD 777

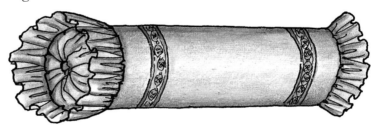

This neck roll has deep, gathered ends that are embellished with ruffles. The face is decorated with two bands of wide decorative tape.
CD 778

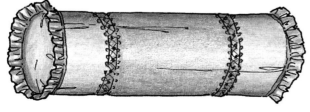

Decorative tape separates contrasting fabrics on this simple neck roll with ruffled edges.
CD 779

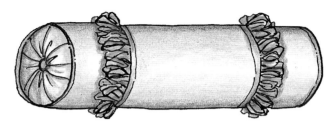

Looped ribbon fringe is inserted between
the end and center panels of this neck roll.
CD 780

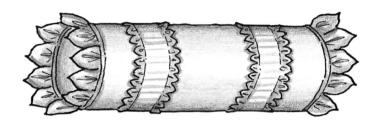

Pleated zigzag ruffles decorate the ends
of this pillow, which is decorated with
lace-edged fabric bands.
CD 781

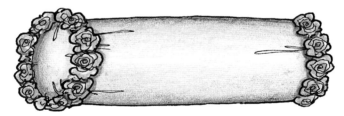

A plain neck roll is adorned with luxurious
silk rosettes along the end-cap edge, creating
a sumptuous design.
CD 782

Long ruffles extend well beyond the end
caps of this banded design.
CD 783

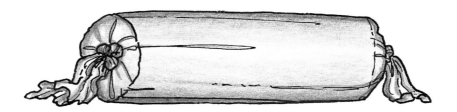

The end caps of this neck roll extend into a
long tail, which is bound with a faux knot.
CD 784

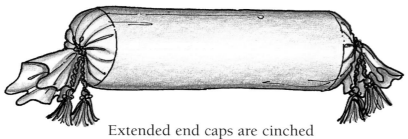

Extended end caps are cinched
in with a pair of chair-tie tassels.
CD 785

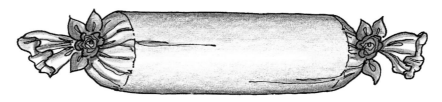

Rosettes and velvet leaves adorn the
tails of this neck roll.
CD 786

The long tails at each end of this neck roll
are secured with a ruched band.
CD 787

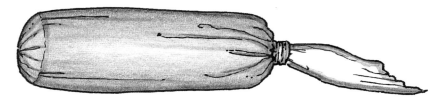

An extended tail at one end is cinched in
with a ruched fabric sleeve.

CD 788

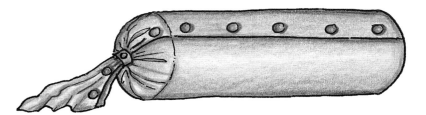

A faux opening is buttoned down and runs the full
length of this neck roll and its one-sided tail. A small
looped tab with a button holds the tail together at the
end of the pillow.

CD 789

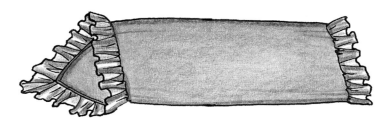

The unique triangular shape of this pillow is
accentuated by ruffles at each end.

CD 790

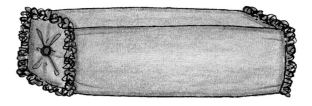

An elongated cube-shaped pillow requires
a firm foam insert to maintain its shape.

CD 791

Specialty Shaped Pillows

Decorative pillows can be made in a myriad of shapes and sizes.

- Circles
- Triangles
- Octagons
- Crescents
- Flowers
- Hearts
- Fans
- Balls
- Stars

Use your imagination to come up with unique and eye-catching designs.

Specialty Shaped Pillows

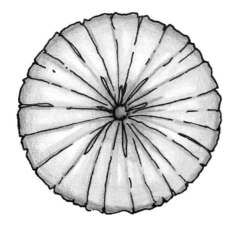

This round, shirred pillow is tufted at the center with a single button.
CD 792

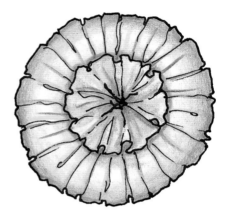

The face fabric of this gathered pillow is pulled up in the center to create a large pouf.
CD 793

Extra-long extensions of the face fabric of this round pillow are pulled up and folded back over the face. A rosette marks the center.
CD 794

This scallop-edged pillow is separated into eight sections by decorative cording radiating out from the center.
CD 795

Scallops form the edge of this round pillow constructed of eight separate sections. A large ribbon ruffle and fabric rosette mark the center.
CD 797

A cloverleaf pillow is tufted in the center and decorated with a large pouf.
CD 796

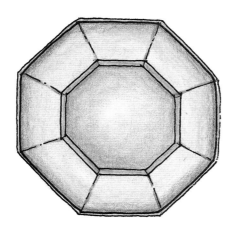

Eight separate sections make up the border of this octagonal pillow. A single center section completes the pillow face.
CD 799

This pillow has six angled sides and face sections that are tufted in the center.
CD 798

The five sections of this fan-shaped pillow are delineated by contrasting welt applied between sections.
CD 800

Nine shallow scallops form the profile of this fan pillow. The face is constructed of nine separate pieces in this version, but it can also be made with a single face piece.
CD 801

This fan-shaped pillow has seven points at the edge.
CD 802

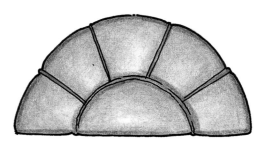

Contrasting welt creates a pattern on this half-circle fan pillow.
CD 803

A center-scalloped, fan-shaped panel serves as a base for the outer border of this pillow.
CD 804

The fabric covering this fan pillow is shirred and gathered to the center. A large pouf covers the gathering point.
CD 805

This shirred fan pillow has a separate banner at the center that wraps over the top and appears to tie in a large bow at the base. The bow is attached separately.
CD 806

This flower-shaped pillow looks best when edged with thick fringe or bullion.
CD 808

The four sections of this pointed pillow come together at the center.
CD 809

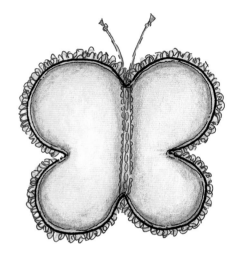

Whimsical shapes like this butterfly add a personal touch.
CD 810

This leaf-shaped pillow is hand tufted to mimic the veins in a real leaf.
CD 811

Short fringe adds emphasis to the angled lines of this pyramid-shaped pillow.
CD 813

Upholstered Headboards

An upholstered headboard is a shaped plywood panel frame that is covered with padding and fabric and placed at the head of a bed.

Using an upholstered headboard has the following distinct advantages:

- It provides soft, comfortable support for the user.

- It creates a softer look than a wood or metal bed frame.

- It creates a focal point at the head of the bed.

- It provides an opportunity to add style, pattern, and color to the bedding design.

- The proportions and balance of the bed can be manipulated by the size and shape of the headboard.

- The shape can reinforce existing lines in the room or conform to the shape of patterns in the fabric.

- Headboards can be constructed to be freestanding, to hang directly on the wall, or to attach to the bed frame. No matter what their construction, they should be securely attached to the wall to prevent movement and to add stability to the bed.

- Many headboards can be easily fitted with slipcovers for additional flexibility of style.

- The height and scale of a headboard can be modified to fit the scale of your particular bed. When specifying the overall height of your design, take into account the height of the mattress and box spring with the bed frame and the height of the pillows to be used.

✦ A headboard is smaller and lighter than a full bed frame and can be moved and installed easily. It is a good option for spaces with limited access, such as tight corners or small doorways.

✦ To create the look of a full platform bed using only a headboard, specify the bed skirt to be made in the same fabric. This gives the appearance of a full frame.

✦ The upholstered headboard is an element that provides a great opportunity to exercise your creativity. Almost any shape is possible, depending on the skill and experience of the upholsterer.

Common Types of Headboards

Single Panel: A single-panel headboard is composed of one section of padded surface that is covered with a flat layer of the face fabric. It can be embellished with trim, cord, or flat borders and other elements as long as the face remains flat.

Combination: A sectioned headboard is composed of more than one section of padded surface that is covered by one or multiple face fabrics. Each section is upholstered individually and is separated from the other sections by the tucking of face fabrics between the padded sections.

Shirred: A single-panel or sectioned headboard is one in which the face fabric is shirred before being applied to the surface. It can be used in combination with sections of flat face fabric.

Tufted: A tufted headboard is composed of single or multiple padded sections that are covered with a flat layer of face fabric that is pinched back toward the backboard, creating indentations and padded mounds on the surface. It is constructed by stapling through the face or by running a thread through the backboard to the face and securing it with a button or other similar decorative implement.

Slipcovered: A slipcover added to a single-panel headboard gives detail and style.

Embellished: An embellished headboard incorporates decorative elements such as ties, bows, or ribbons and decorative hardware such as finials, ironwork, or grommets into its design.

Single-Panel Headboards

Almost any single-panel or sectioned headboard shape can be personalized by adding borders, shirring, pleating, welting, nail heads, etc. These drawings illustrate the multiple looks you can achieve by adding different details to a single shape.

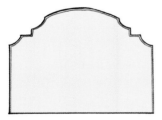

Single Panel with Welting

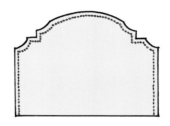

Single Panel with Nail heads

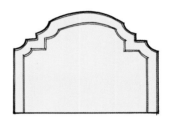

Single Panel with Interior Welting Border

Single Panel with Contrasting Fabric Border and Welting

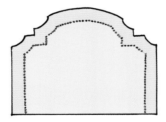

Single Panel with Contrasting Fabric Border and Nail Heads

Single Panel with Double Contrasting Fabric Border and Welting

Single Panel with Shirred Contrasting Fabric Border and Welting

Single Panel with Contrasting Fabric Outer Border, Shirred Inner Border, and Welting

Single-Panel Headboards

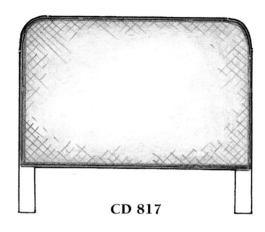

CD 817

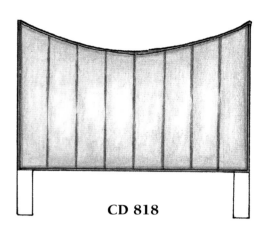

CD 818

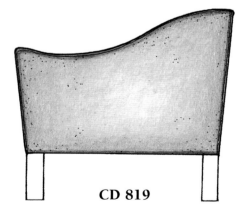

CD 819

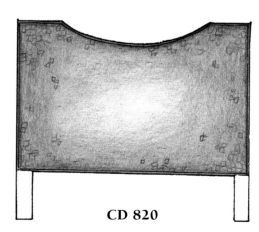

CD 820

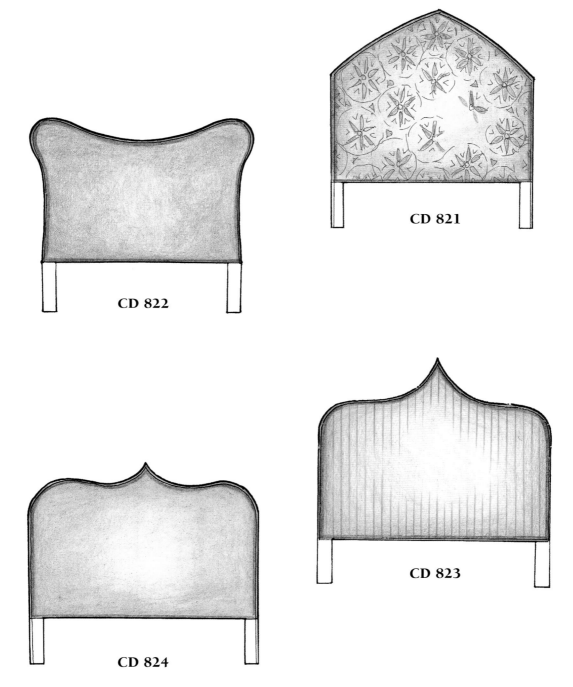

CD 821

CD 822

CD 823

CD 824

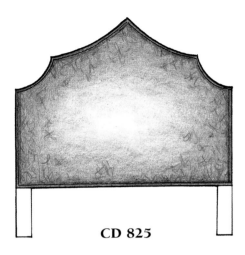

CD 825

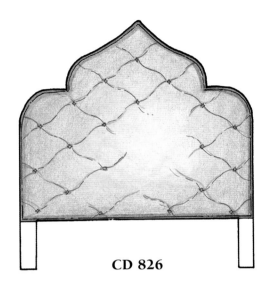

CD 826

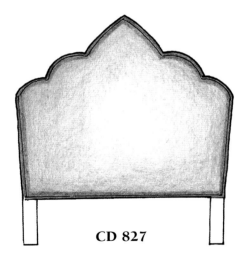

CD 827

CD 828

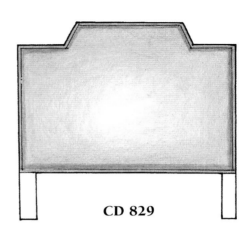

CD 829

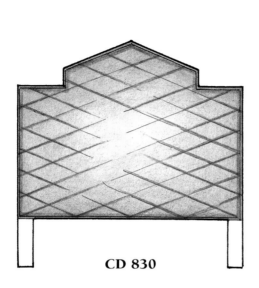

CD 830

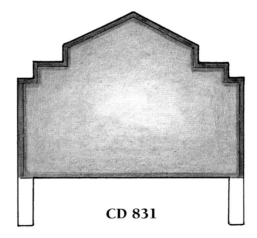

CD 831

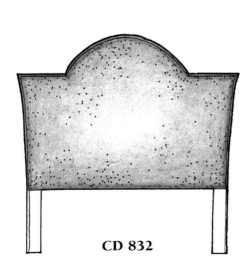

CD 832

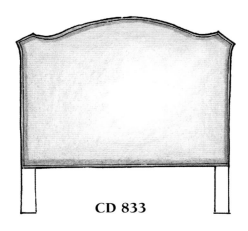

CD 833

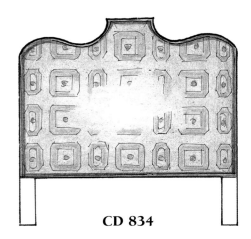

CD 834

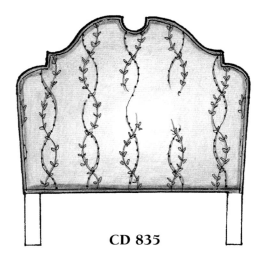

CD 835

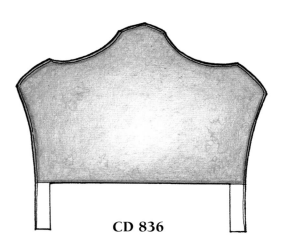

CD 836

CD 837

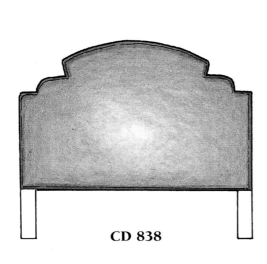

CD 838

CD 839

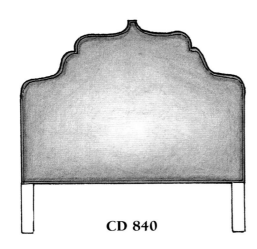

CD 840

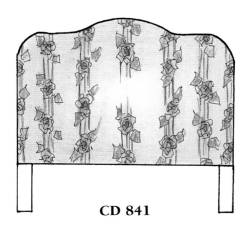

CD 841

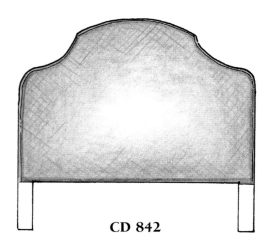

CD 842

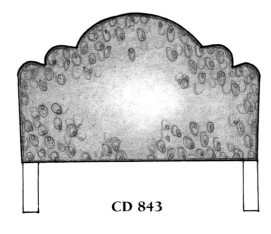

CD 843

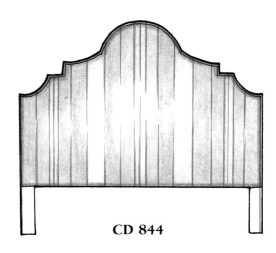

CD 844

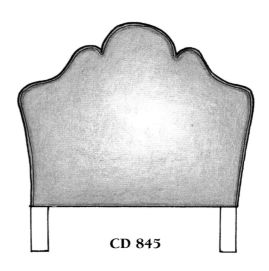

CD 845

CD 846

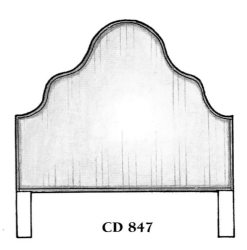

CD 847

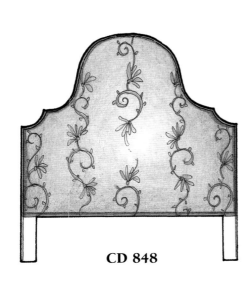

CD 848

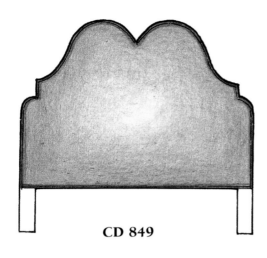

CD 849

CD 850

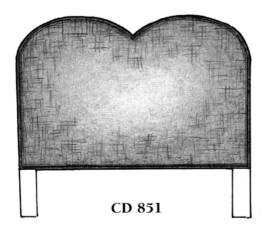

CD 851

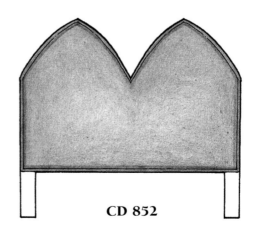

CD 852

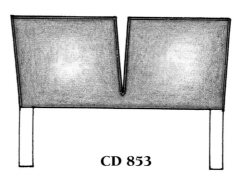

CD 853

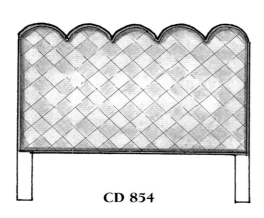

CD 854

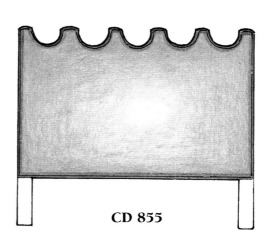

CD 855

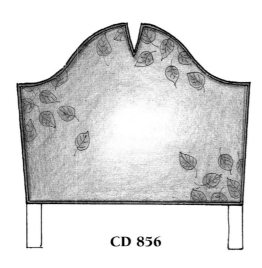

CD 856

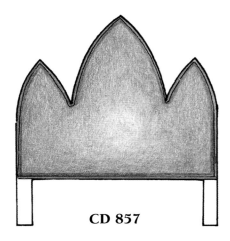

CD 857

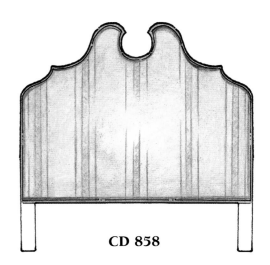

CD 858

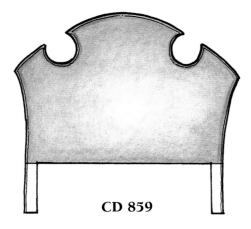

CD 859

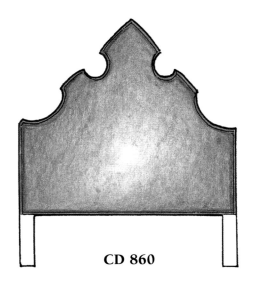

CD 860

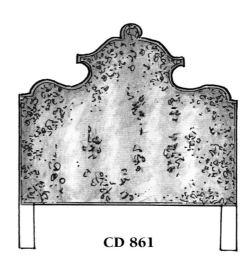

CD 861

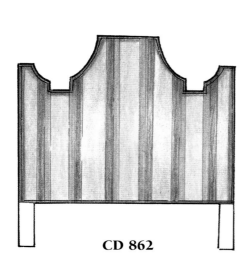

CD 862

CD 863

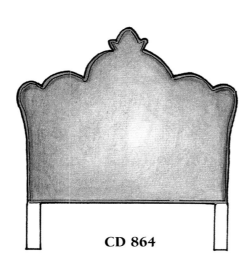

CD 864

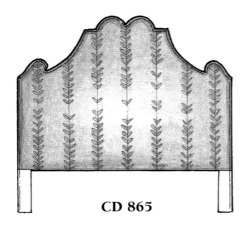

CD 865

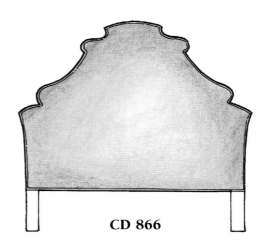

CD 866

CD 867

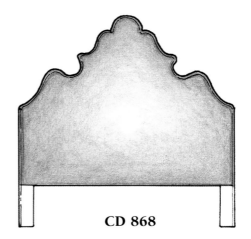

CD 868

CD 869

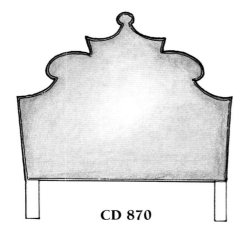

CD 870

Combination Headboards

A sectioned headboard is composed of more than one section of padded surface that is covered by one or more face fabrics. Each section is upholstered individually and is separated from the others by the tucking of the face fabrics between the padded sections.

✦ The separate sections of a combination headboard can vary in thickness and projection, as well as in fabric choice.

✦ Sections can be rounded or squared off, depending on the desired effect.

✦ Consider alternating textures as well as colors and patterns for variety and drama.

✦ Inserting decorative cording, braid, welting, or ruching between sections will emphasize the separation.

✦ Shirring the fabric on selected sections of the headboard can add depth to the design.

Combination Headboards

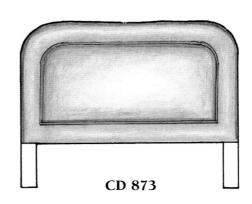

CD 873

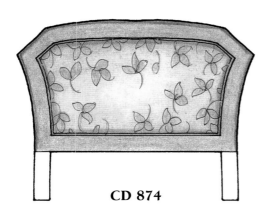

CD 874

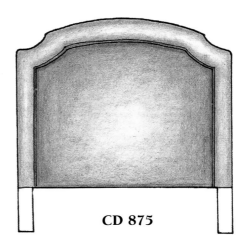

CD 875

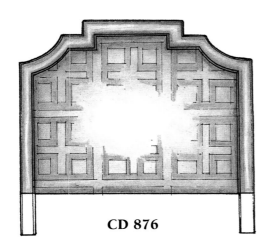

CD 876

CD 877

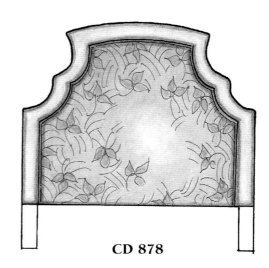

CD 878

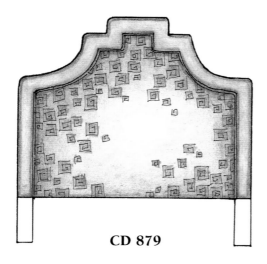

CD 879

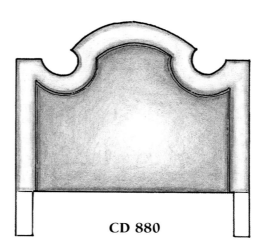

CD 880

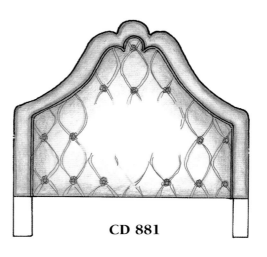

CD 881

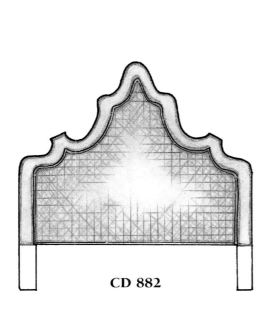

CD 882

CD 883

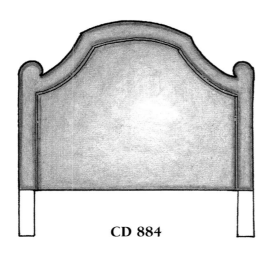

CD 884

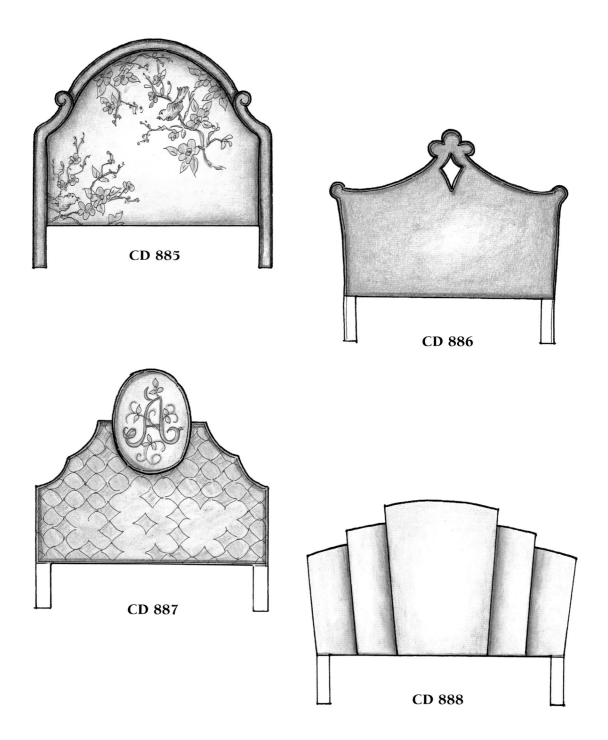

CD 885

CD 886

CD 887

CD 888

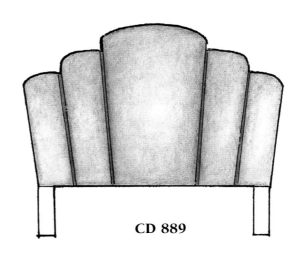

CD 889

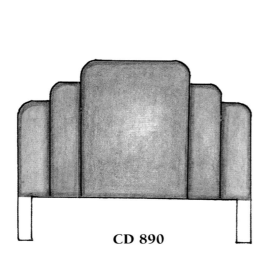

CD 890

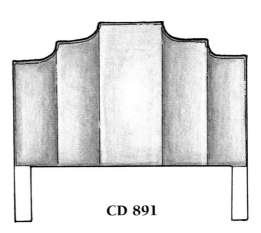

CD 891

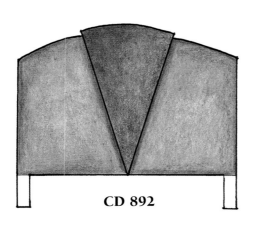

CD 892

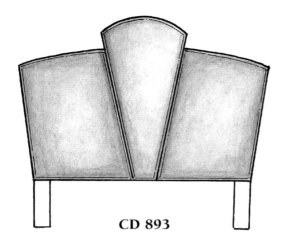

CD 893

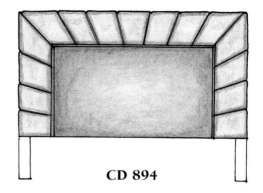

CD 894

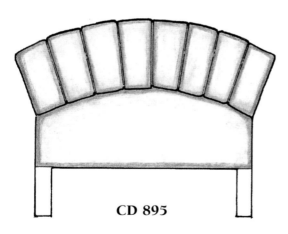

CD 895

CD 896

Shirred Headboards

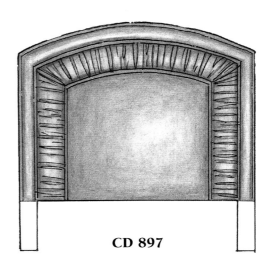

CD 897

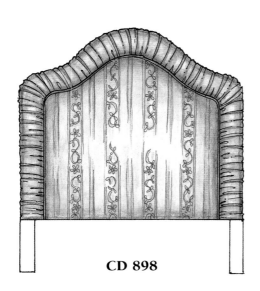

CD 898

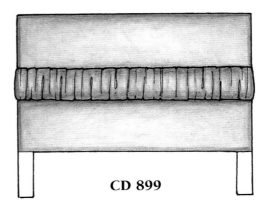

CD 899

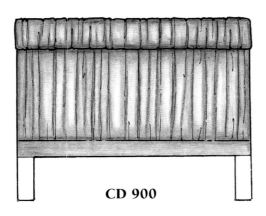

CD 900

Tufted Headboards

Almost any flat headboard can be tufted to add more depth and texture to the design.

There are three common tufting methods:

+ Float-Button Tufting: A button is pulled down lightly and left to float on the surface of the fabric and batting, creating a shallow indentation.

+ Deep-Button Tufting: A button is pulled down through the face fabric and batting close to the base of the headboard, creating a deep-pleated diamond.

+ Channel Tufting: The batting is separated into strips and the face fabric is stapled down in between them, creating a series of deep channels.

Tufted Headboards

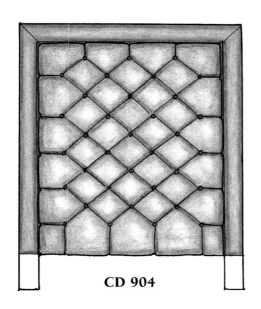

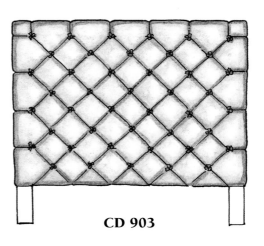

CD 903

CD 904

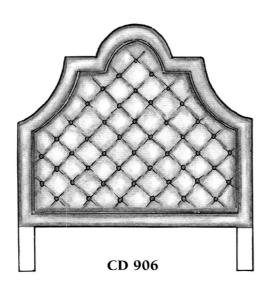

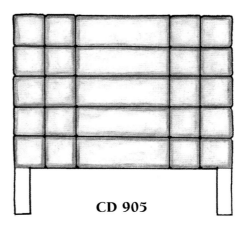

CD 905

CD 906

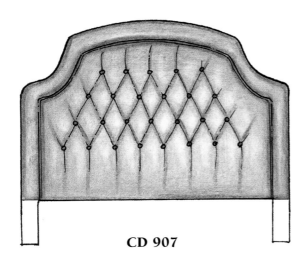

CD 907

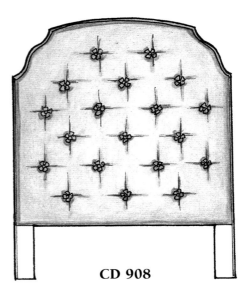

CD 908

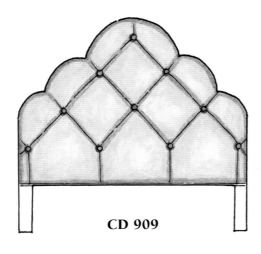

CD 909

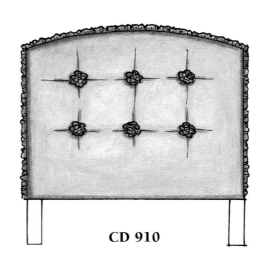

CD 910

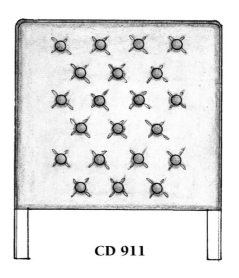

CD 911

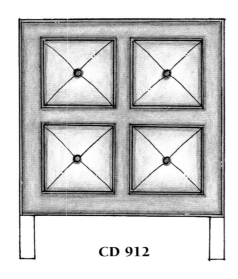

CD 912

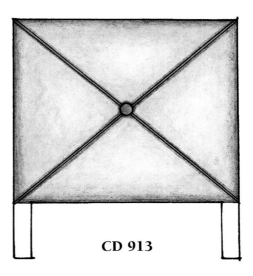

CD 913

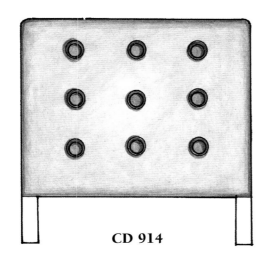

CD 914

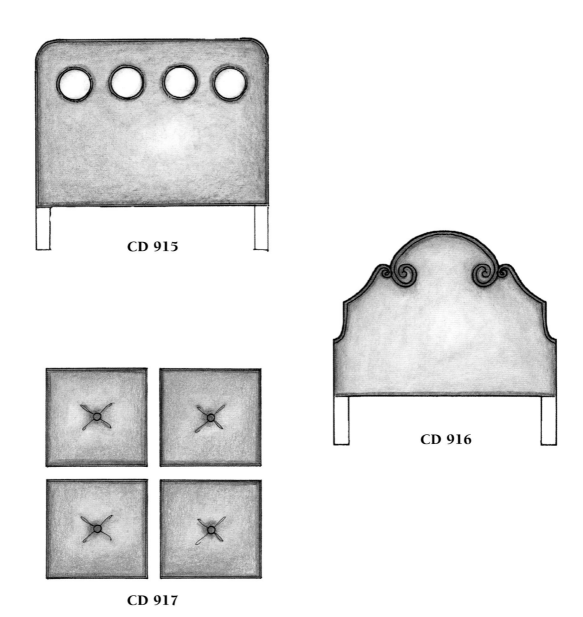

CD 915

CD 916

CD 917

Slipcovered Headboards

A slipcovered headboard is fitted with a second separate or integrated layer of fabric that appears to hang over or on top of the headboard.

✦ A true slipcover is completely independent from the headboard and can be removed.

✦ A faux slipcover gives the appearance of a separate slipcover but is actually permanently attached to the headboard.

✦ Fabric to be used as a slipcover should be prewashed and preshrunk before construction.

✦ When using light-colored or sheer fabrics as the top layer, be sure to consider pattern and color bleed-through from the base layer.

Slipcovered Headboards

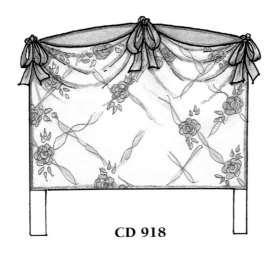

CD 918

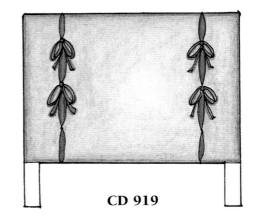

CD 919

CD 920

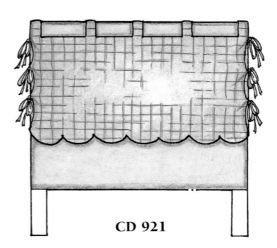

CD 921

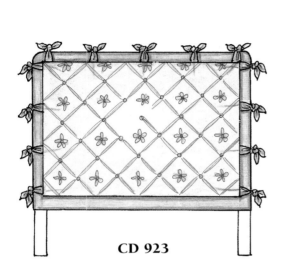

CD 923

CD 922

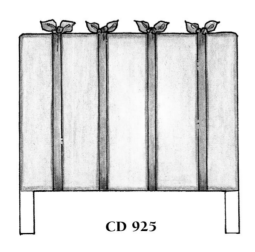

CD 925

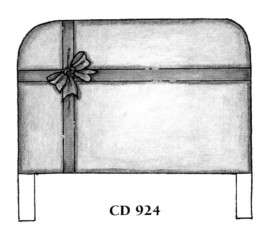

CD 924

Embellished Slipcovered Headboards

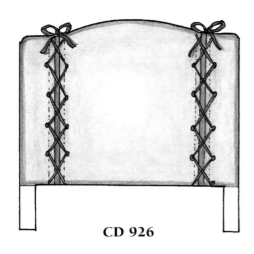

CD 926

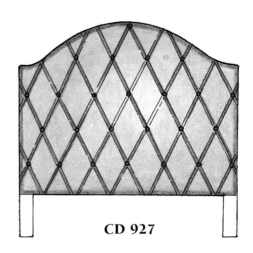

CD 927

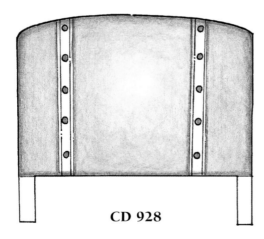

CD 928

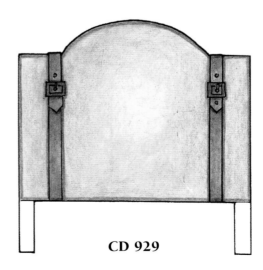

CD 929

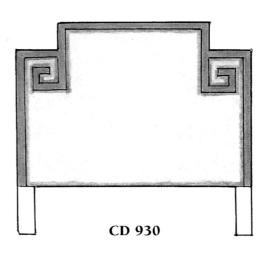

CD 930

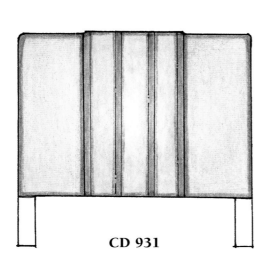

CD 931

CD 932

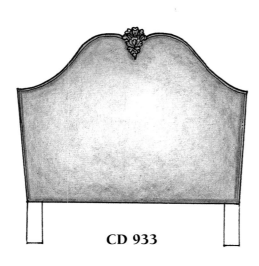

CD 933

CD 934

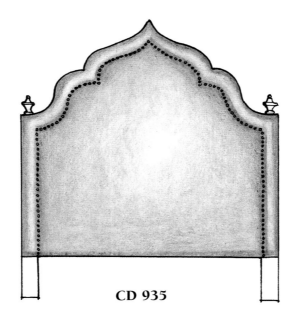

CD 935

Alternative Headboards

One of the most important talents a designer can possess is the ability to think beyond the norm to create truly unique environments for their clients or their own homes. There are many alternatives to the typical headboards, such as:

- Antique gates and doors
- Framed mirrors
- Decorative frames
- Screens
- Tapestries
- Window frames
- Fabric-covered cork or ribbon boards
- Stained glass panels
- Shutters
- Iron grillwork
- Wallpaper panels
- Murals
- Wall hangings

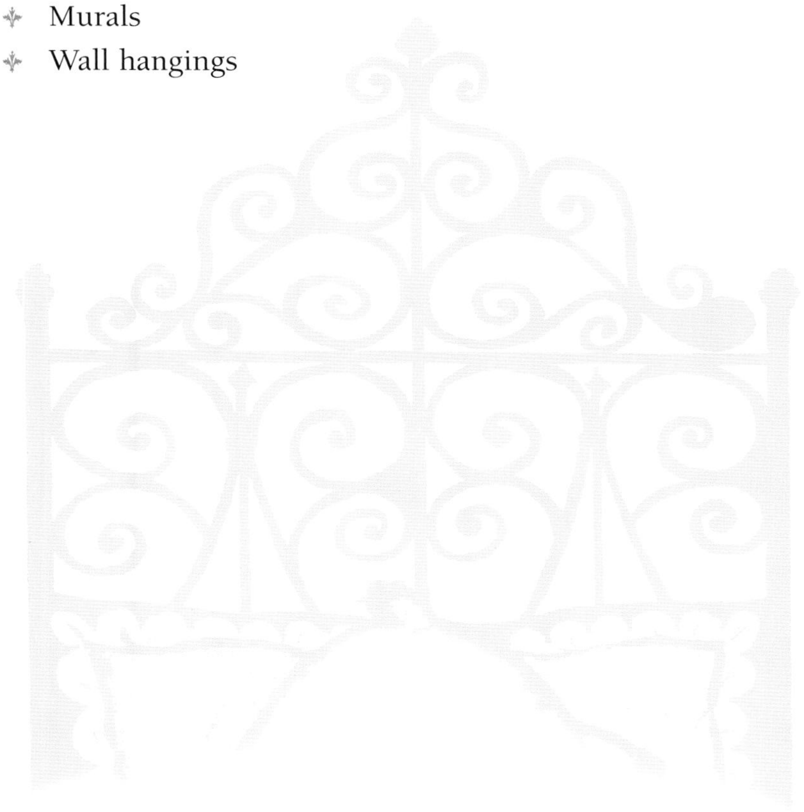

Alternative Headboards

Art

Traditional Japanese painted panels create a striking focal point for this bed. The Asian motifs in the paintings are repeated in the bedding design, with frog closures on the full-bed-width bolster as well as flared flanges at each end. The center of the round pillow is embellished with a cut-stone medallion, while the bolster is finished with long stone-beaded tassels.

CD 936

Screens

A decorative screen makes a fabulous backdrop for almost any bed. Here, a simple classic screen forms a private alcove for this comfortable bed. Consider adding Euro shams or bolsters when using an alternative headboard for additional padding and emphasis at the head of the bed.

CD 937

Decorative Frames

A decorative frame from a mirror or a piece of old furniture can make a bold impact as a headboard. Leave the mirror in place or upholster the opening to add warmth and softness. Frames can also be fitted with ribbon to create a ribbon board. This application works very well for teen rooms.

CD 938

Window Frames

Antique window frames can be versatile elements to use as a headboard. You can drape fabric behind them or drape it over them in a faux curtain. Insert wallpaper behind the glass for a different look. Paint or stain the glass to coordinate with the bedding. The options are limited only by your imagination.

CD 939

Shutters

Shutters come in a large variety of shapes and sizes and are easily found at hardware stores. Antique shutters are readily available at architectural salvage yards. They come in flat-panel, louvered, and combination styles that can mimic a much more expensive wood headboard.

CD 940

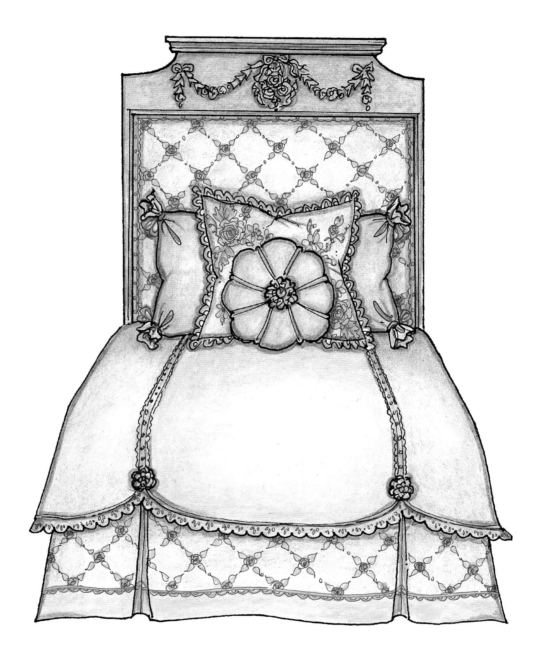

Architectural Salvage

Many bits and pieces of furniture or decorative molding can be easily made into a headboard frame. This frame is made with a decorative header from an old piece of furniture. The thin frame at each side and bottom is a new addition. The center is upholstered to finish the piece.

CD 941

Ironwork

Decorative ironwork or iron gates are a unique way to create a focal point. Many times it is possible to find a single piece that will fit your design. An alternative method is to combine several pieces to complete the desired size and shape. Custom shapes and designs can be commissioned through most iron foundries at very reasonable prices.

CD 942

Bed Drapery

Bed drapery describes any method of design in which fabric is draped over, behind, on, or about a bed independent of the bed frame.

- Bed drapery can be used on almost any type of bed—full frame, wood, iron, and upholstered beds, beds with a headboard only, or a plain mattress with no frame at all.

- Draping the bed adds softness and a sense of privacy and intimacy to the bedroom.

- Bed drapery promotes a look and feel of luxury and opulence.

- It provides an opportunity to add color, pattern, texture, and style to the room.

- It is an element that allows you to add architectural detailing to a bland room.

- It creates a strong focal point in the room.

- It can provide acoustic benefits such as noise reduction.

- It can serve as an effective tool to delineate space in a large room by highlighting the sleeping area.

Bed Drapery Categories

Crown: A small, compact, circular or semicircular decorative frame from which a bed drape can be hung.

Corona: A one-piece upholstered, semicircular or rectangular frame that is wider than it is high. Fabric is hung from the frame to drape a bed.

Pediment: A hard-surfaced, three-sided wall- or ceiling-mounted frame that is wider than it is high. Fabric is hung from the frame to drape a bed.

Cornice: A three-sided upholstered frame, with or without an open top, that is usually close to or as wide as the bed. It can be suspended from the ceiling or mounted on the wall behind the bed, and fabric can be draped from it.

Drapes: Drapery swags or panels hung using drapery hardware or other methods behind a bed. The drapery can be attached at the ceiling or on the wall.

Tented Drapes: A drapery treatment that resembles a tent or awning having high and low points and usually a raised ceiling. It can be suspended from the ceiling or mounted on the wall behind or above the bed.

Crowns

A bed crown is a small, compact, circular or semicircular decorative frame from which a bed drape can be hung.

✦ A bed crown can resemble an actual royal crown or can be of another design as long as it is small in size.

✦ A full crown forms a full circle and is finished on all sides. It can be hung from the ceiling.

✦ A partial crown is shaped in a semicircle and has one unfinished side at the back. It must be hung on the wall.

✦ Many crowns have a drapery ring already in place inside the bottom border of the crown to accommodate drapery panels.

Classic Bed Crown Designs

There are several good retail and wholesale sources for bed crowns in the resource directory of this book.

Classic Bed Crowns

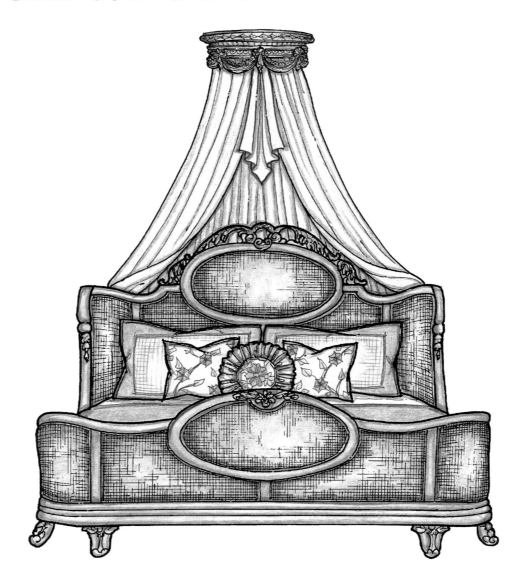

The informal cascade hanging from the center of this crown repeats the draped motif on the crown itself. The drape is lined in a contrasting fabric and hung from a drapery ring mounted inside the crown.

CD 950, 951

A swagged valance is the focal point of this crown treatment. The side panels barely wrap around the front, creating a very open-back drape. Ties attached to the leading edge of the back drape are looped into bows around the head posts of the bed. Beaded trim adds a whimsical touch to this rather traditional treatment.

CD 952, 953

A fixed pleated back panel serves as the backdrop for the sweeping side panels of this crown treatment. Long tassel fringe is added to the perimeter of the crown to integrate it into the drapery. Formal tiebacks are used to hold back the puddle side panels.

CD 954, 955

Suspended from the ceiling, this full crown supports four separate panels that drape down to the head and foot posts of this bed. The panels are secured to the posts at the finials and drape down to the floor.

CD 956, 957

Simple gathered panels cross over at the center of the crown, allowing for extra volume in the drapes. Shirred ruffles are used as trim to embellish the sheer fabric at the leading edge, giving the side panels a dramatic look that highlights their gentle swag.
CD 958, 959

The shape of this crown provides the inspiration for its drapery design. The small swag at the center highlights its curved edge. The side panels are draped from the high points of the curve to accentuate this feature. In order to achieve the correct proportion for the back drape, the sides are pulled back higher than usual.

CD 960, 961

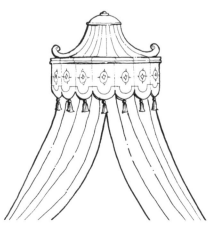

Crown drapery can be extremely simple in design and still deliver a dramatic impact. This one-piece panel is shirred onto the rod, which is integrated into the design of the crown. It is pulled back and secured to hidden tiebacks with large tassels.

CD 962, 963

Rod pocket draperies with a single long ruffle at the heading are shirred onto this iron crown. The leading edge below the heading is embellished with a single contrasting ruffle. Matching tiebacks finish the romantic look.

CD 964, 965

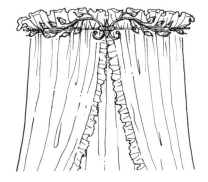

Metal Crowns

A metal crown or cornice is a decorative wrought-iron or cast-metal framework from which a bed drape can be hung.

+ Unlike traditional circular crowns, metal crowns are flat.

+ They are typically mounted to the wall with L brackets.

+ The distance that they project from the wall can usually be adjusted.

+ Fabric can be hung directly from the crown or it can be mounted behind it, depending on your preference and the design you have chosen.

+ Metal crowns can be used alone or in combination with other coordinating pieces.

Metal Crowns

Two swagged panels are topped with a separate swag and hung by tabs from the frame of the crown. A separate double flourish is tied onto the upper medallion of the crown to create additional height and volume at the center to balance the design.

CD 968, 969

A swagged back panel is pleated to create volume at each high point and topped with a double cascade. It is tied to the brackets that support the frame at the wall. Tassels are hung from the long point of each cascade to accentuate their vertical lines.

CD 970, 971

A single self-lined scarf or length of fabric is used to drape this crown and matching scroll brackets. It is pulled up with loops of decorative braid hung over the wall brackets of the crown. A length of decorative braid runs the width of the swags, ending in a long tassel hung from the wall bracket under the last swag.
CD 972, 973

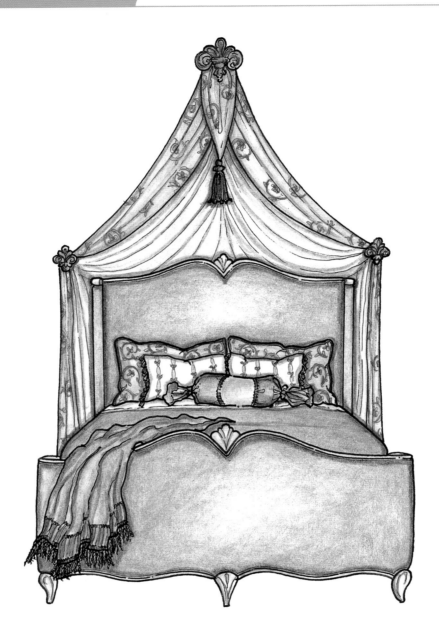

This design is constructed with four separate sections: a center-gathered jabot, two overlapping shirred side panels that end at the tieback, and a separate back panel that is tightly shirred just above the intersection of the jabot and side panels. Mounting the back panel as low as possible allows it to have the maximum possible width at the heading, allowing for more volume in the shirred panel.
CD 974, 975

Coronas

A corona is a one-piece upholstered semicircular or rectangular frame that is wider than it is high. Fabric is hung from the frame to drape the head of the bed.

✦ A traditional corona can be mounted to the wall or from the ceiling.

✦ The frame of the corona must be mounted flush with the wall.

✦ A corona is considerably narrower than the bed is wide.

✦ It can be semicircular or rectangular in shape.

✦ The drapes that are hung from a corona are decorative only, not functional.

✦ The interior and ceiling of the corona should be finished and lined in appropriate fabric.

✦ Side panels and draperies should be lined in a coordinating or contrasting fabric.

✦ Unlined sheer panels should be sewn with French seams for a finished, professional appearance.

✦ When designing large coronas or pediments, make sure there is adequate structural support in the wall and/or ceiling for the weight of the treatment.

Corona Variations

Variations of the traditional corona include:

Pleated

A traditional corona shape frame covered with pleated fabric.

Shirred

A traditional corona shape frame covered with shirred fabric.

Swagged

A traditional corona shape frame covered with swagged fabric.

Boxed

A three-sided wall- or ceiling-mounted upholstered frame that is wider than it is high. Fabric is hung from the frame to drape a bed.

Tented

A corona with the addition of a raised portion at the top that slopes back to meet flush with the wall. It may or may not have a peak at the center.

Finishing Details

Ceiling Panels

The ceiling of a corona, cornice, or pediment should be finished in an appropriate manner for the style of treatment.

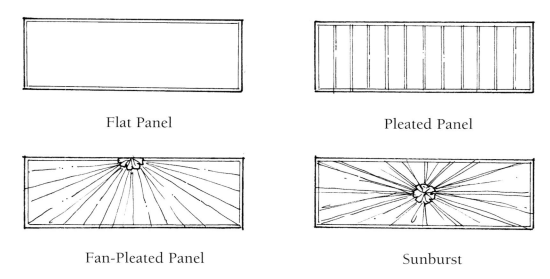

Flat Panel

Pleated Panel

Fan-Pleated Panel

Sunburst

Ceiling panels should be finished with decorative braid, cording, or welting around the perimeter of the panel.

Back Panels

Many of the bed drapery designs shown in this book can be made with one lined panel that makes up the back and side panels of the treatment, but in some cases a separate back panel is necessary. In this case, the back panel is attached directly to the wall and the side panels are joined to it at the side seams.

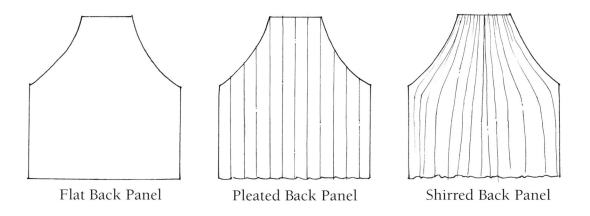

Flat Back Panel

Pleated Back Panel

Shirred Back Panel

Traditional Coronas

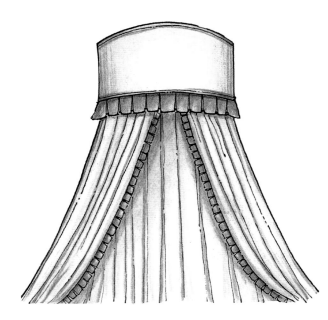

This half-circle corona is trimmed at the bottom with box pleats in a contrasting fabric. That fabric is repeated in the drapery panels and box-pleated border. The panels are lined in the fabric that is used on the face of the corona.

CD 975

A row of sheer pleated ruffles borders the scalloped bottom edge of this arched half-circle corona. The same ruffle edges the scallops of the side panels. Notice the different lengths of the two ruffles. Many times it is necessary to adjust the length or width of ruffles to maintain good proportions in a design.

CD 976

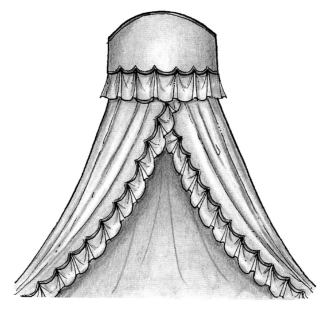

This unique corona has a wooden base with an upholstered half dome at the top. Pleated side panels crisscross at the center and tie back to reveal a flat, upholstered back panel.

CD 977

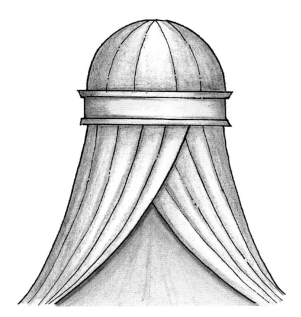

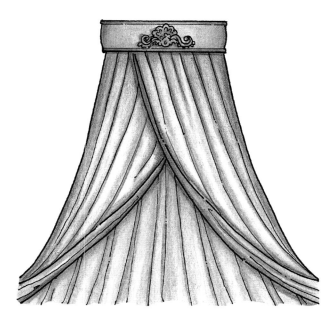

A simple upholstered corona is embellished with an iron medallion. The pleated drapery is rolled back at the leading edge to expose the contrast lining.

CD 978

A center medallion showcasing a large monogram is the highlight of this raised corona. The side panels are wrapped around the finials of the headboard bedposts for an elegant yet casual look. The back panel is a separate piece attached to the wall. Matching monogrammed linens finish this modern, classic design.

CD 979, 980

Multiple fabrics and trims combine for an eclectic mix in this design. The side panels are joined to the back panel only to the low point of the swag, allowing them to be lifted and threaded through the ring tiebacks at each side of the treatment. The remaining lengths of the panels cover the edges of the back panel, making it appear to be one piece. The side panels must be considerably longer than the back panel for this treatment.

CD 981, 982

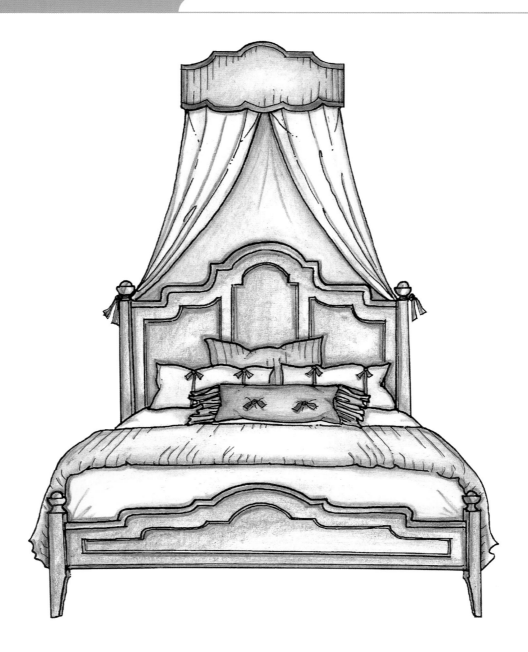

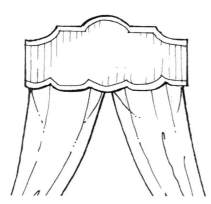

The shape of the panels on this bed frame is the inspiration for the outline of the corona. Repeating shapes and motifs throughout your design creates balance.

CD 983, 984

Pleated Coronas

Contrasting triangles are placed between goblet pleats on this corona. Fabric ties and a bordered hem in another color balance its proportions. The outer side panels and back panel are made in the main fabric, while the interior of the side panels is made of the contrasting fabric used for the triangles.

CD 985

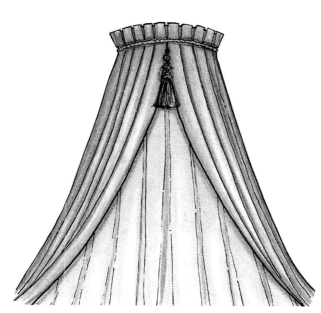

Crisp box pleats are the main design element of this simple corona. Decorative braid separates the top row of pleats from the panels, and the center is finished with a heavy tassel.

CD 986

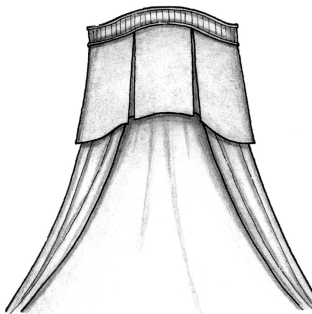

A long box-pleated valance is hung from the arched base of this corona. The base is upholstered in a contrasting fabric and trimmed in welting. The curved lines are repeated in the hemline of the long pleats.

CD 987

A classic design, the simple box pleats of this corona have a slight curve in the hem. The side panels are spaced apart at the center and are hung to appear to fall straight from the pleats at either side of the center.

CD 988

Crisp box pleats are held together a few inches from the top by contrasting fabric-covered buttons. Below the buttons, the pleats open up.
CD 989

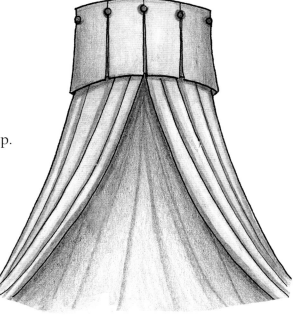

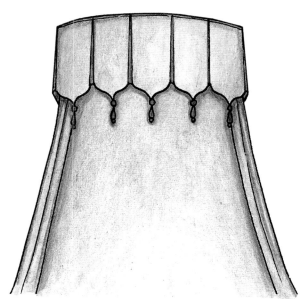

The box pleats of this extra-wide corona end in Moroccan points that are trimmed with beads. The side drapes are minimal and wrap to the front just enough to create a frame for the flat back panel.
CD 990

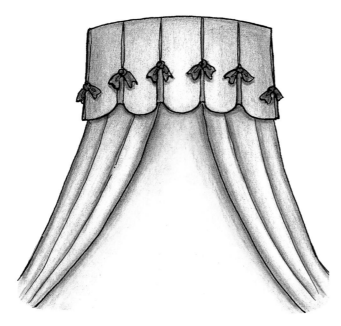

Scalloped box pleats are open from the top welt. They are held closed with contrasting ties placed at approximately two-thirds the length of the corona. The side panels are placed at either side of the center pleated section.

CD 991

A simple box-pleated corona is given a new look by adding lacing that threads through grommets at the pleat edge and ties into bows. The side panels are embellished with a contrasting border that continues the laced theme. The placement of the laces at the center of the border continues the line of the laced pleats.

CD 992

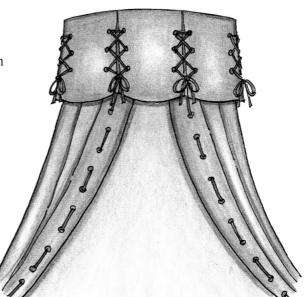

A strong center line is created by the placement of a jabot and a long bow at the raised middle point of the corona and a deep pleat running along the same line in the back panel. Matching bows are placed at the top of both side pleats, which are lower than the center bow, creating a visual peak at the center of the treatment.

CD 993, 994

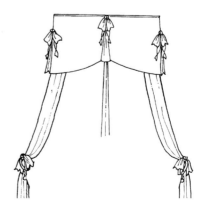

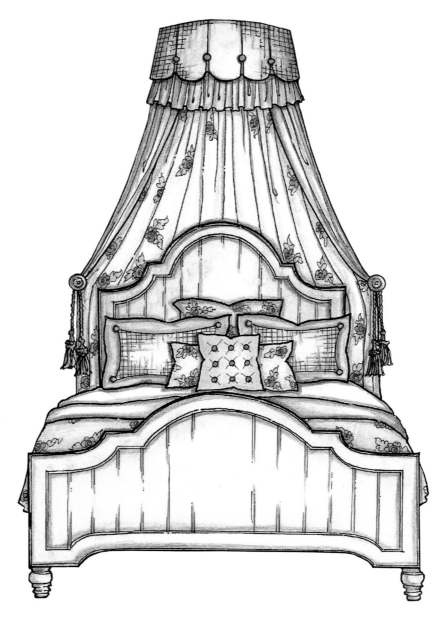

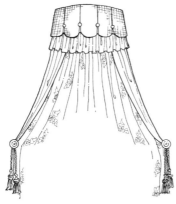

This tailored box-pleated corona has a scalloped hem and a ruffled underskirt that create a nice contrast in styles. Buttons covered in the underskirt fabric are placed approximately one-third of the way up the face of the corona to tie the two sections together.

CD 995, 996

The flat face of this corona is bordered by two deep pleats at each side that are held together with contrasting ties. Adding a detailed shape to the bottom hem gives height and interest to the design. The side panels are rolled back and casually tucked behind the head-post finials of the bed.
CD 997, 998

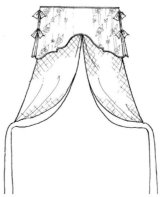

Pelmet Coronas

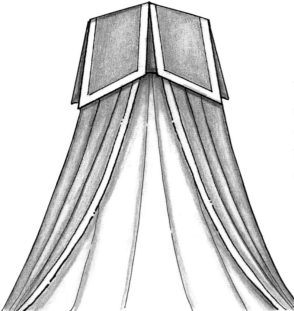

The angular lines of this pelmet corona are accentuated by the bold contrast of the banding and interior panel fabric.

CD 999

Buttons are the focal point of this design, with a center panel on the corona whose fabric is repeated on the back drapery panel. Alternating the fabrics between sections adds contrast and depth to the treatment.

CD 1000

A pleated header is the base for long, straight pelmets that are banded with contrasting fabric. The sections placed underneath the top pelmets are considerably shorter, which gives emphasis to the shape of the top sections.

CD 1001

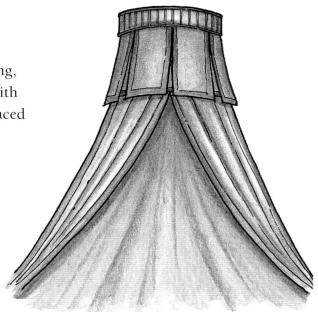

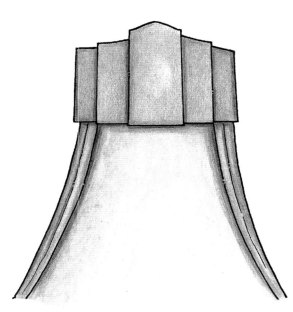

This unique design is made up of a series of stepped layers. The center section projects out from the middle section and the middle from the base. In addition to the different levels of projection, the angles of the head of each section rise in height toward the center.

CD 1002

Shirred Coronas

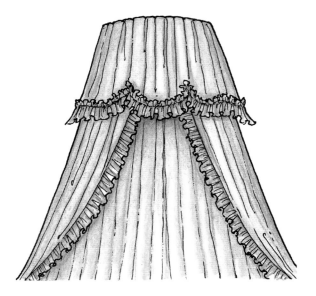

The shirred heading of this corona is concealed by attaching it to the ceiling of the frame. The gathered valance is allowed to cascade over the edge. The shape of the bottom hem is highlighted by the double-sided ruffled edge, which is reinforced by the single ruffle at the leading edge of the side panels.
CD 1003

A smocked heading is the highlight of this shirred corona. The gentle scallop of the hem is finished with a short ruffle.
CD 1004

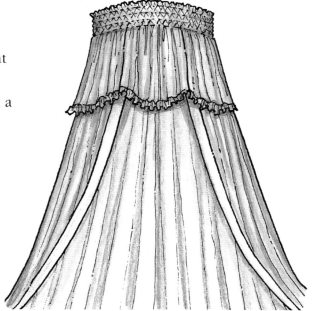

The side panels of this design are shirred to accommodate the maximum amount of fabric, but the header is finished with goblet pleats for a more tailored look. Decorative braid separates the two, and the center is highlighted with a metal crown.

CD 1005

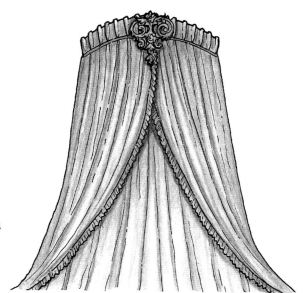

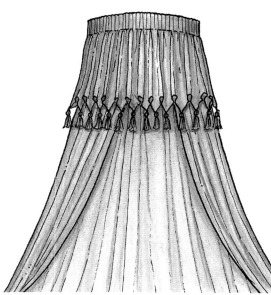

A zigzag hem is the focal point of this pencil-pleated corona. A tassel hangs from each long point. The side panels are spaced apart to expose the contrasting back panel.

CD 1006

Ruffles bordering the rounded leading edges of this corona appear to cross over one another at the center. A matching ruffle tops the corona and trims the leading edge of the side panels. Tiebacks are threaded through a buttonhole or grommet placed in the side panels to hold them back in a unique way.
CD 1007, 1008

This fun design is achieved by alternating different bands of fabric and trim. The first band is shirred and hemmed with a beaded fringe. The second band lays flat and is topped with tassel fringe. The final band is a gathered ruffle. The beaded fringe used on the second band is repeated at the leading edge of the panels.

CD 1009, 1010

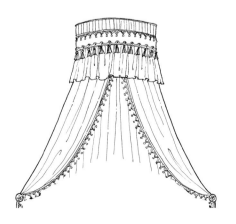

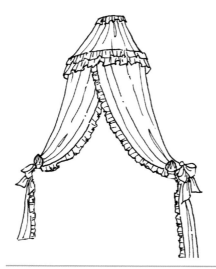

The sloping profile of this shirred crown makes it unique. Rows of alternating ruffles in contrasting colors add variety and unify different parts of the treatment. They are used to separate a wide band of contrasting fabric at the bottom of the side panels.

CD 1011, 1012

Swagged Coronas

Formal swags create the leading edge of this corona. A rounded pelmet done in a contrasting fabric fills the gap at the center and leads down to the scalloped side panels. The scallops and the center pelmet are edged in welt matching the swagged section of the corona.
CD 1013

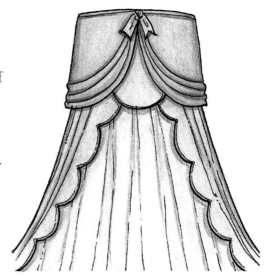

A swagged valance is hung from the pleated base of this classic corona. The leading edges of the side panels are folded back at the header to expose the contrasting lining on the face.
CD 1014

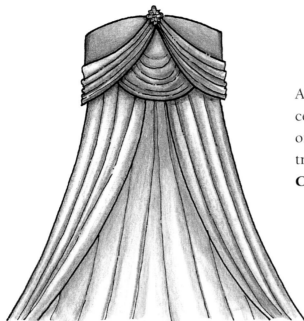

A decorative medallion marks the center and creates a peak at the apex of a turban swag in this treatment. A traditional swag fills the center gap.
CD 1015

Scooped swags are draped over an open frame that is the base of this corona. Both the base and the swags are trimmed with coordinating beaded tassel fringe. The side panels are mounted flat over the back panel at the wall.
CD 1016

Balloon swags are pulled up at two points to create a center focal point in this design. The hem is trimmed with brush fringes and the two pull-up points of the swags are highlighted with ruched fabric cording that ends in a key tassel.

CD 1017, 1018

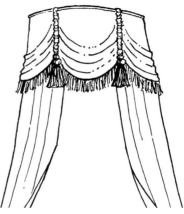

Two open swags are suspended on top of this corona by decorative medallions. The swags at each side of the treatment are half swags and only one end is attached to the medallion. Jumbo welting borders the top and bottom edge of the corona. The side panels are held back with tiebacks that match the medallions used to hold up the swags.

CD 1019, 1020

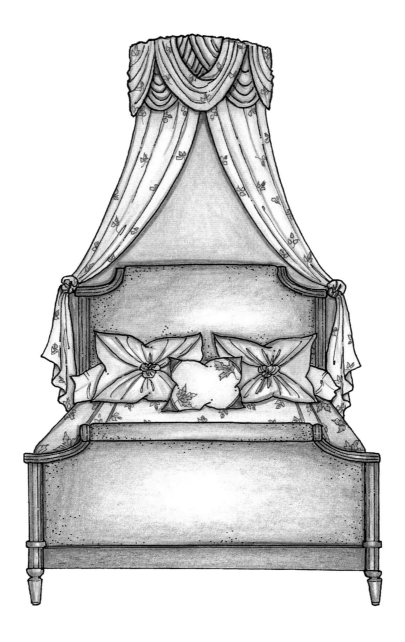

This corona is covered with scooped swags and half swags in contrasting fabrics that overlap each other. A flat back panel is separate from side panels that are cut at a steep angle to create cascades when they are pulled back. A faux knot is used to disguise the tieback.

CD 1021, 1022

Boxed Coronas

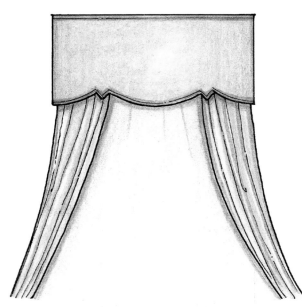

Simplicity is the key to this boxed design that has a distinctive hem shape that corresponds to the placement of the side panels at its long points.
CD 1023

Bottom-edge shapes can be accentuated by the addition of braid, gimp, or fringe. This curved design is highlighted by multicolored bullion fringe and matching braid.
CD 1024

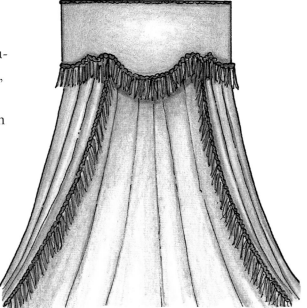

Appliqué can be a powerful tool to create pattern and the sense of shape to a straight boxed corona. A bold motif softens the hard lines of the treatment.

CD 1025

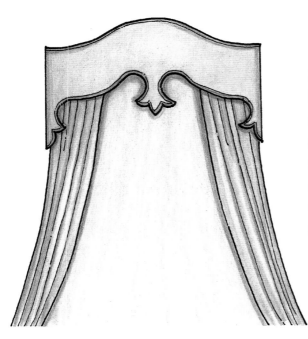

Intricate shapes and cutouts can be dramatic but should always correspond to some other pattern or architectural detail in the room. Look to fabric or wallpaper motifs and lines of furniture and wood-work for inspiration.

CD 1026

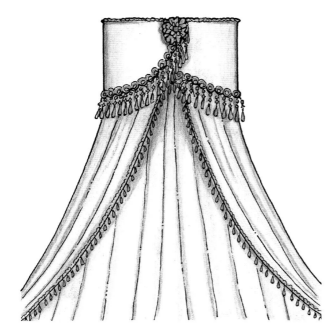

A boxed corona can have straight side panels and a curved front panel, as in this design. The leading edges of this corona appear to overlap and are trimmed in long beaded fringe. A fabric rosette centers the overlapping layers.
CD 1027

The flared sides of this corona are a unique element. The curved bottom edge is trimmed with a short contrasting ruffle that is repeated at the leading edge of the shirred side panels. A contrasting scarf is looped over the front of the corona and tied in a bow to unify the separate components.
CD 1028

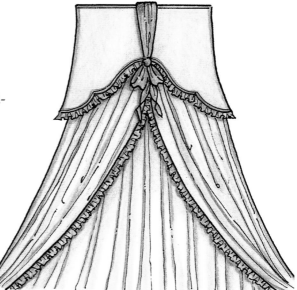

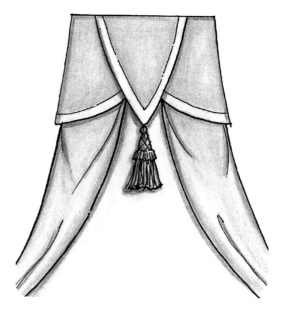

A single-pointed pelmet is mounted over the peaked base of this boxed corona. Contrast banding unifies the separate sections, while a single large tassel adds emphasis to the center point of the treatment.

CD 1029

The intricate shape of this design allows the base fabric of the corona to show through. Contrast banding accentuates the curves and angles of the design.

CD 1030

Soutache braid or gimp can be used to create intricate designs and motifs to embellish bedding, as in this striking design. The shape of the bottom edge of the corona is determined by the outline of the appliqué. The shallow projection of this boxed corona makes side panels unnecessary. A pleated back panel hangs flat against the wall.

CD 1031, 1032

The top and bottom edges of this corona have two distinctly different shapes that correspond to each other, creating a balanced whole. The border of the side panels and the face of the corona are embellished with contrasting appliqués.

CD 1033, 1034

Tented Coronas

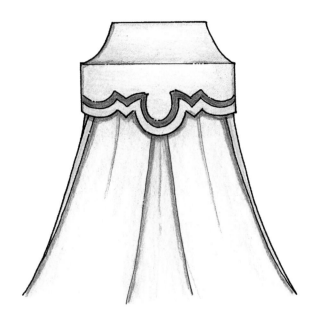

The detailed edge of this tented corona is enhanced by applying a contrasting border a distance in from the edge equal to the border's width. The contrast of the base fabric on both sides of the border increases its visual impact. A deep center box pleat adds interest to the center of the back panel, which is flanked by minimal side panels.

CD 1035

A decorative finial tops this tented corona with flared sides. The center peak of the face draws the eye up to the finial, while the small points at the bottom edge direct it back down to the bed, creating a sense of balance.

CD 1036

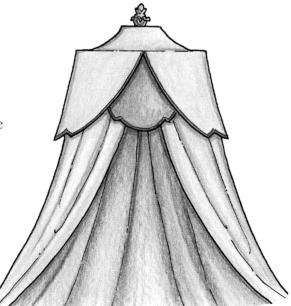

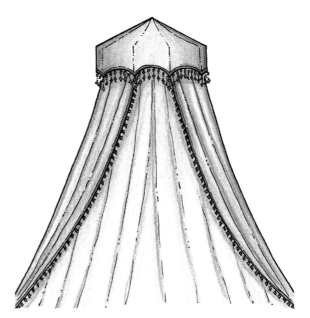

This corona resembles a parasol, with its angled sections culminating at a central point at the top. The skirt is also separated into sections that are accentuated by an arched hem. Beaded fringe adds a whimsical touch to the design.

CD 1037

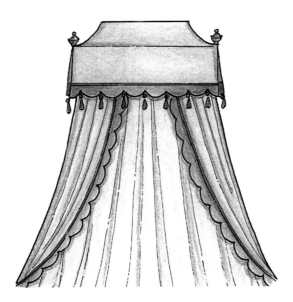

Pleats at either side of this design are topped with decorative finials that highlight the sharp points created by the sloping roof. Scalloped borders trim the bottom edge and side panels. Chandelier crystals are hung at the high point of each scallop on the corona for the final touch.

CD 1038

Cornices

A cornice is a three-sided upholstered frame, with or without an open top, that is usually close to or as wide as the bed. It can be suspended from the ceiling or mounted on the wall behind the bed, and fabric can be draped from it.

A series of pelmets run across the flat face of this arched-top cornice. A contrasting border on each pelmet draws attention to their unique shapes. The side panels are hung to correspond to the break in the border at the last pelmet on each side.

CD 1039

This arched cornice projects out from the wall in a bowed profile. Gathered jabots add volume and texture to the design. A contrasting line of welting runs across the pleat line of the jabots and the face of the cornice.

CD 1040

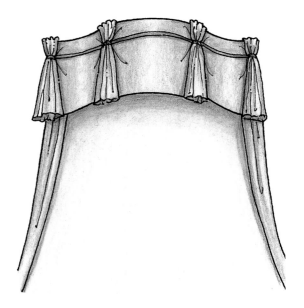

Cornices

An undulating profile is the key feature of this cornice. Two classic swags flank the center and lay over the top of the shirred side panels, which are wound around the tiebacks for a casual touch. A separate flat back panel finishes the design.

CD 1041, 1042

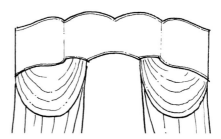

The complex outline of this peaked cornice is made even more powerful by the front and back draping of contrasting swags and cascades. By applying luxurious trim only to the center swag and the ends of the cascades, the eye is drawn to the center of the treatment.
CD 1043, 1044

Angled top and bottom edges of this cornice create sharp lines and points, while cascades frame the back drape and open swags meet at the center of the bowed cornice. A flat box-pleated back drape continues the crisp lines of the design.
CD 1045, 1046

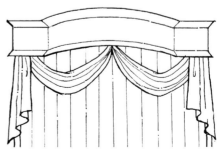

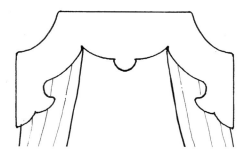

This elaborately shaped cornice is technically a lambrequin, as it has legs, or vertical extensions, at each side of the cornice box. Its overall scale and shape make for a dramatic design. The leading edges of the side panels are positioned to hang from the short points of the cornice.

CD 1047, 1048

The bowed center of this boxed cornice projects out over the bed. Long wide box pleats hem the cornice box. The side drapes are hung from the side panels of the cornice box, creating a frame around the bed.
CD 1049, 1050

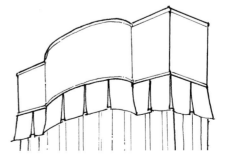

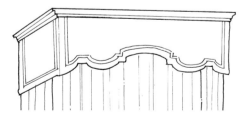

This wooden cornice, or half tester, projects out over the bed by about a third of its length. The center sections of the cornice box are upholstered with a fabric that coordinates with the fabric on the panels of the bed.

CD 1052, 1053

Curved and stacked sections of this cornice bow out from the flat base to create a rolling profile. Full-length side panels are limited to the boxed corner of the base of the cornice, while a shorter contrasting scarf falls from the first bowed section. The flat back drape allows the large print on the fabric to be seen without distortion.

CD 1054, 1055

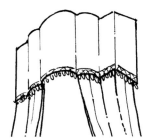

Pediments

A pediment is a hard-surfaced, three-sided, wall- or ceiling-mounted frame that is wider than it is high. Fabric is hung from the frame to drape the head of a bed.

+ A fabric valance, swags, or pelmet can be attached to the frame, as well as bed drapery.

+ The frame can be mounted on the wall or from the ceiling, depending on the design.

+ The frame can be made of materials such as wood, resin, or metal. It can be painted, stained, or covered with wallpaper.

+ The back of the frame must be mounted flush with the wall.

+ In most cases, the ceiling of the pediment will be seen by the occupant and should be finished in an appropriate manner for the design.

Traditional Pediments

Traditional Pediments

This antique pediment is draped with pleated panels that overlap the full width of the pediment frame. The panels are tied back just below the finials of the head posts.

CD 1061, 1062

A wall shelf with a cutwork valance serves as the frame for this pediment. The side panels have a pleated, scalloped heading with fabric ties that are used to hang it from the shelf. The panels are draped over tiebacks that have been painted to match the pediment.

CD 1063, 1064

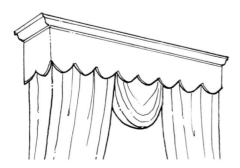

Many classic pediments are constructed of a crown molding header with a shaped apron. This pediment has a scalloped edge that has been painted with a scalloped border to match the fabric used. The swag at the center of the side panels reinforces the theme.
CD 1065, 1066

A classic center-arched pediment is draped with balloon swags. The center section is constructed with two raised half swags that cross over each other. The ruffled trim creates a vertical center line that accentuates the height of the arch.

CD 1067, 1068

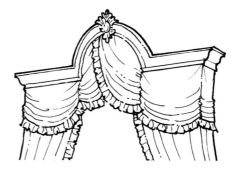

The swags hung from this simple pediment are pulled up with ties that are threaded through casings sewn into the fabric. Their excess length is tied into bows. Matching bows are used to tie back the side panels.
CD 1069, 1070

A traditional Amish peg board—with wooden dowels extending outward from a wooden base board—is a great alternative to a fancy pediment. In this design, a pleated back panel is tied onto the pegs, allowing for extra space between pegs to create droop at the heading.

CD 1071, 1072

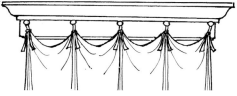

Although this treatment has the look of a complicated design, it is actually achieved by using a very simple pediment made of crown molding that has been embellished with an ornate medallion at the center. Swags and jabots hung from the pediment give it a formal appearance.

CD 1073, 1074

Drapery

A draped bed has a section, or sections, of drapery hung flat against the wall behind or on either side of the bed. It can include other drapery elements such as a valance, swags, or pelmets as long as they lay flat against the drapery or the wall.

Bed drapery is usually hung using traditional window drapery hardware components, such as:

- Decorative Rod with Brackets and Finials
- Drapery Tiebacks
- Drapery Swag Holders
- Hooks or Rings
- Ceiling Hooks
- Mounting Boards

Bed drapery should be constructed with the same high standards as conventional window drapery.

Drapery

A preserved tree branch might be an unlikely candidate for a drapery rod, but it is perfect in this situation. The branch is hung by long ties looped through rings in the ceiling. The sheer drapery panels are shirred and bound with a contrasting fabric that ends in long ties that are tied to the branch at each end.

CD 1075, 1076

This bordered panel is tuck-pleated at each flat tab. The tab is fitted with hook-and-loop tape so it can be folded over a large ring and secured at the back of the panel. The rings are hung from large decorative wall hooks.
CD 1077, 1078

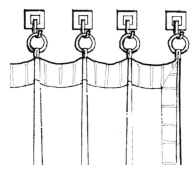

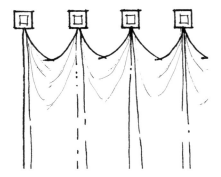

This slouched drapery panel is designed with an inverted pleat at each hanging loop to add volume and to create a strong vertical line. The loops are hung over evenly spaced decorative square medallions, creating a dramatic treatment.

CD 1079, 1080

Swags and jabots are the main features that make up the design of this valance. Long fabric loops are used to hang the treatment from decorative ceiling hooks. The loops are then threaded through buttonholes or grommets in the heading of the valance and are tied into bows. Beaded fringe accentuates the lines of the valance.

CD 1081, 1082

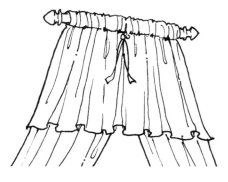

This design features a rod pocket heading with a long integrated valance edged with a wide contrasting border. The treatment is hung from a traditional drapery rod and pulled back to expose the contrasting interior lining. The simple knotted tie at the center of the valance draws the eye down to the bed.

CD 1083, 1084

Although this swagged design might look simple, some serious planning has gone into its construction to achieve the finished look. Separate pole swag sections are attached to the pole, while individual side panels hang to the floor in perfect columns.

CD 1085, 1086

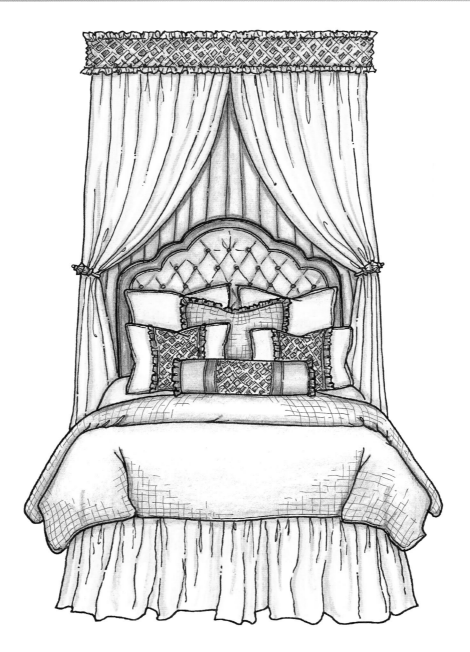

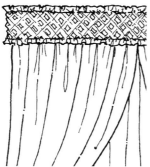

In this design, a smocked header is bordered with short ruffles on either side and mounted on a board that is attached directly to the wall. Shirred side panels are pulled back to expose a contrasting back panel.
CD 1087, 1088

As an alternative to a typical drapery panel, a tapestry is used in this design. Coordinating tabs are sewn to the tapestry, which is hung from decorative scarf holders.

CD 1089, 1090

Tiebacks can be used to hang drapery as well as hold them back. A slouched panel is hung from each tieback with an extra-long tie. Glass beads are tied to the end of each tie for impact.

CD 1091, 1092

The simplest of designs can be very effective when done properly. Here, a pair of tabbed, self-lined panels with inverted box pleats are folded back into a tuxedo opening and secured to decorative knobs.

CD 1093, 1094

Tented Drapery

Tented drapery has panels that are hung from the ceiling or from a drapery rod projecting out from the wall, which creates an overall look of a tent or awning.

Tented Draperies

The sinuous shape of the hem on this tented panel reinforces the lines of the bed. A rod pocket is sewn into the end of the panel and a decorative rod is inserted. When specifying this type of design, always tack rods in place to prevent slippage.

CD 1095, 1096

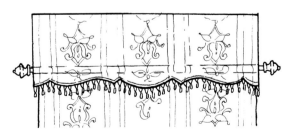

Here, two decorative drapery poles are suspended from the ceiling by long hooks to hold a single shirred panel of fabric. The panel must be secured to the poles to prevent slipping and sagging. When using medium- to heavy-weight fabrics, it is best to sew a rod pocket on the underside of the panel at the appropriate position for both poles. Lightweight fabrics can be secured by self-adhesive hook-and-loop tape.

CD 1097, 1098

In this design, three decorative drapery rods are used to suspend a series of flat ceiling panels, a valance, and a back panel by rod pockets sewn into the fabric. This tented treatment is hung from the ceiling with metal hooks and loops.
CD 1099, 1100

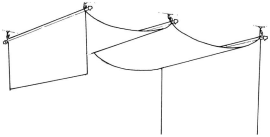

Two projecting rods suspend this casual tented valance with side panels. An inverted box pleat at the center of the valance and tucks at each corner allow for flexibility.

CD 1101, 1102

This unique treatment is hung from the ceiling and supported by a central drapery rod. The treatment is two-sided with self-lining, a separate valance, and side panels on each side of the rod. The treatment is hung on rings and splits down the center to tent over the bed.
CD 1103, 1104

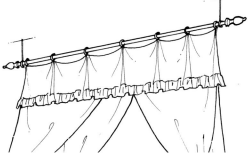

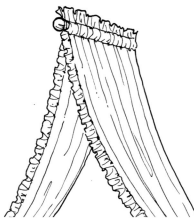

A double ruffle and rod pocket form the heading of this tented drape. A pole projecting out from the wall serves as the focal point at the apex of the tent. When specifying this type of pole, it is best to use fishing line suspended from the ceiling to support the end of the rod.

CD 1105, 1106

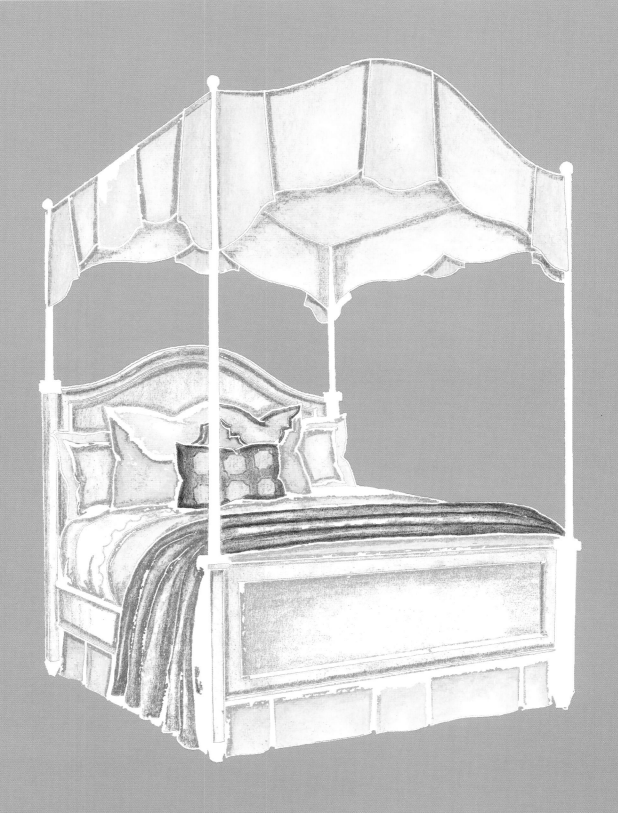

Canopy Beds

A canopy bed is a bed structure or frame that is designed to be draped with fabric to provide decoration or privacy.

✦ Canopies look best in large rooms with above-average ceiling heights. Keep in mind that canopies can have a shrinking effect on the ceiling height of a room.

✦ Canopy beds and four-poster beds, which are commonly used with canopies, pose specific challenges when designing bedding, such as splitting the end corners of the bed covers and designing a pieced bed skirt. Make sure you address all of the specifics of your bed frame in the planning stage.

✦ The post draperies or panels should be lined with a contrasting or complementary fabric. If a sheer fabric is to be used, it should be finished with French seams and lingerie hems. Back panels can be lined with standard lining fabric.

✦ When specifying operable bed curtains, use rings or a track mechanism for a smooth and easy operation. Tabs are not suitable for operational panels. Drapery wands can be helpful for opening and closing heavy drapes.

✦ Consider the finished weight of your canopy treatment and drapes. Be sure the bed frame is sturdy enough to support the weight.

✦ Interlining should be used only when absolutely necessary, as it adds considerable weight and bulk to the finished design.

✦ The underside, or ceiling, of the canopy top panel should be finished in an appropriate manner for the design.

✦ Consider the location of items on the ceiling such as air registers, ceiling fans, and smoke detectors when determining the design and placement of your canopy.

Types of Canopies

- Full
- Partial
- Open
- Scarf-Draped
- Back-Draped
- Raised
- Ceiling-Hung

Full Canopy:

A full canopy is one that possesses all of the traditional canopy options, including:

- Canopy ceiling panel
- Canopy skirt or pelmet
- Head panel or drapes
- Head post panels or drapes
- Foot post panels or drapes

A full canopy is the most traditional of canopy designs and can be the most luxurious, as it requires many yards of fabric to finish.

Partial Canopy

A partial canopy design is one that possesses some but not all of the components of a full canopy.

Open Canopy

An open canopy can have head post and/or foot post panels along with a head panel, but it does not have a canopy ceiling. The ceiling is left open.

Scarf-Draped Canopy

A scarf-draped canopy does not use the traditional canopy components. Instead, it is decorated with long lengths of finished fabric called "scarves."

Back-Draped Canopy

A back-draped canopy places all of the design emphasis at the head of the bed. It can have head post panels or drapes and a head panel or drape. It can even have a partial canopy at the head of the bed, but the foot of the bed is left plain.

Raised Canopy

A raised canopy includes a center portion of its canopy frame raised above the perimeter. The center of the bed is literally raised higher towards the ceiling than the rest of the bed, making it the focal point. The design can include all or some components of the traditional full-canopy bed.

Ceiling-Hung Canopy

A ceiling-hung canopy does not rely on a canopy bed frame to create its draping structure. It has an independent frame or design suspended from the ceiling over the bed.

Canopy Ceiling Panels

The underside, or ceiling, of a canopy is just as important as the design of the rest of the bedding. The ceiling should reflect the same style as the rest of the bedding while providing an attractive focal point for the occupant.

Flat-Panel Canopy Ceilings

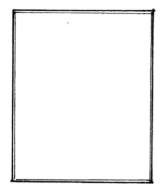

Plain Panel

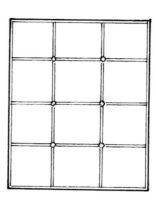

Welted grid with buttons

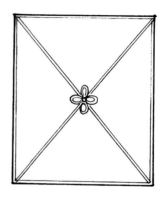

Four-section panel with welt and center flourish

Shirred-Panel Canopy Ceilings

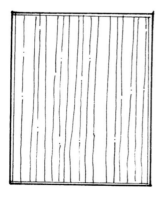

Single shirred panel

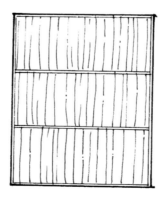

Austrian panel with welt

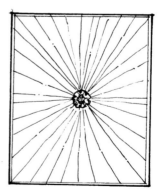

Starburst with center rosette

Full Canopies

This canopy bed has an arched ceiling that is draped with a shirred valance on three sides. Gathered end post panels wrap around the post and are hung from the side and end frames. The side panels at the head of the bed are hung from the side frame only. A matching gathered panel is hung from the head frame behind the headboard. To finish the full canopy, the ceiling is shirred in a starburst pattern and centered with a large rosette.

CD 1111

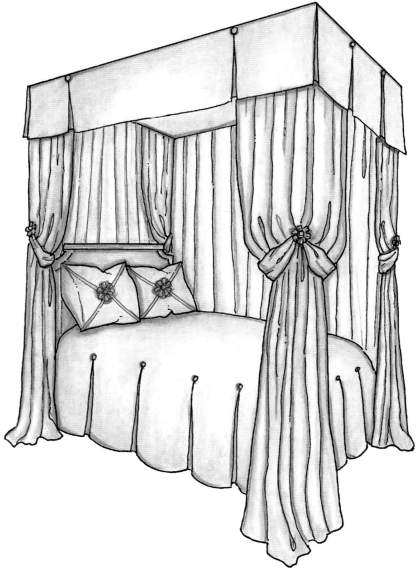

A canopy bed placed against a wall provides an opportunity to create a very cozy retreat. Full pleated wall panels are hung from the ceiling of this canopy at the head and side of the bed. The pleats in the canopy valance correspond to the widths of the post panels, and pleats are repeated in the bed cover. The side panels are pulled back with a contrasting tieback and secured to the posts with a ribbon floret, allowing it to swag in reverse at the back of the post.

CD 1113

Partial Canopies

The valance of this canopy is draped with traditional swags and bows. Full-length side panels at the head posts frame the shirred panel that hangs behind the headboard. They are tied back to the head posts with matching bows.
CD 1115

Box pleats create strong vertical lines on this canopy. The back and ceiling panel folds over the end of the canopy frame to create a valance. It is edged with an inverted scallop border that matches the border of the bed skirt. The borders soften the hard lines of the pleats and replicate the curves of the bed frame itself.

CD 1117

Swags and cascades make up the valance of this traditional treatment. The back panel is split at the center and pulled back at each head post. The swagging of the pulled-back head panels repeats the lines of the swagged valance, creating balance. Beaded trim is added to update the design.

CD 1119

For many canopy beds, the frame can be so elaborate or commanding that little embellishment is needed. Here, the shirred-fabric ceiling and back panels serve as a background to draw attention to the impressive framework of the bed itself.

CD 1121

This canopy design is an updated version of the traditional pelmet valance found on many Victorian-era beds. In this treatment, simple banding and contrasting fabrics are used to create a pattern. The elaborate trims and bullions have been removed, and the shapes of the pelmets themselves become the focal point of the design.

CD 1123

Colorful borders are the star of this design. They follow the lines of the bed to accentuate its shape and to create unity between the separate pieces. The ceiling panel is attached to the side frame with long ties that match the border, and the end of the panel folds over the end frame to create a valance.

CD 1125

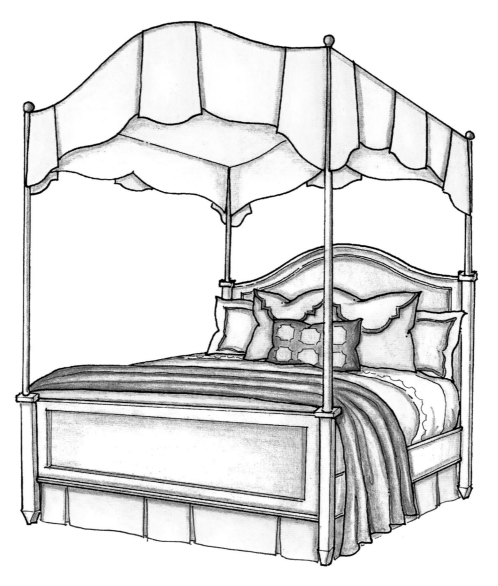

Overlapping pelmets shaped to reflect the
outline of the headboard alternate in color to
highlight the high and low points of this
arched-canopy bed. The pleats in the bed skirt
correspond in location to the pelmets of the
valance. Subtle color variations can be just as
dramatic as strong ones in the right design.
CD 1127

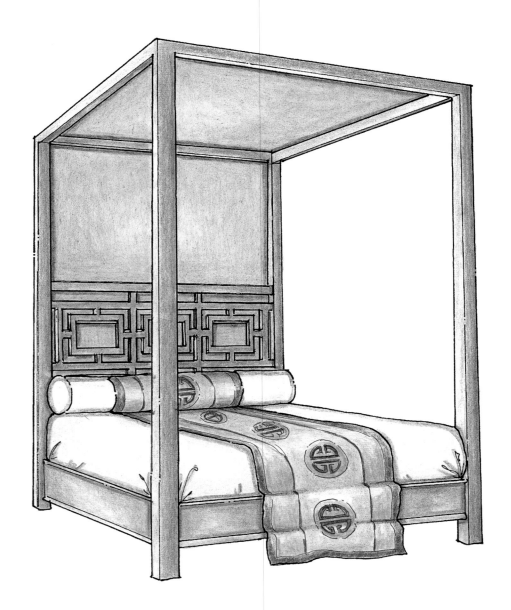

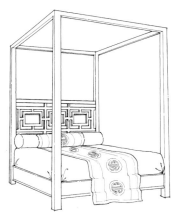

Asian design motifs are the focus of this dramatic treatment. The canopy is draped with a flat ceiling and back panel that show off the intricate latticework of the headboard. The vibrant appliquéd runner flowing down the center of the bed to the floor is repeated at the center of the bolster at the headboard. This gives the illusion of it being constructed in one piece.

CD 1129

A tightly shirred valance with a deep zigzag hem tops this pretty canopy bed. Long, shirred ruffles are repeated on the pillow shams and the foot warmer at the end of the bed to lend balance and unity to the design.

CD 1131

Open Canopies

Crisp pleats and long lines create a feeling of tailored sophistication in this design. Tab panels are hung at each corner of the bed, with a matching panel being hung from the back. The ceiling is left open, and a full-length pleated bed cover completes the treatment. When using tab panels, secure them in place at equal intervals with self-adhesive hook-and-loop tape.

CD 1133

Rod pocket panels can be used only on beds with removable canopy rails, as they must be threaded over the rail itself. If you really want this look but your bed does not accommodate it, you can achieve it by lacing ties through a series of grommets or buttonholes laid out in two lines running the width of the rail placed at the heading of the panel.
CD 1135

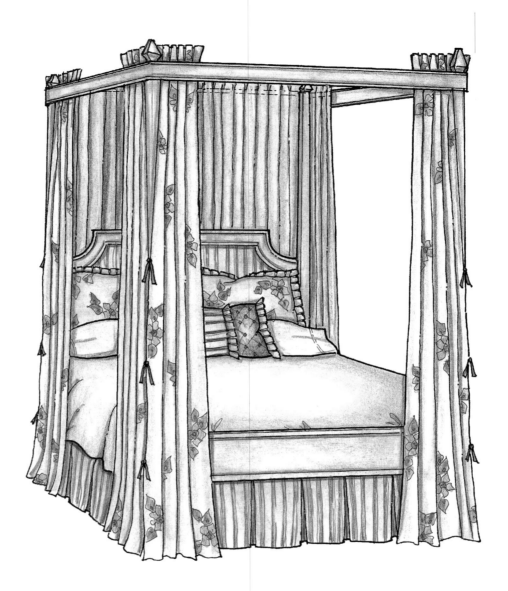

The pleated drapery panels on this open-canopy bed are hung on the inside of the bed frame, and the heading projects up above the top of the frame, creating a backdrop for the finials at each corner. The separate side panels are joined together at the front of the post with contrasting ties.

CD 1137

The voluminous panels of this canopy are shirred at the heading and tied onto the frame with wide contrasting ties that come to a point at the end. The ties are placed close together to prevent the panels from sagging between ties.
CD 1139

Bishop's sleeve panels form the legs of this pretty peaked canopy. Each sleeve is gathered at the top and is hand tacked into a large ruched flourish at the top. Twill tape is hung inside the sleeve from the top to the desired length, where the bishop's sleeve will be gathered in and pulled up to create its distinctive poof. This stabilizes the length of each sleeve and ensures conformity throughout the design.

CD 1141

Full panels taper in at the top and form a long-lined heading. They are cinched in by a tie threaded through a casing sewn into the heading and tied securely to the posts. The valance is allowed to flop over the tie, creating a long flounce. The panels are made with two sections of fabric. The bottom section has godets inserted to add volume and flair to the profile of the panel. The seam is covered with decorative trim.
CD 1143

Scarf-Draped Canopies

You can't get simpler than this design that consists of three lined lengths of fabric casually draped over the canopy frame. One length drapes from the head frame to the foot frame while the other two are draped around finials at opposite corners of the bed. Although this design looks random, it should be dressed and then secured in place with self-adhesive hook-and-loop tape or another fastening method to prevent the drapes from slipping or sagging.

CD 1145

Iron-on metal tape or flexible wire sewn into a casing in the fabric can allow you to achieve this sinuous look. Long lengths of fabric are sewn into tubes and bent around the canopy and posts of the bed. Here, two very long fabric tubes cross over one another and wind around the bed frame, eventually puddling on the floor. This design is especially suited to accordion-pleated, perma-pleated, or crinkled fabrics.

CD 1147

There is something very romantic about a casually dressed bed. This canopy is created by a single length of lined fabric that is cut at an angle in the opposite direction at each end. Hand-tied fringe accentuates the sharp angle. Be sure to secure the scarf in place after it is dressed.

CD 1149

While it may appear that this treatment is created by tying long scarves to the frame of the bed, it is actually constructed with separate scarf swags and cascades that are joined together by a series of faux knots that tie to the bed frame. It is almost impossible to achieve this look using a single scarf.

CD 1151

Rather than follow the arched lines of this raised canopy, this design uses swagged scarves to oppose them, which, in turn, has the effect of highlighting them. The scarves are tied to the posts and pulled up to meet at the center, where they are threaded through a ring at the top of the canopy. They are tied into a bundle at the center and finished with a bow.

CD 1153

The center ring of this canopy is fitted with a ruffled heading that is attached to the interior of the ring with hook-and-loop tape. Four long scarves are hung from the same tape at the center and supported at regular intervals by long fabric loops and bows.

CD 1155

Back-Draped Canopies

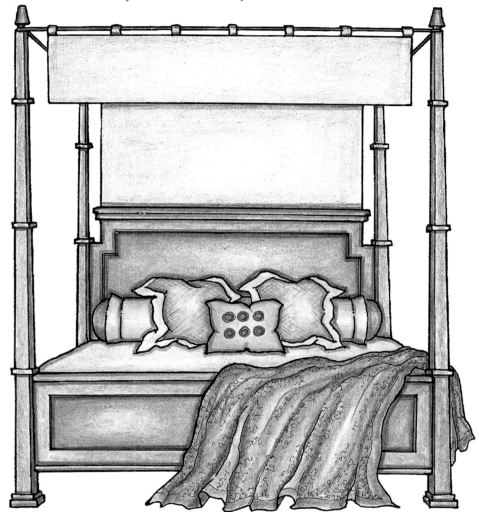

The flat sections of this canopy are stiffened and hang from tabs at the top of each panel. The ceiling panel is reinforced with a board to maintain its shape and prevent sagging.

CD 1157

This unique bed frame has a hoop canopy at the head post only. In this design, a double-layered shirred panel with a ruffled heading is threaded through each side of the hoop to achieve the look of a separate set of side panels and a contrasting back panel. Tassel fringe borders the leading edge of the top panels, which are pulled back to expose the second layer of fabric. A large key tassel hangs from the apex of the hoop.

CD 1159

The side panels of this back-draped canopy have a double integrated valance with a ruffled rod pocket heading. A matching panel with a one-sided valance hangs at the back of the bed. Keep in mind that many canopy bed draperies cannot be hung using a rod pocket heading. To modify this design, you would eliminate the ruffled heading and hang the panels using ties or loops or button-down tabs.

CD 1161

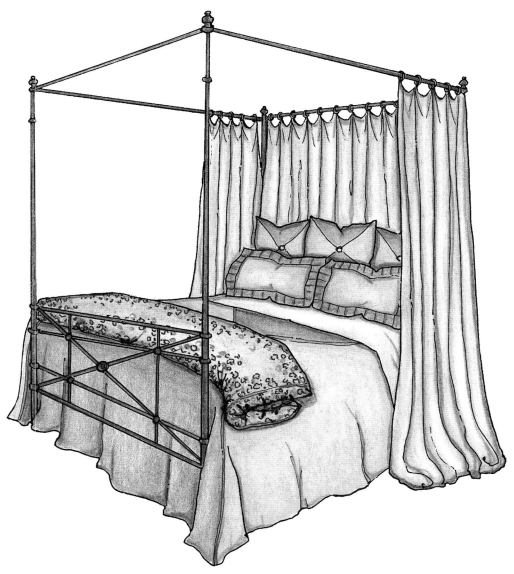

The panels of this design are hung by
drapery rings placed at equal intervals
along the head and side frames of the
canopy. Rings should be fixed in place to
prevent having to constantly straighten
them. The side panels are puddled on the
floor at either side of the bed.

CD 1163

A padded cushion is attached to the headboard of this bed with long ties. Matching panels of fabric are also tied to the back panel and the side and foot rails of the bed. The back panel should be secured firmly at each side to the head posts to prevent gapping. Use self-adhesive hook-and-loop tape for a tight fit.

CD 1165

Raised Canopies

Eight separate panels of sheer fabric are gathered and sewn to the top panel of this raised canopy. The back sections are very long and swag back to the head posts, where they are tied back. They fall to the floor in a long column of fabric. The front sections are also tied back at the foot posts but are cut to hang in double cascades, ending at the top of the footboard. When using sheer fabric, always specify French seams for a professional look.

CD 1167

This raised canopy has side panels that have a similar appearance to bishop's sleeves. The shirred lengths of fabric are draped over the canopy frame and secured to the side posts. A specific length of the panel is gathered into a bunched section and tied in place, creating a floret that is embellished with a long tie. A separate ruffled heading is attached to the interior of the center ring.

CD 1169

Ceiling-Hung Canopies

This ceiling-hung canopy is reinforced at the heading seams with tension wire to help maintain its sharp lines and prevent sagging. Side panels are split in pairs on all sides of the bed and tied back to the bed posts. A flat valance tops the treatment.

CD 1171

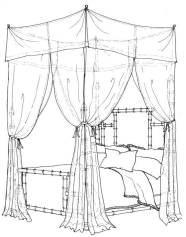

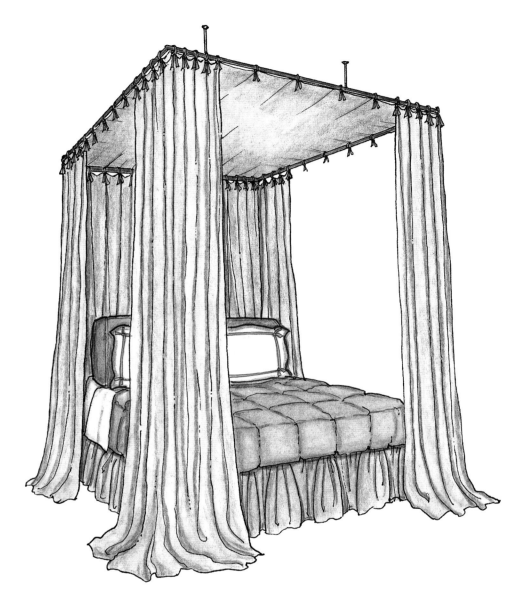

A free-hanging metal frame is the base for this canopy, which features a flat ceiling panel attached to the frame with short ties. The side and back panels are tied to the frame and generously puddle on the floor.

CD 1173

This canopy is supported by a hidden wooden frame that hangs from the ceiling on chains covered with a ruched fabric sleeve. Crisp panels appliquéd with contrasting banding make up the valance of the canopy. The side panels have a matching appliquéd band at the hem.

CD 1175

The gathered valance and side panels of this light and airy canopy are bound at the heading with fabric bias tape that ends in long loops at each corner. The loops hang from ceiling hooks. The panels are cinched together at each corner. **CD 1177**

Daybeds

A daybed is a bed or sofa that can be used as seating during the day and for sleeping at night.

- Most daybeds are built to accommodate a standard twin-sized mattress and box spring. Some can hold only a twin mattress.

- Many daybed frames are designed to be placed lengthwise against a wall.

- Daybeds can be covered with traditional decorative bedding or fitted covers more suitable for seating than for sleeping, depending on how the bed is to be used.

- Antique daybeds may require a custom-sized mattress or seat cushion.

- Many daybeds can accommodate a separate trundle bed, which fits underneath the frame and pulls out to accommodate another sleeper.

Common Structural Components

- Two matching side panels or arms support the base of the daybed at each end.

- A base or platform supports the mattress. This base usually includes additional legs or feet for support.

- A back panel holds the mattress in place and provides back support.

Daybeds

This antique French daybed is dressed formally with an upholstered seat cushion rather than a mattress. The back of the daybed is draped with a scarf swag treatment hung from a center pole and swagged back behind two matching sets of tiebacks.

CD 1181

Placed in a corner of the room, this iron
daybed is watched over by a set of bird-
shaped resin scarf holders. A long scarf is
draped over them, creating a whimsical
treatment. The daybed is made up as a
traditional bed, with a bolster used at
the head of the bed to cushion the hard
iron frame.

CD 1182

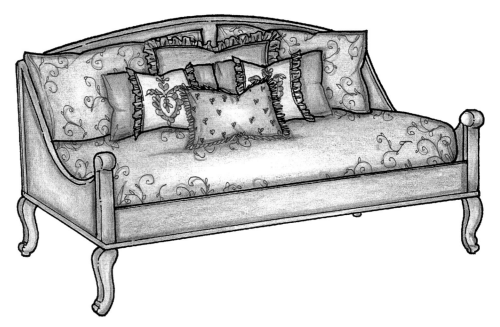

When designing bedding for a daybed that has low arms or no arms at all, use large back pillows that will not fall off the bed. Accent with smaller throw pillows for variety.

CD 1184

The overstuffed bolsters at each arm of this bed add comfort by padding the otherwise hard angles of the arm rails. Additional pillows are added for back support.

CD 1185

The pointed-arch back panel of this daybed provided the inspiration for the cornice treatment that hangs above it. A shirred bed ruffle and duvet cover make up the bed, and a multitude of overstuffed down pillows provide back support and luxurious comfort.

CD 1186

This antique cast-iron bed frame would probably require a custom-made mattress or seat cushion. An antique coverlet is used to cover the seat and is topped with an assortment of eclectic pillows.

CD 1188

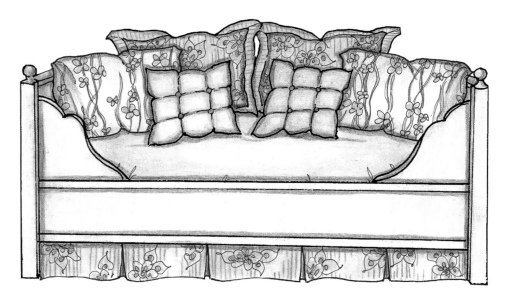

When designing for a frame that surrounds the mattress, consider a fitted mattress cover with elastic binding similar to a fitted bottom sheet. It will make dressing the bed less of a challenge.

CD 1189

This beautiful canopy daybed doesn't need elaborate coverings to show off its attributes. Simple scarves or self-lined lengths of fabric are knotted at the center crown of the canopy and draped to each corner, where they are knotted in place again and allowed to fall to the floor. Large round bolsters provide support at either end of the mattress.

CD 1190

A matching corona frame hangs above this sleigh-shaped daybed. The frame is draped with a box-pleated valance ending in sharp points. The long drapery panels drape over the sides of the daybed and puddle on the ground.

CD 1192

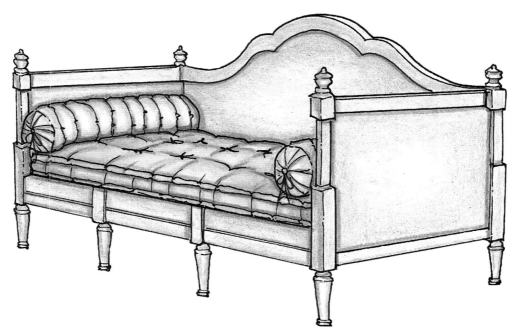

A hand-tufted and tied mattress and matching bolsters add a rustic, casual flair to this traditional daybed.

CD 1194

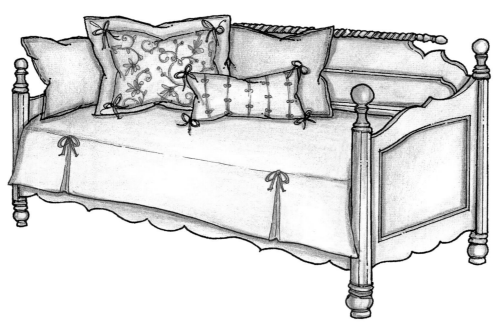

The front flap of the coverlet on this daybed has two inverted box pleats at each side that are embellished with ribbon bows. The bows are carried through the design on the accompanying throw pillows.

CD 1195

Sheer mosquito netting is hung from a natural bamboo frame suspended from the ceiling above this Asian-inspired bed. The heading of the netting drape is tacked in at each ring to create volume and is allowed to swag between rings. The mattress is covered with a tight-fitting cover. It is topped with extra-large decorative pillows.

CD 1196

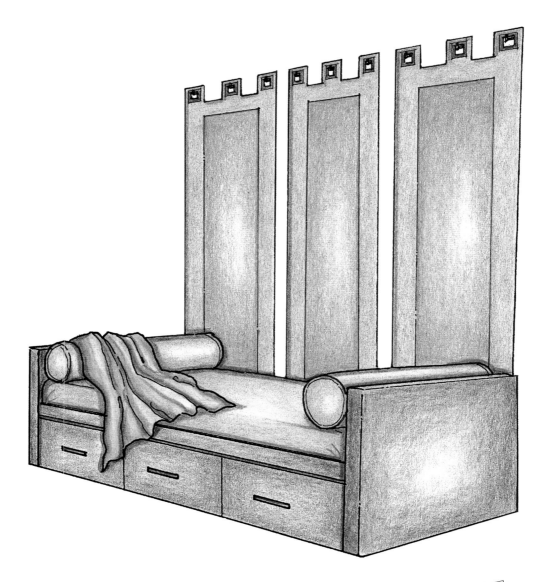

This contemporary campaign bed is high-lighted by three bordered panels hung behind it. The panels are fitted with square grommets at each large tab so they can be hung with decorative wall hooks.
CD 1199

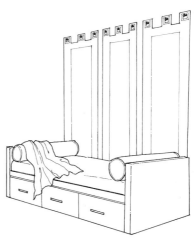

The canopy of this antique wicker daybed is covered with a scalloped valance embellished with a ribbon quatrefoil at the top of each pleat. Box pleats also border the mattress cover and throw pillows. Shirred back and side panels hang straight to the floor, creating a luxurious, comfortable retreat.

CD 1200

A cabinet-framed canopy creates a very
formal alcove in this design. The interior
of the cabinet is lined with shirred panels,
and drapes at each side of the opening
can be drawn closed for privacy and
warmth. The bolsters at each side of the
opening have long tails that drape over
the side of the mattress.

CD 1203

Sheer fabric is used to create the dramatic canopy treatment for this daybed. A short box-pleated valance drapes over the front and back of the canopy frame, while the side panels hang down over each side of the frame and puddle on the floor. An informal bed throw covers the mattress, and a large assortment of pillows provides comfort and back support.

CD 1205

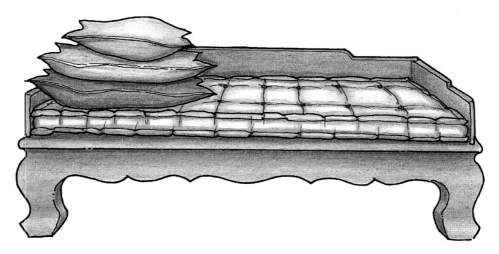

Stacking pillows vertically rather than arranging them across the back of the bed can impart a contemporary look to your design.

CD 1206

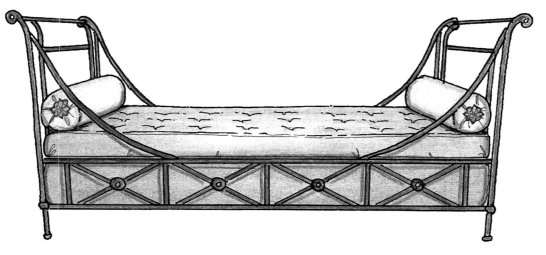

Oftentimes less can be more when specifying bedding. The style of this vintage campaign bed calls for minimal, small-scale elements.

CD 1207

The tented canopy on this daybed is supported by an integrated iron frame attached to the back of the bed. A flat scarf is draped over the frame and tied in place with long bows. A pleated skirt adorns the front of the bed, and the long tails of the bolsters hang down over the mattress.
CD 1209

This daybed frame is designed to fit into a corner of the room. Sloping side and back-rests come together at a high point in the corner. Matching bolsters run along the sides and back of the bed. The corner behind the bed is draped with panels that have a deeply scooped heading bound with ribbon. The ribbon is also used to tie the drape to medallions mounted on the wall in long bows.

CD 1211

In this design, a fully upholstered daybed is flanked by a pair of drapery panels. The panels have rod pocket headings with a single ruffle. They are shirred on short lengths of decorative rod with finials at each end and hung on matching brackets.
CD 1213

Finishing Touches

Paying close attention to the small details is the key to creating beautiful bedding.

The following elements are important to consider:

- Welting
- Banding
- Rosettes
- Medallions
- Ties and Bows
- Functional Fasteners
- Decorative Fasteners

Fasteners

Many bedding components and treatments require a decorative or functional fastening element as part of the overall design. The choice of type and style of fastener can dramatically alter the appearance of the design.

Common Fastening Elements

- Buttons
- Bows
- Knotted Ties
- Rosettes
- Medallions

Fasteners can be a functional element of your design, or they can serve a purely decorative purpose.

Functional Applications

- Button tufting
- Fastening surfaces together
- Fastening components in place
- Creating functional openings and closures

Decorative Applications

- Creating focal points
- Introducing color and texture
- Establishing rhythm and balance
- Creating faux openings and closures
- Disguising seams and gather points

Make sure these elements are sewn on with heavy-duty button twist thread that has been knotted several times during sewing. This may prevent them from coming loose or falling off with use.

Use a fabric-marking pen that has disappearing ink to mark an element's placement. If an element does fall off, there will be no obvious mark present on the face of the treatment.

Hard Buttons

Fabric-Covered Buttons

CD 0155

CD 0156

Knotted Ties

CD 0157

CD 0158

CD 0159

CD 0160

CD 0161

CD 0162

Bows

CD 0163

CD 0164

CD 0165

CD 0166

CD 0167

CD 0168

Florettes

CD 0169

CD 0170

CD 0171

CD 0172

CD 0173

CD 0174

Rosettes

CD 0175

CD 0176

CD 0177

CD 0178

CD 0179

CD 0180

CD 0181

CD 0182

Medallions

CD 0183

CD 0184

CD 0185

Border Options

Many times the edge or border of an item holds the greatest interest and detail. The addition of an interesting border can set the tone for the whole design.

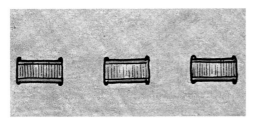

Grosgrain ribbon threaded
through buttonholes

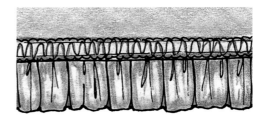

Ruched sleeve ruffle with
decorative gimp

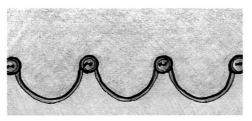

Inverted scallop overlay
with buttons

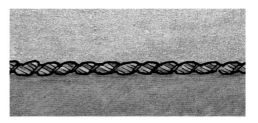

Contrast banding with
lip cord insert

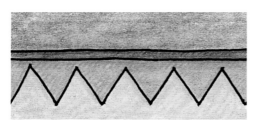

Contrasting banding with
zigzag overlay and flat welt

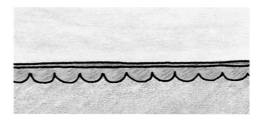

Contrasting band with
scalloped overlay and welting

Alternating threaded
ribbon and bows

Floral appliqués with
round button centers

Hemmed edge with
blanket stitching

Zigzag edging with a contrast
band and double welting

Accordion-pleated scalloped ruffle

Flat tape or gimp with
ribbon rosettes

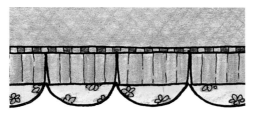

Scalloped edge with contrasting
inverted box-pleated ruffle
and welting

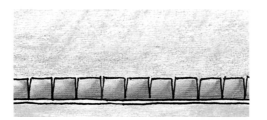

Straight edge with zigzag banding
and alternating zigzag panel edge

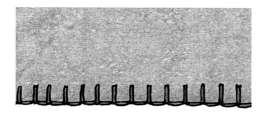

Back-facing inverted box-pleated
ruffle with welting and
contrast banding

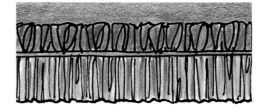

Ruched sleeve ruffle with welting
and ribbon-loop fringe

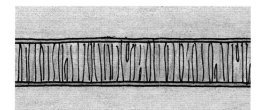

Shirred banding with
contrasting welting

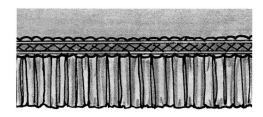

Ruched sleeve ruffle with
decorative braid

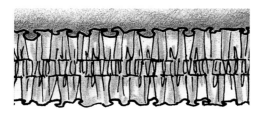

Flat lace trim with welting

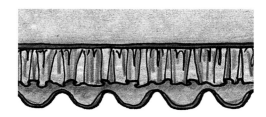

Scalloped banding with welted edge
and contrasting ruffle with welting

Double ruffle with center shirring

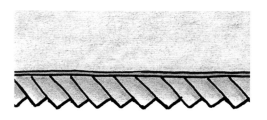

Zigzag angled knife-pleated
edging with welt

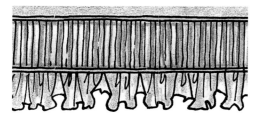

Ruffle with shirred banding
and contrasting welt

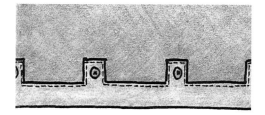

Shaped banding with topstitching
and contrasting buttons

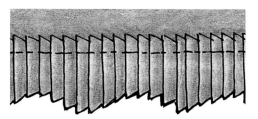

Scalloped knife-pleated ruffle

Scalloped wedge with welting
and soutache braid design

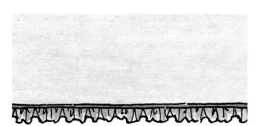

Small ruffle with contrasting welt

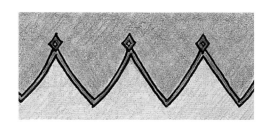

Shaped overlay with contrasting
welted edge and appliqués

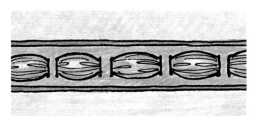

Inset contrasting band with welting
and scarf threaded through
buttonholes

Banding with ribbon threaded through
buttonholes, welting on both edges
and a single ruffle at the bottom edge.

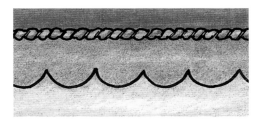

Contrast banding with scalloped
overlay and cords with lip insert

Tapestry ribbon with inverted
box-pleated ruffle

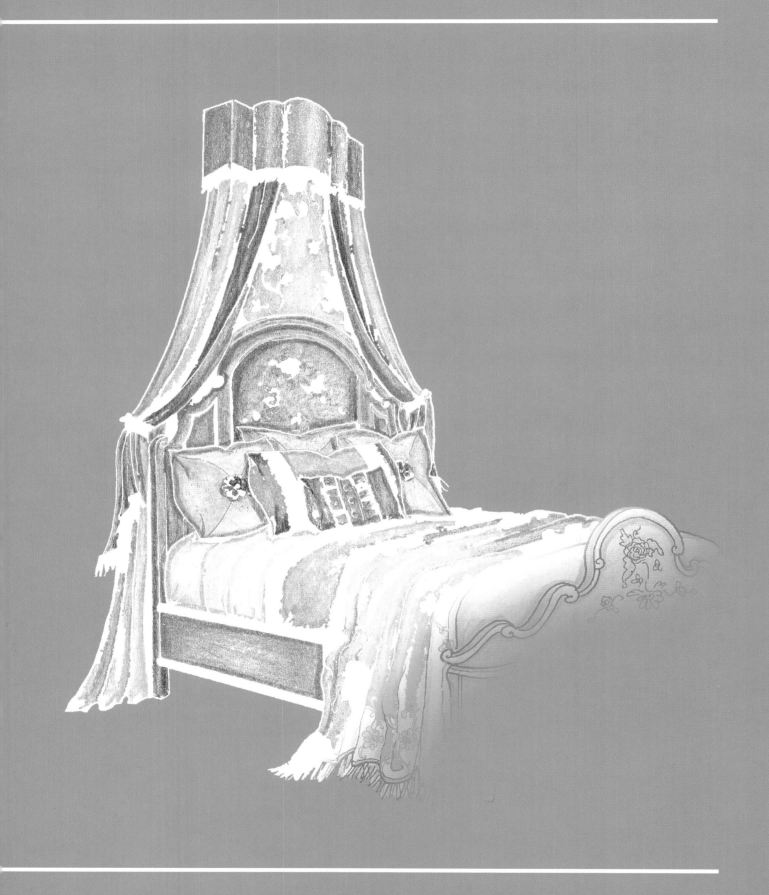

The Workroom

A workroom is a professional business specializing in the manufacturing of custom soft furnishings. Many workrooms provide services to designers and to the public, while some are exclusive to the design trade. The following are some tips on how to work effectively with your workroom to achieve your desired results.

✤ Always double check your yardage estimates with the workroom. Their methods of construction might require additional yardage that you are not aware of. Better to be safe than to run short of materials at the last minute.

✤ No two workrooms are the same. Find out what your workroom's individual standards are. Be prepared to specify your preferred options if their standard option does not fit your requirements.

✤ Discuss your design ideas with your workroom professional because she/he might have great tips and cost-saving techniques that can be applied to your design. The professional might also prevent you from making some costly mistakes.

✤ Always sketch a scale drawing of your design to visualize its proportion and scale. It doesn't have to be a work of art—just sketch it out on 4 x 4-inch-square graph paper at $1/4"$ scale.

✤ Always provide the workroom with a professional worksheet that has a color-coded scale drawing of your design, including complete specifications.

✤ Tag your C.O.M. (customer's own material) and trims clearly, in at least two places, with your contact information and job specifications to avoid your products being misplaced.

✤ Identify your work. Order dressmaker labels online with your name and contact information, and ask your workroom to sew them inside your treatments. This adds a couture touch and lets future owners of the home know who provided the treatments.

✤ Most workrooms are run in a very professional manner. Ask your workroom for a copy of their business license and proof of liability insurance to keep them on file. This will assure you and your clients that you are using a legitimate business and that your products are insured while on their premises.

Worksheets

Once you have completed the design process and chosen all of the materials to be used in the construction of your treatment, you must be able to communicate your design clearly and effectively to your workroom.

• You can never provide too much information.

• Always use the same worksheet format so the workroom can become familiar with your system.

• Many workrooms will provide you with a worksheet system that they have found works well for them.

• Always go over each worksheet in person with your workroom and have them sign a copy.

• Always provide detailed to-scale drawings showing key measurements.

• Always provide a separate color-coded drawing.

Create a color system by choosing a different highlighter color for each fabric and trim to be used. Use the highlighter to color the areas on the drawing that correspond to fabric or trim for that color. This gives the workroom a quick visual reference that can cross language barriers and is easy to understand.

- Whenever possible, do not ship fabric or trim directly to your workroom. It is better to receive the goods yourself, make sure it is the correct product, and check it for flaws. Once the product is cut, it cannot be returned. The inconvenience of having to deliver it to your workroom yourself is well worth avoiding a costly mistake.

- Do not be afraid to visit your workroom periodically during construction of your treatments. Ask questions and take a good look at the work. Your workroom is just as invested as you are in producing an error-free product. Mistakes cost everyone time and money. Good communication is the key to avoiding them.

- Be prepared to make concessions. There are many times when a design looks great on paper but cannot be produced exactly as shown in reality. If your workroom tells you that a change in your design is necessary, there is usually a very good reason why.

CUSTOM BEDDING WORKSHEET

Customer: **Phone:** **Room:** **Phone:** **Workroom:** **Wrksht #:**

Drop Off: **Pick Up:**

Euro Shams	Qty.	Size:	Inserts:
Front:		Back:	Style:	Border:	Welt:	Trim:
Pillow Shams	**Cases**	Qty.	Size:	Inserts:	Style:
Front:		Back:		Border:	Welt:	Trim:
Pillow Shams	**Cases**	Qty.	Size:	Inserts:	Style:
Front:		Back:		Border:	Welt:	Trim
Duvet	**Comforter**	**Coverlet**	Qty.	Size:	Length	Width	Insert:
Closure:		Duvet Ties:	Quilting / Batting:
Style:					Front:
Back:		Border:	Welt:	Trim:
Dust Ruffle	Qty.	Size:	Length:	Style:	Fabric:
Notes				

Fabric 1

Fabric 2

Fabric 3

Trim 1

Trim 2

Drawing:

Drawing:

Drawing:

SOFT TREATMENT WORKSHEET

Customer:

Phone:

Wrksht #:

Phone:

Window:

Room:

Workroom:

Drop Off:

Quantity:

Pick Up:

Install:

Scrf Hldr	Spcng	Extsn	Tie Back	Length	Width	Return	IM / OM	L/R	# PLTS	Rod Diam	Rings	Tabs	Ties	Pins

Hardware:

Spcng	Extsn	Crown	Wdth	Extsn

Notes:

Drawing:

Fabric 1:   Yds.

Fabric 2:   Yds:

Trim 1:   Yds:

Trim 2:   Yds:

Lining: Yds:

Interlining: Yds:

CUSTOM UPHOLSTERY WORKSHEET

Customer:		Location:		Workroom:		PO #
Phone:			Delivery:		Address:	Drop Off:
Quantity:	Sections:		Style #		Phone:	Ready Date :

FAB 1   YDG: **FAB 2**   YDG:

Drawing:

TRIM 1   YDG: **TRIM 2**   YDG:

SEAT - # of cushions	BACK - # of cushions
Fill Options	Fill Options
Nail Heads	Tufting
Welting	Buttons
Notes:	

DEPTH	LENGTH	BACK HT	SEAT HT	ARM HT	CUSHION HT
SEAT WDTH	ARM WIDTH	RADIUS	ANGLE	FEET	LEGS

www.designdirectory4u.com

Copyright © 2007 Jackie Von Tobel

C.O.M.

C.O.M. is an abbreviation for "customer's own material" and is the term used to identify any fabric trim or hardware belonging to you or your customers that has not been provided by the workroom or manufacturer.

- Always mark your fabric, or C.O.M., clearly and in multiple locations. Use a C.O.M. tag like the one shown below and staple a small cutting of the fabric to the tag in case it should come loose from the bolt. Make an extra tag with a cutting for your files.

- Workrooms will always assume that the face of the fabric is rolled to the inside of the bolt, which is how fabric is usually shipped from the mill. If you are buying fabric from a fabric store, it might be folded or rolled to the outside. In this case, always mark the face clearly and note it on your worksheet and C.O.M. tag.

- Trims such as braids, tapes, galloon, ribbon, and cord have a face side. If it is not clear which side is which, mark it clearly. Many times multicolored bullions and fringes can look very different from side to side. One color will dominate on one side more than the other. Mark the side you want to face up.

- Always ask that your workroom save any unused fabric and trim for you. It may come in handy later on, or it can be used for pillows or throws.

```
┌─────────────────────────────────┐
│           COM  TAG              │
│                                 │
│  DESIGNER:_____  │
│                                 │
│  JOB: _____   │
│                                 │
│  ROOM: _____   │
│                                 │
│  WORK ORDER #: _____   │
│                                 │
│  PO#: _____   │
│                                 │
│  VENDOR: _____   │
│                                 │
│  PATTERN:_____   │
│                                 │
│  NOTES:_____   │
│                                 │
│  _____   │
│                                 │
│  _____   │
│                                 │
│  _____   │
│                                 │
└─────────────────────────────────┘
```

Subcontractor Agreement

Working with subcontractors such as workrooms and installers should be approached in the same manner as with any business. You should always enter into a written agreement that identifies the scope of services to be provided as well as conditions of the relationship between yourself and the vendor.

Sub-Contractor Agreement

This agreement is made this _____ day of _____ , 20____ ,

By and between _____ and _____

With it's principal place of business at _____

For a term of _____ months from the date above.

The parties above agree to as follows:

1. Work to be preformed. The subcontractor shall perform work and provide materials as set forth specifically on written purchase orders signed by the company. No other work shall be preformed unless in written change order.

2. Payment: Company shall remit payment within 30 days of receipt of payment from client for work preformed by subcontractor. If client objects to work preformed, or materials provided by subcontractor, and results in credit to customer, sub-contractors payment shall be accordingly adjusted.

3. Workmanship: All work preformed and materials provided by sub-contractor shall be in a quality manner and as is standard to the trade. Company alone shall determine if work and materials comply with requirements.

4. Insurance: Sub-contractor shall obtain and maintain insurance and hold harmless the company from any claims that may arise out of his / her or employer's work, for example:
    a.   Any and all workman's compensation claims
    b.   Any personal Injury claims
    c.   Any claim arising from damages from injury or property damage
    d.   Any claims to damage of use of a vehicle
    The above-required insurance shall be written for not less than limits of liability specified in a contract or required by company in the amount of 1 million dollars.

    Insurance Co: _____   Policy # _____

5. Independent Contractor, Sub-Contractor relationship with company shall be an independent contractor.

6. The Sub-Contractor is independently established in his/her own business of
    _____ for persons other than the company.

7. The Sub-Contractor will not solicit or provide any services or product directly to the Company's clients. All bids must be presented by the Company only. This applies to any current and future bids or contracts.

In witness whereof, the parties have signed this agreement the day and year written above.

_____   _____
Contractor   Company

_____   _____
Address   Phone

_____   _____
License # (type)   Expiration / Renewal Date

The CD-ROM

The companion CD-ROM attached to the back cover contains individual JPEG images of black-and-white illustrations of every drawing and worksheet included in the book.

These JPEGs can be printed directly using the image viewing program on your computer, or they can be dragged into a photo editing program such as Photoshop to be resized or edited. You can also drag the image into Microsoft Word to resize it and print it. Use the images as they are, or color them to reflect your finished design.

The drawings are organized on the CD-ROM in separate folders by bedding type and illustration number.

- Bed Skirts 100–138
- Bed Covers 201–266
- Pillowcases 300–398
- Pillow Shams 400–438
- Pillows 441–813
- Headboards 817–935
- Drapery 950–1106
- Canopy Beds 1111–1177
- Daybeds 1181–1213
- Finishing Touches 0155–0185
- The Worksheet System

The images in this book are meant to inspire your own unique creations. Explore the many possibilities of each design by adding your own colors or patterns to the black-and-white drawings. Combine drawings together with the worksheet system to create accurate, easy-to-understand working drawings for your workroom.

Please keep in mind that these drawings are provided for your personal use only. They are copyrighted, and resale of the images is prohibited.

Glossary

Baffle box: Three-dimensional box or divider sewn into the body of a comforter that is made of fabric and allows maximum thickness for the fill while maintaining even distribution of filling within the comforter. It minimizes shifting and migration of fill for maximum comfort and support.

Bed frame: A typical metal frame that supports the mattress and box spring independent of a headboard or footboard.

Bedposts: Decorative posts at the head of a bed or at the head and foot of a bed. They may or may not support a canopy over the bed.

Bed rails: Wood or metal rails that rest on top of and between the two side rails in order to support the mattress and box spring.

Bed skirt: A length or lengths of fabric that are hung from the bed frame or over the box spring to the floor in order to cover the gap between the bed frame and the floor.

Bias cut: Fabric cut that is a 45-degree angle of the fabric weave. This cut of fabric will have give to it, allowing swags to drape better and cording to hug curves better. Prints should be checked before cutting on the bias. Some upright prints cut on the bias will look great, while others won't.

Blend: A combination of two or more different types of fibers woven together to make a distinct cloth, e.g., polyester blended with cotton so the sheet is warmer and less prone to wrinkling than cotton alone.

Brushing: A mechanical fabric-finishing process that raises the nap of the fabric, sort of like combing, giving it a softer feel. Flannel is a brushed fabric.

Canopy: A framed rooflike structure suspended over the bed by the bed rails.

Canopy crown: The uppermost portion of a raised canopy frame.

Casters: Wheels attached to the bedpost or feet.

Center supports: Additional supports placed underneath the bed rails for large beds to provide additional support at the center for the mattress and box spring.

Chamber: In pillow, comforter, and featherbed construction, "chamber" indicates walls of fabric sewn inside the basic shell that contains down or feathers separate from other filled portions, enabling various support characteristics.

Coil count: The number of innerspring coils in a mattress.

Coil gauge: The thickness of the wire used in innerspring mattresses.

C.O.M. (aka COM): Customer's own material.

Combing: A yarn preparation for removing all short fibers and impurities from cotton. Combed yarn is superior to carded yarn, as it is more compact and has fewer projecting fibers. The finest cotton fabrics are made from combed yarns.

Comfort layers: Foam, padding, and fibers added to an innerspring system to provide cushioning; also called upholstery layers.

Cotton: Vegetable seed fiber grown all over the world. The length of the fiber is the major determining factor in the relative quality of the cotton. The best-quality cottons are Egyptian, supima, and pima cotton.

Crinoline (aka buckram): A heavily sized or stiffened fabric used as a foundation for pleats in draperies.

Crosswise grain (aka fillers, woof, weft): The threads of a woven fabric that run perpendicular to the selvages. The fabric has a slight give in the crosswise grain.

Crown: The apex of a raised canopy.

Cut allowance: The amount of fabric added to finished measurements for hems and headings.

Cut width: The complete amount of fabric needed for treatment width, including hems, and/or any other allowances.

Down: Soft, fluffy tufts of down under the breast feathers of ducks and geese.

Down comforter: A fabric shell filled with down tufts from either geese or ducks.

Drapability: The ability of a certain fabric to hang in pleasing folds.

Drop match: When the width is cut straight across by the print, the pattern will not line up perfectly to be seamed at the selvage. The pattern repeat does not match until down half of the vertical pattern repeat. Therefore, additional yardage is required. Add one-half pattern repeat per cut. This is commonly found in fabrics that coordinate with wallpaper. It is usually designated in the sample books (but not always) as a drop match.

Duvet: A fabric shell filled with synthetic or natural insulating fibers.

Duvet cover: An envelope-type fabric cover into which a duvet or comforter is inserted. The duvet cover protects the insert and prolongs its life.

Dye lots: A batch of fabric printed at the same time. Each time a new printing is done, the fabric is classified with a new dye lot. Fabrics from different dye lots can vary in color. If color matching is important for your project, always get a cutting of the dye lot you will order from.

Egyptian cotton: The longest staple cotton fiber, grown only in Egypt.

Fabrication: The process of manufacturing raw goods into a finished product.

Face fabric: The decorative fabric on a treatment that "faces" into the room. The lining is behind it.

Facing: A piece of fabric stitched to a raw edge and turned to the back side to form a finished edge. The diagonals of jabots or cascades are sometimes faced to show a contrast in the angles.

Featherbed: A fabric shell that is filled with goose or duck feathers and down and laid on top of a mattress as a mattress topper.

Featherbed cover: An envelope-type cover for a featherbed to protect it from body oils and dirt.

Fill power: The measurement in cubic inches that one ounce of down will fill when placed in a glass tube and allowed to loft for up to three days.

Finial: A decorative end cap for the bedpost, used to hold a canopy in place on a canopy bed.

Finish: Product applied to fabric as a protection against watermarks and fading.

Fitted sheet: A sheet that is tailored to fit tightly over the mattress. It is secured at the bottom hem with elastic.

Flame-retardant fabric: Fabric that will not burn. It can be inherently flame retardant, which means the actual fiber from which it was made is a flame-retardant fiber; e.g., polyester, or it can be treated to become flame retardant, which usually changes the fibers and makes the fabric stiff.

Flat sheet: Also called the top sheet, a flat sheet is placed on top of the fitted sheet and is typically tucked around the mattress at the sides and bottom of the bed.

Foot: The foot of the bed is the portion of the bed at your feet. It is the base of the bed and usually faces out into the room.

Footboard: The solid or upholstered secondary focal point of the bed attached at or to the foot of the bed.

Foot posts: The bedposts at the foot of the bed.

French seam: A way of stitching fabric together with the seam hidden from view. Used on sheer fabrics.

Grain: The direction of threads in a fabric. Can be crosswise or lengthwise.

Half-drop match: One in which the pattern itself drops down half the repeat on the horizontal but does match at the selvage. It is a concern when planning cuts for horns, pelmets, empire swags, box pleats, etc., when the same design or motif is needed on each piece. It is usually designated in the sample books as a half drop.

Hand: The tactile feel of fabric.

Head: The head of the bed refers to the portion of the bed that you lay your head on. It is usually the anchor of the bed and is placed against a wall or focal point.

Headboard: The solid or upholstered focal point of the bed attached at or to the head of the bed.

Head posts: The bedposts at the head of the bed.

Hemstitch: A straight or decorative topstitching used at the hemline of linens.

Innerspring unit: A coil-and-wire unit that makes up the supportive heart of a mattress.

Latex foam: A natural body-conforming material often used to increase softness and relieve pressure points.

Lengthwise grain (aka warp): The threads in a woven fabric that run parallel to the selvages. Fabrics are stronger along the lengthwise grain.

Nap: A fabric with a texture or design that runs in one direction, such as corduroy or velvet. A fabric with a nap will often look different when viewed from various directions. When using a fabric with a nap, all pieces must be cut and sewn together so the nap runs in only one direction.

Open construction: Comforter construction that does not have baffle boxes or channels. The filling is loose within the cover.

Pattern repeat (aka repeat): The distance between any given point in a design and where that exact point first appears again. Repeats can be horizontal or vertical.

Percale: A closely woven plain-weave fabric, generally 180 thread count or better. Percale is soft, cool, and light to the touch.

Pilling: Loose and weak fibers fray at the face of the fabric and matt together, forming little balls, or pills. This typically happens with cotton or cotton-blend fabrics that have not been constructed of combed cotton fibers.

Pillowcase: A functional pillow cover that protects the pillow from body oils and wear and tear.

Pillow protector: A close-fitting fabric cover usually with a zipper closure at one end. Used to cover a bed pillow to protect it from wear and tear.

Pillow sham: A decorative pillow cover that is enclosed on all four sides and has an opening in the back to insert a pillow form.

Platform: A boxed base for a mattress and sometimes a box spring and mattress.

Preshrink: To wash and dry fabric prior to fabricating it into bedding to avoid shrinking and fading after construction.

Railroad: To turn fabric so the selvage runs across the treatment instead of up and down. One-hundred-eighteen-inch sheer is made to be used this way so that pinch pleats are put in across the selvage end instead of across the cut end. This can eliminate seams on some treatments.

Right side: The printed side of the fabric that is used as the finished side of an item. The right side generally has the most color and the most finished look.

Risers: Extensions made to raise the bed frame to add height to the bed.

Seam: The join where two pieces of fabric are sewn together.

Seam allowance: An extra amount of fabric used when joining fabric.

Selvage (also selvedge): The tightly woven edge on the length of the fabric that holds it together.

Side rails: The support rails that anchor the headboard of the bed to the footboard.

Straight grain: The lengthwise threads of the fabric running parallel to the selvages.

Tabling: To measure a treatment and mark it to the finished length before the final finishing.

Thread count: The actual number of threads going in either direction in one square inch of cloth.

Turn of cloth: The minute ease of fabric that is lost from making a fold.

Viscous memory foam: Synthetic material that responds to body temperature and weight.

Warp and weft: Refers to the direction of threads in a fabric. Warp threads run the length of the fabric. Warp threads are crossed by the weft threads, which run from selvage to selvage across the width of the fabric.

Width: A word to describe a single width of fabric (from selvage to selvage). Several widths of fabric are sewn together to make a panel of drapery.

Wrong side: The back of the fabric; the less-finished side, which might have stray threads or a rougher look to it.

Resource Directory

Beds and Bedroom Furniture

American Drew
4310 Regency Dr., Ste. 101
High Point, NC 27265
www.americandrew.com

American Iron Bed Company
1613 Chelsea Rd., #355
San Marino, CA 91108
800.378.1742
www.antiqueironbeds.com

Amy Howard Collection
3664 Cherry Rd.
Memphis, TN 38118
901.547.1448
www.amyhowardcollection.com

Artifacts International
9340 Dowdy Dr.
San Diego, CA
858.693.6000
www.artifactsinternational.com

Avery Boardman
6 Empire Blvd.
Moonachie, NJ 07074
800.634.6647
www.averyboardman.com

Baker
800.592.2537
baker.kohlerinteriors.com

Bernhardt
P.O. Box 740
1839 Morganton Blvd.
Lenoir, NC 28645
866.527.9099
www.bernhardt.com

Brighton Pavilion
Jane Keltner Collections
Memphis, TN 38112
800.487.8033
www.paintedfurniture.com

Carriage House
1500 River Dr.
Belmont, NC 28012
704.829.9204
www.carriagehousefurniture.com

Century Furniture, LLC
P.O. Box 608
Hickory, NC 28603
828.328.1851
www.centuryfurniture.com

Charles P. Rogers
800.582.6229
www.charlesprogers.com

Claudio Rayes
800.884.9202
www.claudiorayes.net

Dino Mark Anthony
10040 Geary Ave.
Santa Fe Springs, CA 90670
562.946.3387
www.dinomarkanthony.com

Drexel Heritage Furniture
1925 Eastchester Dr.
High Point, NC 27265
866.450.3434
www.drexelheritage.com

Eddy West
High Point Showroom
#P102B
Union Square
410 English Rd.
High Point, NC 27262
www.eddywest.com

Edward Ferrell, Ltd.
685 Southwest St.
High Point, NC 27260
336.841.3028
www.ef-lm.com

EJ Victor
P.O. Box 309
110 Wamsutta Mill Rd.
Morganton, NC 28680
828.437.2608
www.ejvictor.com

The Farmhouse Collection
P.O. Box 3089
Twin Falls, ID 83303
208.736.8700
www.farmhousecollection.com

Ferguson Copeland
www.fergusoncopeland.com

French Heritage
650 S. San Vicente Blvd.
Los Angeles, CA 90048
800.245.0899
www.frenchheritage.com

Harden Furniture, Inc.
8550 Mill Pond Wy.
McConnellsville, NY 13401
315.245.1000
www.harden.com

Henredon
800.444.3682
www.henredon.com

Hickory Chair
www.hickorychair.com

Hickory White
www.hickorywhite.com

Highland House Furniture
www.highlandhousefurniture.com

Ironies
2222 Fifth St.
Berkeley, CA 94710
510.644.2100
http://ironies.com

Jeffco
www.jeffcofurniture.com

Lewis Mittman, Inc.
685 Southwest St.
High Point, NC 27260
212.888.5580
www.ef-lm.com

Marge Carson
9056 E. Garvey Ave.
Rosemead, CA 91770
www.margecarson.com

Oly Studio
2222 Fifth St.
Berkeley, CA 94710
775.336.2100
www.olystudio.com

Pieces
3234-A Roswell Rd., NW
Atlanta, GA 30305
404.869.2476
http://piecesinc.com

Plantation
www.plantationla.com

The Platt Collections
P.O. Box 3397
11119 Rush St.
South El Monte, CA 91733
626.444.6149
www.theplattcollections.com

Pulaski
www.pulaskifurniture.com

Ralph Lauren Home
888.475.7674
www.ralphlaurenhome.com

Stanley Furniture
276.627.2540
www.stanleyfurniture.com

Wesley Allen
www.wesleyallen.com

Woodland Furniture
Thomas & Company
8425 N. 90th Street, Ste. 5
Scottsdale, AZ 85258
480.922.4960
www.woodlandfurniture.com

Bed Crowns, Coronas, and Pediments

Amore Drapery Hardware
12121 Veteran's Memorial Dr., Ste. 2
Houston, TX 77067
281.440.0123
www.amoredraperyhardware.com

Antique Drapery Rod Co.
2259 Valdina St.
Dallas, TX 75207
214.653.1733
www.antiquedraperyrod.com

Artifacts International
9340 Dowdy Dr.
San Diego, CA 92126
858.693.6000
www.artifactsinternational.com

Brighton Pavilion
Memphis, TN 38112
800.487.8033
www.paintedfurniture.com

Crayon Castles, LLC
P.O. Box 3149
Sugar Land, TX 77487
www.crayoncastles.com

Design Source, Ltd.
2506 Sinclair Ave.
High Point, NC 27260
336.841.1650
www.designsourceltd.com

Friedman Brothers Decorative Arts
9015 NW 105th Wy.
Medley, FL 33178
800.327.1065
www.friedmanmirrors.com

Hickory Manor House
1200 Hickory Chapel Rd.
High Point, NC 27260
800.752.6629
www.hickorymanor.biz

House Parts
479 Whitehall St. SW
Atlanta, GA 30303
404.577.5584
www.houseparts.com

J-Art Iron Company, Inc.
9435 Jefferson Blvd.
Culver City, CA 90232
310.202.1126 (voicemail)
www.jartiron.com

King Architectural Metals
800.542.2379
www.kingmetals.com

Outwater Plastics Industries
P.O. Box 500
24 River Rd.
Bogota, NJ 07603
800.631.8375
www.outwater.com

The Well Appointed House
www.thewellappointedhouse.com

Bedding and Bed Linens

Anichini
800.553.5309
www.anichini.com

Ann Gish
599 Eleventh Ave., 8th Fl.
New York, NY 10036
212.969.9200
www.anngish.com

Aribesque Fine Bedding
P.O. Box 7511
High Point, NC 27264
336.474.7455
www.aribesque.com

Austin Horn Collection
2331 Tubeway Ave.
City of Commerce, CA 90040
323.838.7808

Bella Notte Linens
www.bellanottelinens.com

Bella Rose by Chateau
4601 N. Santa Fe
Oklahoma City, OK 73118
800.783.7317
www.bellarosebychateau.com

Bellino Fine Linens
18 West Forest Ave.
Englewood, NJ 07631
201.568.5255
www.bellinofinelinens.com

Dwell Studio
155 – 6th Avenue, 7th Fl.
New York, NY 10013
212.219.9343
http://dwellshop.com

Eastern Accents
Feathersound
4201 W. Belmont Ave.
Chicago, IL 60641
800.397.4556
www.easternaccents.com

Frette
800.353.7388
www.frette.com

Home Treasures
5150 Ashley Ct.
Houston, TX 77041
713.937.7716
www.hometreasureslinens.com

Legacy Linens
14140 Parke Long Ct., Ste. N
Chantilly, VA 20151
703.830.6818
www.legacylinens.com

Leontine Linens
1589 Newtown Pike
Georgetown, KY 40324
800.876.4799
www.leontinelinens.com

Libeco Linens
Libeco-Lagae, Inc.
230 Fifth Ave., #1907
New York, NY 10001
212.764.6644
www.libeco.com

Lulu DK Matouk
www.luludkmatouk.com

Mario & Marielena
616 Design Dr.
Cookeville, TN 38501
800.551.1441
www.mariomarielena.com

Mystic Valley Traders
106 Cummings Park
Woburn, MA 01801
781.933.0666
www.mvtbedding.com

Peacock Alley
2050 Postal Wy.
Dallas, TX 75212
800.275.0784
www.peacockalley.com

Pierre Frey
979 Third Ave., Ste. 1611
New York, NY 10022
212.421.0534
www.pierrefrey.com

Pratesi
829 Madison Ave. (at 69th St.)
New York, NY 10021
212.288.2315
www.pratesi.com

Sferra Fine Linens
877.336.2003
www.sferralinens.com

Signoria di Firenze
5400 NW 161st St.
Miami, FL 33015
305.626.7889
www.signoria.com

Sweet Dreams
1300 East Upas
McAllen, TX 78501
956.687.2737
www.sweet-dreams.com

Tomasini Fine Linens
323.231.2349
www.tomasinifinelinens.com

Pillow and Duvet Inserts

Czech Feather and Down Company, LLC
72 – 16th Ave. SW
Cedar Rapids, IA 52404
319.364.0952
www.czechfeatherdownco.com

Harris Pillow Supply, Inc.
3026 Trask Pkwy.
Beaufort, SC 29906
800.845.8240
www.harrispillow.com

Lee's Decorative Showcase
16531 Saticoy St.
Van Nuys, CA 91406
800.347.5337
www.leesdec.com

Pacific Coast Feather Company
1964 – 4th Ave. South
Seattle, WA 98134
888.297.1778
www.pacificcoast.com

Rowley Company
230 Meek Rd.
Gastonia, NC 28056
800.343.4542
www.rowleyco.com

Scandia Down
800.438.2431
www.scandiadown.com

Soft-Tex
428 Hudson River Rd.
Waterford, NY 12188
800.366.2324
www.soft-tex.com

United Pillow Manufacturing
5365 NW 35 Ct.
Miami, FL 33142
877.374.5569
www.unitedpillow.com

Bedding Workrooms—Custom Quilting

Carole Fabrics, Inc.
P.O. Box 1436
Augusta, GA 30903
706.863.4742
www.carolefabrics.com

Kasmir Fabrics
P.O. Box 565507
Dallas, TX 75356
800.527.4630
www.kasmirfabrics.com

Kay & L Draperies
602 Industrial St.
Waverly, IA 50677
800.553.1788
www.kayandl.com

Lafayette Interior Fashions
P.O. Box 2838
3000 Klondike Rd.
West Lafayette, IN 47996
765.464.2500
www.lafvb.com

Mrs. Goodstitch
1606 Bridge St.
St. Matthews, SC 29135
800.833.5359
www.goodstitch.com

Randall K Designers Express
6640 Cobra Wy.
San Diego, CA 92121
800.243.4223
www.randallk.com

Robert Allen
225 Foxboro Blvd.
Foxboro, MA 02035
800.333.3777
www.robertallendesign.com

Wesco Fabrics, Inc.
4001 Forest St.
Denver, CO 80216
www.wescofabrics.com

Fabric Companies

Ado Corporation
851 Simuel Rd.
Spartanburg, SC 29301
800.845.0918
www.ado-usa.com

Arc-Com Fabrics, Inc.
33 Ramland South
Orangeburg, NY 10962
800.223.5466
www.arc-com.com

Artmark Fabrics Co., Inc
480 Lancaster Pike
Frazer, PA 19355
800.777.6665
www.artmarkfabrics.com

Ashbourne Fabrics
215.364.6915

Barrow Industries
8260 NW 27th St.
Miami, FL 33122
800.496.8367
www.barrowindustries.com

Beacon Fabric & Notions
8331 Epicenter Blvd.
Lakeland, FL 33809
800.713.8157
www.beaconfabric.com

Beacon Hill
225 Foxboro Blvd.
Foxboro, MA 02035
800.333.3777
www.beaconhilldesign.com

Bead Industries
11 Cascade Blvd.
Milford, CT 06460
800.297.4851
mmeyer@beadindustries.com
www.beadindustries.com

Benartex, Inc.
1359 Broadway, Ste. 1100
New York, NY 10018
212.840.3250
www.benartex.com

Brimar
28250 Ballard Dr.
Lake Forest, IL 60045
800.274.1205
www.brimarinc.com

Brunschwig & Fils, Inc.
75 Virginia Rd.
North White Plains, NY 10603
914.684.5800
www.brunschwig.com

Calvin Fabrics
2046 Lars Way
Medford, OR 97501
888.732.1996
www.henrycalvin.com

Carole Fabrics, Inc.
P.O. Box 1436
Augusta, GA 30903
800.241.0920, ext. 210
www.carolefabrics.com

Christopher Norman Collection, Inc.
979 Third Ave., Concourse Level
New York, NY 10012
877.846.0845
www.christophernorman.com

Clarence House Fabric
800.221.4704
www.clarencehouse.com

Decoratorland, Inc.
30600 Gratiot Ave.
Roseville, MI 48066
866.723.4357
www.decoratorland.com

Decorators Supply Co.
888.218.5571
207.782.1392

Decorators Walk
Plainview, NY
516.249.3100

Delta Fabrics, Inc.
Atlanta, GA
770.458.7659

Donghia Furniture/Textiles, Ltd.
New York, NY
212.925.2777

Duralee
1775 Fifth Avenue
Bay Shore, NY 11706
800.275.3872
www.duralee.com

Elite Textile, Inc.
Los Angeles, CA
213.689.3247

Fabricade, Inc.
P.O. Box 438
Bohemia, NY 11716
800.645.5540

Fabrics 21, Inc.
Montebello, CA
323.726.1266

Fabricut Fabrics
9303 E. 46th St.
Tulsa, OK 74145
800.999.8200
www.fabricut.com

Fame Fabrics
New York, NY
212.679.6868

F. Schumacher & Co.
P.O. Box 6002
1325 Old Cooches Bridge Rd.
Newark, DE 19714
800.523.1200
www.fschumacher.com

Golding Fabrics
7097 Mendenhall Rd.
Archdale, NC 27263
336.883.9171
www.goldingfabrics.com

Hampshire Printed Fabrics, Inc.
Lawrence, MA
978.683.9910

Highland Court
Duralee
P.O. Box 9179
1775 Fifth Ave.
Bay Shore, NY 11706
631.273.8800
www.highlandcourtfabrics.com

JAB
Stroheim
30-30 – 47th Ave.
Long Island City, NY 11101
718.706.7000
www.jab.de

J. Ennis Fabrics, Ltd.
12122 – 68 St.
Edmonton, AB T5B 1R1
Canada
800.66.ENNIS
www.jennisfabrics.com

J. R. Burrows & Co.
P.O. Box 522
Rockland, MA 02370
800.347.1795
www.burrows.com

J. Robert Scott
500 North Oak St.
Inglewood, CA 90302
800.322.4910
www.jrobertscott.com

Kaslen Textiles
5899 S. Downey Rd.
Vernon, CA 90058
800.777.5789
www.kaslentextiles.com

Kasmir Fabric
2051 Alpine Wy.
Hayward, CA 94545
800.765.3284
www.kasmirfabrics.com

Kast Fabrics, Inc.
P.O. Box 1660
Pasadena, TX 77501
800.733.5278
www.kastfabrics.com

Kirsch Fabric Corp.
Minneapolis, MN
612.544.9111

Kravet Fabrics, Inc.
225 Central Ave. S.
Bethpage, NY 11714
516.293.2000
www.kravet.com

Lady Ann Fabrics, Inc.
St. Petersburg, FL
727.344.1819

Lee Jofa
201 Central Ave. S.
Bethpage, NY 11714
212.688.0444
www.leejofa.com

Libas Limited
4400 S. Soto St.
Vernon, CA 90058
213.747.2406
www.libassilk.com

Lord Jay, Inc.
Miami, FL
305.576.0157

Maxwell Fabric
925 B Boblett St.
Blaine, WA 98230
800.663.1159
www.maxwellfabrics.com

Michael Jon Designs
P.O. Box 59243
Los Angeles, CA 90058
323.582.0166
www.michaeljondesigns.com

Mitchell Fabrics
810 SW Adams St.
Peoria, IL 61602
800.447.0952
www.mitchellfabrics.com

Motif Design
718 S. Fulton Ave.
Mount Vernon, NY 10550
800.431.2424
www.motif-designs.com

Payne
Westgate Interiors, LLC
1517 W. North Carrier Pkwy., Ste. 116
Grand Prairie, TX 75050
800.527.2517
www.paynefabrics.com

Pindler & Pindler, Inc.
P.O. Box 8007
11910 Poindexter Ave.
Moorpark, CA 93021
805.531.9090
www.pindler.com

Plumridge Silks
310.230.0484
www.plumridge.com

Posh Limited
Albuquerque, NM
505.889.8880

Ralph Lauren Home
867 Madison Ave.
New York, NY 10021
888.475.7674
www.rlhome.polo.com

Richard Bernard Fabrics
1810 John Towers Ave.
El Cajon, CA 92020
800.366.9800

Richloom Fabrics Group
New York, NY
212.685.5400

RM Coco
P.O. Box 1270
Cape Girardeau, MO 63702
800.325.8025
www.rmcoco.com

Robert Allen Fabrics
55 Cabot Blvd.
Mansfield, MA 02048
800.295.3776
www.robertallendesign.com

Rockland Mills Div.
Rockland Ind., Inc.
410.522.2505

Sanderson
285 Grand Ave.
3 Patriot Centre
Englewood, NJ 07631
800.894.6185
www.sanderson-uk.com

Scalamandré Fabrics
37-24 – 24th St.
Long Island City, NY 11101
718.361.8311
www.scalamandre.com

Scroll Fabrics
770.432.7228
800.3.SCROLL

S & D Fabrics
Los Angeles, CA
213.748.9200

S. Harris
9303 E. 46th St.
Tulsa, OK 74145
800.999.5600
www.sharris.com

Sierra Textile Company
San Diego, CA
619.550.3880

Silver State Fabrics
1010 W. 2610 S.
Salt Lake City, UT 84119
800.453.5777
www.silverstatefabrics.com

S. L. Textile Corp.
Yonkers, NY
914.375.0800

Soletex Fabrics, Inc.
Weston, ON
Canada
416.747.6797

Spectrum Fabrics
New York, NY
212.684.7100

S & S Fabrics
Miami, FL
305.371.6684

Steven Fabrics
1400 Van Buren St. NE
Minneapolis, MN 55413
800.328.2558
www.stevenfabrics.com

Stout Fabric
3050 Trewigton Rd.
Colmar, PA 18915
800.523.2592

Stroheim & Romann
30-30 – 47th Ave.
New York, NY 11101
718.706.7000
www.stroheim.com

The Thomas Collection
Houston, TX
713.864.8086

Travers
979 Third Ave.
New York, NY 10022
212.888.7900
www.traversinc.com

Trimland
60 E. Jefryn Blvd.
Deer Park, NY 11729
877.TRIMLAND
www.trimland.com

Tritex Fabrics, Ltd.
Vancouver, BC, Canada
604.255.4242

Waverly Fabric
877.292.8375
www.waverly.com

Wesco Fabrics, Inc.
4001 Forest St.
Denver, CO 80216
303.388.3908
www.wescofabrics.com

Westgate Interiors, LLC
418 Chandler Dr.
Gaffney, SC 29340
800.527.6666
www.westgatefabrics.com

Passementerie and Decorative Trim

British Trimmings Limited
P.O. Box 46
Coronation St.

Reddish
Stockport
Cheshire SK5 7PJ
United Kingdom
0161.480.6122
www.britishtrimmings.com

Brimar
28250 Ballard Dr.
Lake Forest, IL 60045
800.274.1205
www.brimarinc.com

Conso
85 South St.
West Warren, MA 01092
800.628.9362
www.conso.com

D'kei, Inc.
P.O. Box 1570
Council Bluffs, IA 51502
800.535.3534
www.dkei.net

Fabricut
9303 E. 46th St.
Tulsa, OK 74145
800.999.8200
www.fabricut.com

Kasmir Fabric
2051 Alpine Wy.
Hayward, CA 94545
800.765.3284
www.kasmirfabric.com

Kast
P.O. Box 1660
Pasadena, TX 77501
800.733.5278
www.kastfabrics.com

Kenneth Meyer Company
1504 Bryant St., 3rd Fl.
San Francisco, CA 94103
415.861.0118

Kirsch
P.O. Box 0370
Sturgis, MI 49091
800.528.1407
www.kirsch.com

Leslie Hannon Custom Trimmings
4018 E. 5th St.
Long Beach, CA 90814
562.433.0161

Lina's
525 S. Main St.
Greenville, MS 38701
800.459.5462

Maxwell
925 B Boblett St.
Blaine, WA 98230
800.663.1159
www.maxwellfabrics.com

M&J Trimming
1008 Sixth Ave.
New York, NY 10018
800.965.8746
www.mjtrim.com

Pierre Frey
979 Third Ave., Ste. 1611
New York, NY 10022
212.421.0534
www.pierrefrey.com

Renaissance Ribbons
P.O. Box 699
Oregon House, CA 95962
877.422.6601
www.renaissanceribbons.com

RM Coco
P.O. Box 1270
Cape Girardeau, MO 63702
800.325.8025
www.rmcoco.com

Robert Allen
225 Foxboro Blvd.
Foxboro, MA 02035
800.333.3777
www.robertallendesign.com

Springs Window Fashions
7549 Graber Rd.
Middleton, WI 53562
800.521.8071

Stroheim & Romann
30-30 – 47th Ave.
New York, NY 11101
718.706.7000
www.stroheim.com

Wendy Cushing Trimmings
Chelsea Harbour
Design Center
London, England
United Kingdom
020.7351.5796

Wesco Fabrics
4001 Forest St.
Denver, CO 80216
303.388.3908
www.wescofabrics.com

West Coast Trimming Corp.
7100 Wilson Ave.
Los Angeles, CA 90001
323.587.0701

Professional Organizations and Industry Resources

American Sewing Guild (ASG)
www.asg.org

**American Society of
Interior Designers (ASID)**
608 Massachusetts Ave., NE
Washington, DC 20002
202.546.3480
www.asid.org

**Council for Interior Design
Accreditation (formerly FIDER)**
146 Monroe Center NW, Ste. 1318
Grand Rapids, MI 49503
616.458.0400
www.accredit-id.org

Drapery Pro
27281 Las Nieves
Mission Viejo, CA 92691
949.916.9372
www.draperypro.com

**Draperies and Window
Coverings Magazine**
840 U.S. Hwy. One, Ste. 330
North Palm Beach, FL 33408
561.627.3393
561.694.6578
www.dwconline.com

**Interior Design Educators
Council (IDEC)**
7150 Winton Dr., Ste. 300
Indianapolis, IN 46268
317.328.4437
www.idec.org

Interior Design Society
164 S. Main St., Fl. 8
High Point, NC 27260
888.884.4469
www.interiordesignsociety.org

**International Furnishings and Design
Association (IFDA)**
World Headquarters
150 S. Warner Rd. Ste. 156
King of Prussia, PA 19406
610.535.6422
www.ifda.com

International Interior
  Design Association (IIDA)
222 Merchandise Mart, Ste. 567
Chicago, IL 60654
888.799.4432
www.iida.org

Window Coverings Association
  of America (WCAA)
2646 Hwy. 109, Ste. 205
Grover, MO 63040
888.298.9222
www.wcaa.org

Window Fashions Certified
  Professionals Program (WFCP)
4215 White Bear Pkwy., Ste. 100
St. Paul, MN 55110
651.293.1544
www.wfcppro.com

Window Fashions Magazine
  Grace McNamara, Inc.
4215 White Bear Pkwy., Ste. 100
St. Paul, MN 55110
651.293.1544
www.gracemcnamarainc.com

Schools and Training

Custom Home Furnishings Academy
13900 S. Lakes Dr., Ste. F
Charlotte, NC 28273
800.222.1415
http://chfindustry.com

Custom Sewing Institute
1318 Sue Barnett Dr.
Houston, Texas 77018
713.697.4110
www.csisews.com

Merv's Upholstery Training Videos
N2758 Shadow Rd.
Waupaca, WI 54981
715.258.8785
www.mervstrainingvideos.com

Slipcover America, Inc.
914 Repetto Dr.
St. Louis, MO 63122
800.267.4958
http://slipcoveramerica.com

Window Coverings Association
  of America (WCAA)
2646 Hwy. 109, Ste. 205
Grover, MO 63040
888.298.9222
www.wcaa.org

Window Fashions Certified
  Professionals Program (WFCP)
4215 White Bear Pkwy., Ste. 100
St. Paul, MN 55110
651.293.1544
www.wfcppro.com

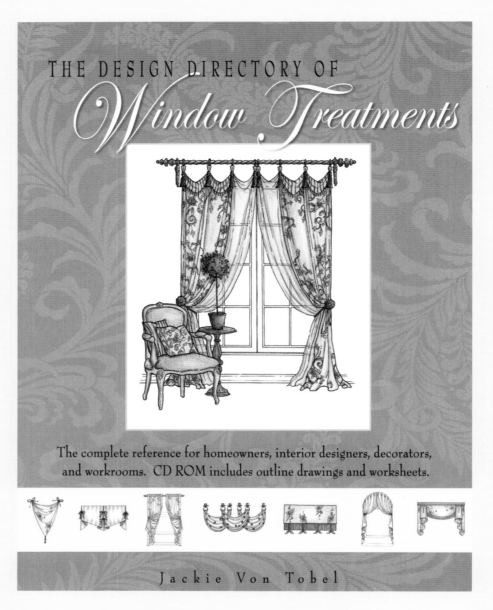

THE DESIGN DIRECTORY OF

Window Treatments

The complete reference for homeowners, interior designers, decorators, and workrooms. CD ROM includes outline drawings and worksheets.

J a c k i e   V o n   T o b e l

8½ x 11 Hardcover, 584 Pages
750 Line Drawings
978-1-4236-0216-3
$60.00

Available at bookstores everywhere
and online at www.gibbs-smith.com

Patterns from DESIGN DIRECTORY OF WINDOW TREATMENTS
are available for purchase at www.minutesmatterstudio.com